DEMOCRACY KILLS

DEMOCRACY KILLS

What's So Good About the Vote?

Humphrey Hawksley

MACMILLAN

First published 2009 by Macmillan
an imprint of Pan Macmillan Ltd
Pan Macmillan, 20 New Wharf Road, London N1 9RR
Basingstoke and Oxford
Associated companies throughout the world
www.panmacmillan.com

ISBN 978-0-230-74408-0

1 3 5 7 9 8 6 4 2

A CIP catalogue record for this book is available
from the British Library.

Typeset by Ellipsis Books Limited, Glasgow
Printed and bound in the UK by
CPI Mackays, Chatham ME5 8TD

Visit **www.panmacmillan.com** to read more about all our books
and to buy them. You will also find features, author interviews and
news of any author events, and you can sign up for e-newsletters
so that you're always first to hear about our new releases.

To my family

TWENTIETH-CENTURY TALK

No one pretends that democracy is perfect or all-wise. Indeed, it has been said that democracy is the worst form of government except all those other forms that have been tried from time to time.

Winston Churchill, 11 November 1947

TWENTY-FIRST CENTURY TALK

I know there has been controversy about the promotion of democracy in recent years, and much of this controversy is connected to the war in Iraq. So let me be clear: no system of government can or should be imposed upon one nation by any other.

Barack Obama, 4 June 2009

Please Imagine

You are with your family sitting around the kitchen table. Across from you is your partner, whom you love very much and with whom you are raising two beautiful children. To your right is your thirteen-year-old daughter, thoughtful, wonderful on the piano and set on becoming a biologist. To your left is your eleven-year-old son, bright, unafraid to speak his mind and often getting into trouble for it at school. Resting away from the table is your mother. She is suffering from diabetes and a little unsteady on her legs.

You are absorbing the most dreadful news. A catastrophic tragedy is sweeping the world. Within days everything will be wiped out and almost everywhere will be uninhabitable. Most people will die.

But there are two countries in the Caribbean that will remain unaffected. You and your family have been a given a special chance to escape there. You don't know much about the two places except that they are within a hundred miles of each other and they are governed by totally different political systems. You have a few moments to see that one country has great mobile phone connection, but the other has far better health care.

Which one would you choose? Cuba or Haiti?

CONTENTS

PREFACE

In late 2008, in Iraq, a US Cavalry sergeant was briefing me before we set out on patrol through western Baghdad. As he finished, I wanted to clarify a small point. 'Excuse me,' I said, 'this might be a stupid question, but . . .'

The sergeant interrupted: 'The only stupid question, sir, is the one we never ask.'

The question – stupid or not – posed by this book is 'What's so good about having the vote?' Many of us living in Western democracies no longer ask it. Indeed, those who do often face an assertion that the question should never arise because the answer is obvious.

For many years, conventional thinking has been that the only way to achieve stability in a society is through democratically elected government. That might be right in the very long term because it is a system that gives each of us a political voice. But as yet there is no road map of how to get there. Indeed, when academics at of Oxford University began working on this issue a few years back he found that no substantive studies had been made of the relationship between the introduction of democracy and political violence.

Much evidence indicates that voting to appoint a government in the developing world can lead to war, disease and poverty. From Pakistan to Zimbabwe, from the Palestinian territories to the former Yugoslavia, from Georgia to Haiti, the holding of elections has produced high levels of corruption and violence. Tribal and religious divisions have become institutionalized into power blocs that have led to ethnic cleansing. Political parties rely on brute force and patronage. Parliaments represent not broad constituencies but vested interests and, amid much fanfare, constitutions are written, but rarely upheld.

Millions now believe that they run more risk of being killed or remaining poor under an electoral system than under a dictatorship. The average income in authoritarian China, for example, is now twice that of democratic India. In the same way, Haitians who are allowed to elect their governments live twenty years less than those in dictatorial Cuba where average life expectancy is seventy-seven years.

At the end of the Cold War, the Western democratic system had an unchallenged opportunity to prove itself, but few understood the complexities. When challenged, Churchill's 1947 maxim that 'democracy is the worst form of government except all those other forms' was often cited.[1] In 1992, the American academic Francis Fukuyama argued that the defeat of communism in the Cold War marked 'the universalization of Western liberal democracy as the final form of human government'.[2] In 2005, the United States declared it was abandoning its policy of supporting stability at the expense of democracy and that it would now support the democratic aspirations of all people.[3]

There are numerous interpretations of 'democracy'. The word itself derives from the Greek – *demos*, meaning 'the people' and *kratia* meaning 'power'. One definition describes

---

1 House of Commons, 11 November 1947.
2 Francis Fukuyama, *The End of History and the Last Man* (Penguin 1992).
3 US Secretary of State Condoleezza Rice, 20 June 2005.

it as 'the doctrine that the numerical majority of an organized group can make decisions binding on the whole group'. Another says democracy is 'a form of government in which the people have a voice in the exercise of power, typically through elected representatives'. Put at its most basic, the people are able to choose between competing political parties an accountable government that will deliver what the society needs to advance. Democracy originated in ancient Greece as opposed to Confucian China with its Mandate of Heaven, or in the Islamic world with its concept of the powerful Caliph. It is unsurprising, therefore, that many in the West should believe that the best way to achieve stability in the developing world is by creating governments similar to their own.

Since the Berlin Wall came down, we have had twenty years to build democracies on a fairly uncompetitive political canvas, and the score card is very mixed. Africa has slid backwards. China has forged ahead. The dictatorship of Saddam Hussein was a catastrophe. Experiments with democracy from Russia to Ivory Coast have resulted in loss of life and social upheaval. The authoritarian governments of Singapore and Malaysia have been successful development stories. Once brutal dictatorships in South Korea and Taiwan have made peaceful democratic transitions – but it took decades of hard work to get there.

The stories in this book span these post-Cold War years, throughout which I have seen the West's democratic mission both welcomed euphorically for the freedoms it brings and bitterly cursed for the bloodshed it causes. I hear from an Iraqi wedding photographer who had lost so many friends and family members that he would have gladly exchanged his right to vote for running water, electricity and safety; from an Argentine shoe maker who bartered trainers for food because his economy has collapsed; and from the African cocoa farmer whose belief in the Western free market left him three times poorer now than he was thirty years ago.

From city slums to arid farmland, I ask the question on the cover of this book –'What's so good about the vote?' Is there is a way that a country can be prepared for democracy? Or is each society with its own particular set of challenges so unique that to lay down any formula at all would be naive and irresponsible? Should there be prescribed benchmarks before a country embarks on the unpredictability of elections? Or do we accept that it's a lottery – some might work, others will end in violence – and do it anyway?

On 4 June 2009, President Barack Obama unfolded his view on imposing Western-style democracy on societies that did not want it. Coincidentally, his speech came twenty years to the day that Chinese troops opened fire on pro-democracy students in Beijing at a time when many in the West clamoured for elections and full democracy in China.

Speaking at Cairo University, President Obama made clear his caution about electoral democracy and his understanding of other cultures. He emphasized that 'no system of government could or should be imposed upon one nation by any other', adding:

> But I do have an unyielding belief that all people yearn for certain things: the ability to speak your mind and have a say in how you are governed; confidence in the rule of law and the equal administration of justice; government that is transparent and doesn't steal from the people; the freedom to live as you choose. Those are not just American ideas, they are human rights, and that is why we will support them everywhere.

Even before his election in August 2008 Obama told *Time* magazine: 'If we think that we can just plunge in and, say, create a democracy from scratch in five years, then we're badly mistaken.' And less than a month later, in Britain, the Conservative leader, David Cameron had agreed, saying: 'Democracy should be the work of patient craftsmanship and not of a uniform mass production line, if the final product is to be of a quality that endures.'

My own curiosity about this began in the early 1990s when I was posted to Hong Kong in the final days of British colonial rule. China was then an international pariah after its troops opened fire on democracy protesters in Tiananmen Square in 1989. As the Berlin Wall came down and millions in Europe and the Soviet Union embarked on the democratic path, China clamped down, convinced that if it allowed more personal freedom the country would be torn apart.

The people of Hong Kong were terrified. In 1997, Britain's tenure would run out and they would be ruled by China. There was no question of them getting the type of full democracy or independence that so many other societies sought by right. But they did not go to the barricades. Instead, they blended peaceful protest marches with keeping their day jobs and making money. The British colonial government and, it turned out, the non-democratic Chinese one gave them enough dignity, wealth and freedom to make democracy a worthy vision, but not one worth dying for.

The title of this book, *Democracy Kills*, was handed to me in a chance conversation in the Middle East. While writing it, I became embroiled in many difficult discussions, often with people who believed I was trying to create an updated version of Hitler's *Mein Kampf* or an apology for Chinese repression in Tibet or the Sudanese government's atrocities in Darfur. I had thought of using a more opaque title such as *The*

Democracy Delusion or a nod to an irritating road repair sign like *Danger – Democracy at Work*. But I opted to address the issue head on when I found again and again that many in the West saw the issue as one that did not merit a debate. To them, it seemed to be more about creating a mirror of our own societies than solving the problems of the developing world. The argument is not whether the end result of establishing democratic government is a good or bad thing. Rather it is the fact that if democracy is not implemented carefully, the process could cause the deaths of a lot of people and fail to deliver dignity and good governance.

The question posed by this book can be put at every stage with every story that follows. There is not a universal answer to what's so good about having the vote. But we should not be afraid to enquire because the only stupid question is the one we never ask.

AFRICA

IVORY COAST – Democracy's Shame

In a tear-wrenchingly poor and fly-blown village near the Ivory Coast town of Oumé, I was taken to see a mud hut, with a thatched roof, dirt floor and holes knocked in the walls for windows.

It was on the edge of the village square, a space of arid, yellow dirt, surrounded by trees. Straw huts stretched back from it towards undergrowth, and on the other side down a slight slope were piles and piles of cocoa, tiny dark brown flat beans speckled like crocodile skin, making the hot air around them smell of bitter musk. Some were in sacks. Some were loose. Women sorted through them.

The hut itself was filled with children, in sun-faded, ragged clothes, with one common injury – hacking scars around their ankles where they had cut themselves on machete blades. Their wounds had come from cutting cocoa and their ages ranged from four to fourteen.

'This is our pilot project,' said George Bredou, the local official showing me around. 'We built this school a month ago.'

Cocoa is the raw material used to make chocolate, and the project Bredou was referring to was meant to be part of a multi-million dollar programme paid for by the global chocolate companies. Their aim, so they said, was to stop cocoa farmers using children in forced labour gangs.

The chocolate industry is worth up to US$70 billion a year

and is synonymous with household brands such as Cadbury, Nestlé, Mars and Hershey, names that many of us grew up with, the currency of childhood parties, presents, little luxuries and a sweet tooth. Almost half of the world's cocoa is grown in the Ivory Coast on what are known as 'plantations', although this is too expansive a word to describe the one or two acres that barely earns enough to live on.

The cocoa-farming families mostly live without sanitation, electricity, telephone or fundamental amenities. The roads are so badly maintained that schools, clinics and shops are often out of reach. Farmers are also unable to get to the markets where they could barter a better price for their beans. The buyer comes to them and dictates the price. Either the farmer sells or starves.

Fresh from London, armed with website printouts from the chocolate companies, I stared dumbfounded at the mud-hut school. The hut would have cost barely a hundred dollars to build. Its walls were of dried, brown mud, the windows square gaps within it. The roof was thatched. The villagers built it themselves. They did not get paid. The desks, books and blackboard had been supplied by USAID, the American government charity organization. Not a penny, from what I could work out, came from the chocolate industry.

Brushing away flies, letting the sweat soak into my shirt, I must have stood for a full five minutes trying to get my head around this. I had almost called off the trip here because I had imagined a village with paved roads, neat gardens, a newly built school, clinic and orphanage and so on – something to show off.

I walked across to Bredou to double-check with him when the school had been built. 'Yes. One month ago,' he said.

The children in the school were tiny, malnourished, in scrappy clothes, but their faces showed the instincts and expressions of a child's hope. Did they like the school? I asked, and all hands shot up amid peals of laughter. What about the cocoa plantations? They fell quiet. Some shook their heads. Most kept their eyes down. One girl screwed up her face and howled as if she imagined a monster intruding into her bedroom. She was five years old.

Bredou took us to see his boss in the local government offices.[1] It was only a few miles away, but the drive took us more than an hour because of the appalling road. The head of the Oumé prefecture was a civil servant named Thomas Lasme, a tall, powerful man who dwarfed the shabby wooden desk he sat behind. His office phones didn't work. Heat seeped into the room, sapping strength. Sunbeams danced through slatted windows onto stacked-up files whose top sheets were being blown about by a fan.

'What happened to the pilot project?' I asked.

'Children aren't working in the cocoa plantations,' he said defensively. 'They're merely taking part in family life.'

'That's not what I asked,' I said. 'What happened to the pilot project in Oumé.'

'It is proceeding as planned.'

'But the school,' I pressed. 'The pilot projects should have started in 2002. Why did it take five years to build a mud hut? And why has so little been done?'

He took off his large spectacles, laid them gently on the desk, rubbed his eyes and made a complete and astounding U-turn. 'Actually,' he said, 'the programme's been halted. It's ended.'

He read my expression of incredulity, nodded and rested his chin on his hands.

---

1 Very often I travelled with a cameraman and interpreter. On those occasions I will use the term 'we'.

'But you've only just opened it,' I said.

'We haven't seen any of their money. We built it ourselves. They didn't do anything.'

'But the promises?'

'Nothing, and we need everything. Money, training, vehicles to take the children from the plantations, places for the children to stay.'

The Ivory Coast cocoa trade is a snapshot, but it encapsulates many of the causes of why Africa is failing – a commodity sought by the West, extreme poverty and a state that collapsed into civil war because its weak institutions could not withstand political pressures. Much is to do with the society itself and how appallingly people treat each other. But this will not move forward substantively until Western democracies examine (as we will shortly) why children are harvesting cocoa for us to eat chocolate.

In the 1960s, as Africa was decolonizing, its raw materials were seen as a source of wealth. Now, they have become a symbol of exploitation. The Cold War allowed multinational companies to continue their trade, while dictators plundered. The Cold War's end ushered in Western-style democracy that bought the free-market system as its ally. Take one and you had to take both – which was how the International Monetary Fund and bankers wrote their loans. But, far from progressing, the continent slipped backward and the United Nations now estimates that between 2009 and 2015 the number of those workers living with their families on less than US$1 a day will actually increase by 20 per cent.

I began visiting Ivory Coast just over ten years after the dictator, Félix Houphouët-Boigny, had died. Houphouët-Boigny was a traditional 'big man' of Africa who, like many of his colleagues, failed to plan for a smooth succession. Under his rule from 1960 to 1993, encouraged by the chocolate companies, the Ivory Coast became the cocoa capital of the world. Now it produces almost half of the global supplies. Drawing on expertise from French technocrats, the country became rich. But Houphouët-Boigny was not a free-marketeer, and he knew only too well that to succeed his people had to be kept happy. He protected his farmers from dramatic falls in prices and always ensured they made a living.

His death left a vacuum that was filled by the fashion of the time – elections and a free-market economy. No leader emerged powerful enough to control the lure of tribal, religious and cocoa-dollar cliques, all of which proved stronger that the institutions Houphouët-Boigny bequeathed. Elections delivered up those who thought victory was the right to take all. It produced losers who became afraid and lashed out. The free market cut down the cocoa farmers' safety net and the price of cocoa plummeted to only a quarter of what it had been forty years earlier. The farmers became so poor they couldn't afford to hire adult workers. So they used children instead who were easier to control and cost far less.

Year by year, the Ivory Coast unravelled. Tribalism, religion and power-grabs were its underbelly and cocoa made the stakes high enough to kill for. By 2002 war had broken out. Cocoa dollars in their tens of millions funded both sides and prolonged the violence.[2] Thousands died. Hundreds of thousands were displaced. More than 40 per cent of the Ivory Coast, once one of the wealthiest and most stable countries in Africa, ended up living in poverty.

As end-users, Western multinationals detached themselves.

---

2 'Hot Chocolate: How Cocoa Fuelled the Conflict in Côte d'Ivoire' (Global Witness, 2007).

They cast their nets toward Indonesia and Bolivia to see if they could secure cocoa supplies from elsewhere.

I first heard reports of child slavery in the cocoa trade back in 2000, six years before meeting Thomas Lasme in Oumé. My automatic reaction then was to ring around the chocolate companies to see what was being done about it. After a couple of calls, I sensed that something truly dreadful was happening. When asking simple questions such as 'Where do you buy your cocoa from?' it turned out they didn't know. When I asked if they thought they should know, they said it was not really their business. One press officer shouted that reports of illegal child labour were all untrue and slammed down the phone. The Ivory Coast embassy wrote to the BBC warning us against covering the story.

Each chocolate company pointed me towards a trade organization called the Biscuit, Cake, Chocolate and Confectionery Association (BCCCA). No executive from any major company would speak on this issue. Nor would I be allowed to film inside a chocolate factory. I have filmed at insurgent training camps and inside nuclear weapons plants, and never had I imagined being banned from filming people making chocolate.

The BCCCA also claimed the issue was now over because the 'industry' – as they called the chocolate companies – had researched the allegations and found there was not a problem. It turned out that this research had been carried out from someone's desk in Britain. No researcher had been to the Ivory Coast.

A few days later, I was in the Malian town of Sikasso close to the Ivory Coast. It was a hot, noisy place with that edgy seediness you get when people and goods move conspiratorially across borders. Minibuses circled the market. The dirt streets were piled with boxes and contraband wrapped in bright cloth. Drivers counted money. Three prostitutes, in bright mini-skirts, smoked in the awning shade of a kiosk. Two policemen, their car door opened for the light breeze, listened to a soccer match on the radio. On a scrap of grassless land, children played football with oil drums as goal posts. It was from here that children had either been sold or kidnapped and sent across the border to work on the Ivory Coast cocoa farms.

The Malian government kept a detailed record of child slavery in files at the Ministry for the Protection of Women, Children and the Family. Its official in Sikasso, Assitan Coulibaly, compiled lists in a huge book of those children who had escaped or been rescued, each entry neatly hand-written with name, age, when they went missing, when they returned and which plantation they worked on.

'Everyone knows that children are working on these plant-ations,' said Coulibaly. 'This is a typical one.' She pointed to a boy who was kidnapped when he was eleven and had only managed to escape six years later aged seventeen. His name was clearly written as Moumino Syllo, with his age, and his home village – Banankomo, just outside of Sikasso.

'And, here,' continued Coulibaly, her finger sliding across the page. 'This is where he was held.' Printed in ballpoint pen in capital letters in French was 'N'peo, Bangalo, near Man' – as precise an address as you would get in the Ivory Coast cocoa belt. Coulibaly promised to help me find him.

'Have any of these chocolate companies been in touch with you at all?' I asked. 'Or been here to help?'

'No,' she said, closing the book. 'No one has been here and spoken to us.'

Abusive child labour, as it's officially known by the International Labour Organization (ILO), has been going on in Africa for thousands of years, and on the cocoa farms at least for the past hundred – since our Western palates developed a taste for chocolate. The chocolate companies would have known about it, but back then children were used as human chimney sweeps in Dickensian London and African-American toddlers were picking lettuces in the American South.

As our democracies developed, two elements of how we raise children became illegal in ILO conventions. A child has to go to school, and the work must not be forced or dangerous. These conventions were not new. The schooling convention was introduced in 1919 and modified in 1921. Forced labour dated back to 1930 and was modified in 1999 to include the 'worst forms of child labour' for anyone under the age of eighteen. Multinational corporations were well aware of their duties to modern democracy – except they claimed they were not responsible for those actually working on the cocoa farms.

Near Coulibaly's office, Save the Children, Canada, ran a sanctuary for children who had escaped or been freed. It was a large warehouse-style building on the edge of town set in a yard surrounded by high walls. The local representative, Salia Kante, became more agitated and angry as he told the story of the centre. In the communal area on the first floor were photographs of the wounds inflicted on the children. Some had bloodied welts on their shoulders where they had been made to carry sacks of cocoa. Others bore scars around the wrists where they had been tied up or chained to posts to stop them escaping.

'People who drink cocoa and eat chocolate should think what they are doing,' said Kante, 'because they're doing no better than drinking the blood of these children. What are they thinking about? Look at the heavy sack that a child is made to carry. It's so heavy that it cuts them and they work with blood dripping down their shoulders.'

A short drive from the centre we found Moumino Syllo, the boy listed in Coulibaly's book. He was now eighteen. He was stacking firewood into a neat pile on the edge of a cluster of huts that made up his family's compound. It was a poor settlement, existing on the very basics. While Syllo worked, two women swept the earth into an elaborate pattern as if it were an exotic carpet. Another cooked on an open fire, with pots arranged in an artistic pyramid, each one spotless. Some men worked with Syllo. Others sat around a draughts game. It was a scene that I would come across time and time again in Africa, one that kept posing that overwhelming question as to why, if the people took such pride in what they had, was the continent failing so badly.

Syllo said he had been playing soccer when he was lured away by someone offering a place in a soccer club in the Ivory Coast. As soon as he was across the border, he was taken to a cocoa plantation.

'They drove me to a remote place,' he recalled. 'When we arrived, I saw it was a cocoa farm. I was very frightened and said I didn't know how to do this kind of work. A man, the owner of the plantation, said I would be paid. Then he took all my papers away from me. I worked until my clothes were rags. At the end of the first year, the other boys and I asked for our salary. But they refused to give it, and said we would be paid at the end of the second year. At the end of the second year, he said he would pay us at the end of the third year. I thought of escaping. But one boy who tried to escape was caught. They beat him and cut the soles of his feet so he couldn't run away again. But he ran away again and this time reached the Malian consul in Bouaké. He was a kind man who came and rescued us all.'

17

The Malian consul's name was Abdoulaye Macko and he was responsible for freeing hundreds of Malian children from cocoa farm slavery. He became the classic whistle blower, exposing an issue that governments and multinationals would have preferred to have kept quiet.[3]

In early 2002, I went back to Sikasso and again sought out Salia Kante and Assitan Coulibaly. In the interim, one of those unique events that combine human suffering, the media and politicians had forced the chocolate companies to concede there was a problem.

In April 2001, human rights groups reported that a tramp steamer, MV *Etireno*, was heading for the Ivory Coast with as many as two hundred children on board destined for forced labour on the cocoa farms. The story played all around the world. Journalists headed for West Africa and found how easy it was to gather evidence of child labour. Two Democratic American politicians, Senator Tom Harkin and Congressman Eliot Engel, drew up a protocol for the chocolate companies to promise to end child slavery in the cocoa trade. They tested congressional reaction and won a 291 to 115 approval for a move to introduce 'slave free' labelling on all cocoa-based products.

The chocolate companies buckled. They pledged to 'identify and eliminate the worst forms of child labour' in 50 per cent of the cocoa farms in West Africa by July 2005. The agreement became known as the Harkin–Engel Protocol, and I had gone back to Sikasso with plans to drive from there through the Ivorian cocoa belt to Abidjan and report on the progress being made under the terms of the protocol.

---

3 Carol Off, *Bitter Chocolate – Investigating the Dark Side of the World's Most Seductive Sweet* (Random House, Canada, 2006).

Coulibaly brought out her huge book again and we sat on the same office verandah as before while she showed me pages of new entries of freed children over the past year.

'Has anybody from chocolate industry come to see you yet?' I asked.

'Not yet,' she said.

'Has anybody written to you?'

'No. Nobody has written to us.'

'Has anybody talked to the children?'

'No.'

'Why is that, do you think?'

'I don't know. Maybe they don't think it's a problem.'

'What about you? Do you think it's a problem?'

She shrugged and dropped her eyes. 'What about you?' she challenged, jabbing her finger at the list of names. 'Do you think it's a problem?'

At the Save the Children centre, Salia Kante took me upstairs to meet four children who had recently been freed. Their names were Souleymane Dembele, aged thirteen; Nouhoum Kone, twelve, Seriba Keita, ten, Karim Sadibe, twelve. I first saw them as four shadows cast by the fierce sunlight on a whitewashed wall. A fan was cooling them, and its breeze blew a sheet of paper off a table. Seriba Keita darted across to pick it up. Then with terror on her face he handed it to a woman who was looking after them.

The woman squatted down and pulled the child to her chest. 'You mustn't be afraid,' she said. 'We are like your parents. Whatever you want to do, do. Whatever is here, belongs to you. This is your home.'

Their stories followed a similar pattern to that of Moumino Syllo. Except Syllo was taken in 1994 and this was eight years later in 2002. 'I was playing football,' said Karim Sadibe. 'This man said I should come with him to the Ivory Coast. He would sign me up for the national team and I would get lots of money and that I shouldn't tell my parents.'

Sadibe was lucky enough to have been intercepted by the Malian police at the border. The man who was with him melted away. As he was telling his story Moussa Doumbia came into the room. He had escaped two years ago and was now twenty and was helping around the centre.

'I don't know how one human being can treat another in the way they treated me,' he whispered. He told how at night he slept on the floor in a locked room. He was given food once a day. If he complained, he was beaten and, as with Syllo, the boys who were caught escaping had their feet cut with razors.

Kante and I sat in a shaded area under the outside steps coming down from the first floor. I showed him a copy of the Harkin–Engel Protocol. We translated key parts of it to him, telling him that the chocolate companies had promised to end child slavery. Surprise and disbelief spread across his face.

'I don't know anything about this,' he said.

'So nobody has been here to talk to you about it?'

'Nobody.'

'Why not, do you think?'

'They must think these children are just slaves and this is a normal situation for Third World countries,' he said. He rubbed his fingers on his forehead and glanced to where the children were chatting above us. 'On these cocoa farms, there are no schools. It is very hard, and if they do anything wrong at all they are treated violently. Those are the conditions that make a child become a terrorist.'

The next day we drove across the border to the Ivory Coast. It was six months after 9/11, and Kante had raised the spectre of a belt of terror breeding across the developing world, an uneducated underclass, their emotions deadened by brutality, lashing out with the self-justification of the victim. In the Middle East it was about Israel. In Afghanistan, it was blow-back from the Soviet invasion. In West Africa, it was about the exploitation of commodities.

I thought Kante might have been taking advantage of the post-9/11 atmosphere to argue his case, ramping things up for the visiting reporter. But I was wrong.

We drove down undulating hill country, a single dark bitumen strip of road, flanked by orange earth and arid undergrowth. Diesel fumes belched from trucks and overloaded buses. We weaved between them while avoiding deep potholes.

Not far inside the Ivory Coast, the checkpoints began. A plank of wood embedded with spikes on wheels was pushed across the road to rip your tyres apart if you crossed without permission.

Ballo, our Malian interpreter and fixer, who had been with me the previous year, immediately sensed the tension. Fred Scott, our camera operator, picked out the different uniforms, army, police, paramilitary – a bad sign that indicated there were rival groups muscling against each other for power and money. Fred hid his camera on the floor of our vehicle, then when past he filmed with a smaller camera, easier to conceal.

But we were caught. At the next checkpoint, we were flagged down, ordered out of the vehicle and up to a shack by the side of the road. A large figure in military fatigues and wrap-around dark glasses sat on a low bamboo stool. Men in different uniforms hung around with him. If Hollywood had wanted to portray decaying and violent Africa, here it was. He asked for our passports and Ballo's papers and spread them out on a low table in front of him.

I took out the business card of the Ivory Coast ambassador I had met in London. Recognizing the flag in the corner of the card, he moved his shades up his forehead to examine it more closely, showed it to a soldier standing next to him, who laughed and handed it back. Our host dropped the business card and ground it into the earth with the heel of his boot.

Ballo, a schoolteacher by profession, talked continuously in a low, relaxed tone, using French and the local dialect, and negotiated for them to let us back to the car. 'I will join you soon,' he said.

When Ballo returned and climbed in, the guards wheeled back the spikes to let us pass. We put the cameras away and arrived at the regional capital of Bouaké by nightfall.

Our hotel happened to be staging the Miss Bouaké 2002 beauty pageant, and we had dinner in the garden watching young women in brightly coloured West African dress walk up and down past us. I paid Ballo for the checkpoint bribe and with a smile he gave me back the card of the Ivorian ambassador from London. It was dirt-smeared and marked with a boot print. 'That chief said it would be more useful to you once we get across the border.'

'I thought we were across the border,' I said.

'Not the Malian border,' said Ballo shaking his head. 'He is a commander of the northern rebels. We are going to the south.'

The beauty queens balanced baskets on their heads to show their posture. Their parents had come to watch. Guests applauded.

'Rebels?' I asked.

'Yes. Soon they will be fighting.'

'What about?'

'The cocoa,' said Ballo. 'Everyone fights over the cocoa.'

*

In the morning, shortly after we left Bouaké heading south the parched bush land turned into deep green jungle, and Ballo announced that we were entering the cocoa belt. We were also crossing the north–south divide that Ballo had described, a frontier of the type that ran through Africa creating complex underbellies. Bouaké marked a tribal, geographic and economic division that was soon to be the front line of the Ivory Coast's civil war. It divided a swathe of Islamic communities to the north and Christian ones that stretched down to the coast. Intermingled were numerous tribes with their own loyalties and grievances. And to the west, Liberia's warlords, who had already destroyed their own country, were looking to expand into the Ivory Coast to get their hands on the cocoa. They were drawing up plans for raiding parties and ethnic cleansing. As we drove south through the cocoa belt, war was only four months away.

The Ivory Coast had a particular set of problems that led it to war. But it was also a mirror of what happens in much of Africa. Substitute cocoa for diamonds, oil or other commodities needed by the West, insert a supply chain disparity of extreme wealth and poverty, ally that to a corrupt government, inject the unpredictability of elections, sprinkle on it historical, tribal and religious prejudices, and you have a mix of lethal ingredients. Those basic needs of food, shelter, dignity and future come face to face with power manipulation that turns human energy into violence, jealousy and revenge. This is what Salia Kante was referring to when he made his grim prediction at his children's sanctuary in Sikasso.

The late dictator Houphouët-Boigny had celebrated the wealth that cocoa gave him by building monuments to himself. He turned his ancestral village of Yamassoukro into the administrative capital where he commissioned the massive Basilica of Our Lady of the Peace, which became the largest church in the world. He created a lake of man-eating crocodiles (no one is quite sure why) and put up the time-warped Hotel President for tourists and dignitaries that we checked into when we arrived. The hotel opened to a fanfare in the 1980s and then stayed exactly as it was, its once lavish designs fading and becoming mouldy from humidity and broken-down air conditioning.

Outside in the car park were huge four-by-fours and black limousines with darkened windows. Inside, there was a conference buzz, men in dark suits, women in bright tribal dress, soldiers watching and conversations in French, English and a cocktail of West African dialects. Music wafted in from the garden, where lights shone over the swimming pool.

We had chanced upon a summit of the New Partnership for Africa's Development (NEPAD), an organization recently set up to try to end African poverty. The idea was to empower people at the grass roots and give them what they needed to solve their own problems. I checked into a cavernous bordello-like room, with a purple bedspread, pink telephone, and dark-blue wallpaper, then collected glossy brochures and statements from chocolate companies that I'd brought from London, and headed down to gatecrash the conference delegates over their dinner.

Dr Francis Appiah, Ghana's representative to NEPAD, asked me to join his table. After graduating from university in Ghana, Appiah did his doctorate in Norway, and had become a substantive figure in promoting African good governance. His suit jacket hung on the back of his chair and he wore a pink shirt and silk tie. Passionate about his subject, he leant forward, elbows on the table and his hands together prayer-like. 'You have to look at the conditions of the poor people who are keeping these multinationals in business,' he said. 'If they were given a fair price for their crops, they could move on. But they are at the mercy of the chocolate industry.'

24

One of his colleagues chipped in: 'If they've had it so good for so long, it's very difficult to give up bad habits.'

'We have given so much,' continued Dr Appiah. 'It's about time they met us halfway.'

'How could they do that?' I asked.

'We began production of cocoa at the turn of the last century. By now we should be producing chocolate in our own country, but the Western governments are putting all sorts of obstacles in the way that prevent us from doing that. Under the present system, we cannot make our own chocolate because the import tariffs would be too high. The tariff on a raw cocoa bean is a fraction of the tariff on a wrapped bar of chocolate.'

'And what happens if they don't meet you halfway,' I asked.

'Nobody wants to create the conditions that lead to another 9/11,' he said. 'They have to understand that they must improve the conditions of those who have kept them in business for almost a century.'

I pulled out a statement from Cadbury-Schweppes that said the previous year it had launched an ethical trading initiative in Ghana with a number of pilot studies. I had pressed the company as to where the studies were and what exactly they were doing, but Cadbury-Schweppes had refused to say. As Appiah read the statement he tightened his lips and cupped his hand against his chin. Ghana supplied Cadbury-Schweppes with 60 per cent of its cocoa, which made up half the country's export revenue.

'Has anybody told you about these initiatives?' I asked.

'No,' he said.

'If they had been happening, would you have known about them?'

'I would certainly have known about them,' he replied.

*

We weren't sure how difficult it would be to find children working. Would the farms be guarded? Would our white faces be an impediment? How long would it take to get off the beaten track and deep enough into the cocoa belt? Should we just use the small camera? Should Ballo go on a recce first? Where exactly should we go? We reckoned we had one shot only before the police cottoned on and stopped us.

Each option had its flaw. None was safe, so in the morning – armed with a plantation name from Coulibaly's book – we just headed off, the three of us and the driver, along the main road toward a town called Sinfra. Just beyond it, we turned down a dirt track and came to a settlement where a group of men were walking across the road swinging machetes. Wooden huts were set around a tree. Men sat on the tree roots that had sprung out of the ground. Others squatted on stools. Ballo got out and asked. The men pointed for us to drive further along the track. They were uninterested. They had come back from a morning's work and were sheltering from the sun.

Once past the huts the track narrowed into a single lane with deeply ridged potholes that scraped the bottom of the vehicle. The driver slowed and then a work gang of children came around a corner. Some wore sandals. Some had rubber boots. Some were bare-chested. One had a khaki waistcoat torn into strips. One wore a yellow shirt, its logo too faded to read. One had a Nelson Mandela T-shirt. Most were bare-headed, but one had a floppy baseball cap decorated with red flowers. An older one, who turned out to be the gangmaster, was pushing a bicycle. I counted ten others and reckoned the youngest must have been six or seven. All of them carried machetes.

As Ballo talked to them, another gang of children passed. After that came a group of women with baskets on their heads.

'Some are from Mali,' said Ballo. 'Some are from Burkino Faso. 'The gangmaster says they are working on his mother's farm.'

The gangmaster's name was Bakary Diarra; he was slightly better dressed in a freshly laundered red sports shirt. But he was only fifteen, legally a child himself. At first he was arrogant, then defensive, then his face filled with confusion – a boy who should have been at school with teachers was charged with forcing children to work.

First he said the children were all his brothers. As we pushed him, he claimed they were part of a school field trip. Then the children themselves chipped in, saying it wasn't true.

'We work the whole day in the field,' said one, wiping his face with the bottom of his filthy shirt. 'In the sun. Bent over. It is terrible.'

The others nodded. Ballo asked if they got paid. They shook their heads, and Diarra tried to correct them.

'He says they are paid about . . .' He broke off to calculate. '. . . a dollar fifty or a pound a day.' One of the older boys shouted over and Ballo's forehead creased. 'He says that's between all of them, and they have never been paid.'

Whatever the truth about their work and their payment, it was a Wednesday morning, and under the ILO convention 182 they should have been in the classroom – including Diarra. Under ILO convention 138 they should not have been carrying machetes because of the risks of injuring themselves. We were less than an hour's drive from the NEPAD conference at our hotel.

I took a note of their names.[4] Only one said he knew his age – thirteen. The younger ones were confused about who

---

4 Kone Duissa, Berthe Dio, Konate Issouf, Dagniko Salif, Diarra Moussa, thirteen (the only one who knew his age), Sonogo Yacouba, Sonogo Abou, Brou Kouame Honore, Sanogo Sioka and Kone Lassima.

their parents were. Their eyes went blank or fell to the ground.

After talking to them, it was a strange moment. Pushing his bicycle, Diarra led them off down the track. Ballo advised us not to follow, but to leave before someone alerted the police and our tape was confiscated. We filmed them disappearing around a corner, the path narrowing with high green vegetation on both sides. Two boys lingered to look back. I guessed they were about ten. It was as if they were wondering who we were and what world we came from. For a few moments, they stared straight at us, then with a swing of their machetes, they turned decisively and vanished into the bush.

Back in London, I gave their names to the Ivorian embassy and to Bob Eagle from the BCCCA, who had agreed to be interviewed. Once again, Nestlé, Mars, Cadbury and the others had refused to take part. We sat in Eagle's central London office looking at the photographs of the children. It was unacceptable, he said.

I told him that we had found them by going through Coulibaly's records in Sikasso. I showed him photocopies I had taken from her book, and asked why nobody from the chocolate industry had been to see her.

'The objective of the surveys is to look at what is going on in the field, in the cocoa-growing areas themselves, right now,' he said.

'Not to see the children themselves,' I ventured.

'I think if we look at the detail and objectives it is very much about what is going on in the villages and towns.'

I told him about Appiah's view from NEPAD that the poverty of the cocoa farmer was keeping the multinational in business – paying Bob Eagle's salary, for example.

'What we need to do is to make sure we can deliver as much

cash into the pockets of the farmers as we possibly can,' he said.

'All right,' I asked, 'have you got a price in your mind that needs to be paid to do that?'

'The world market price is the world market price,' he said, stumbling on the words as he spoke. 'And it varies according to whether or not demand is exceeding supply or supply is exceeding demand.'

So often we hear the mantra of free trade and the world market price, cited with an ideological fervour comparable to that of Red Guards waving Mao Zedong's *Little Red Book* – as if reform would ruin life as we know it.

Five years later, I set off for the Ivory Coast again. The chocolate companies had failed to meet the protocol deadline of July 2005, claiming conditions, including the war, had made it too difficult. They had negotiated a new deadline with Harkin and Engel in Washington in July 2008.

This was the first time I had returned since meeting Bakary Diarra and his child-labour gang near Yamassoukro. War had broken out. The country was now divided. Bouaké was the capital of the rebel breakaway north. French troops were deployed to keep the peace.

My original plan had been to retrace our journey from Sikasso in Mali to the Ivory Coast's commercial capital, Abidjan, dropping in on Coulibaly with her register of child slaves on the way. But we wouldn't have made it past Bouaké. So I flew to Abidjan with Keith Morris as cameraman. We linked up with Ange Amboa, an Ivorian who covered the cocoa beat for Reuters, to work as our fixer. Because of the numerous dialects we would encounter, Ange brought along Kone, a linguist, to act as our interpreter.

Before leaving London, I had called around the chocolate

companies, hoping for a changed attitude. I was disappointed. There was still no filming in a chocolate factory and still no interviews with any executives. But the BCCCA did point me to a new organization called the International Cocoa Initiative, which I was told would speak on behalf of the industry.

Its head, Peter McAllister, was a veteran of aid agencies and the developing world, and happened to be in Abidjan when we got there. When we met, he quickly distanced himself from the role of chocolate industry representative.

'We've had some very difficult discussions with industry,' he said, 'trying to educate them to the reality, trying to help them think through their role and trying to encourage active engagement over many years. We've won some of those battles, but sometimes we're frustrated.'

'You mean they don't quite get it?'

'I was told very early on "We don't do development" and I said you have to learn because you have supply chains that enter developing countries. You have to have a better understanding of the issues.'

Some chocolate companies built cradle-to-grave communities in their own countries, ensuring safeguards for workers that were denied in many other industries. In Britain in 1879, Cadbury began to create Bournville just outside Birmingham, and in the early twentieth century Hershey created a town in its own name in Pennsylvania with schools, orphanages and so on. But, as Peter McAllister found out, there appeared to be a line drawn between caring for staff who processed chocolate and the farmers and their families who grew the cocoa beans.

If Western multinationals didn't get it, it seemed the Ivorian government didn't either. That evening we met two officials in the prime minister's secretariat handling the child slavery issue. They worked in a guarded, whitewashed, high-ceilinged

French colonial building in Abidjan whose shabby corridors smelt of rain. Youssoof N'Djore was a slim, athletic man in his early forties and Acquah Assouan Amouan was a matronly figure with a striking blue and white dress, a woman of great presence.

I had brought a carrier bag filled with various chocolate bars that we spread out on a table to make the interview more visual. I asked when we would see the certification on the wrapper as promised in the Cocoa Protocol.

'They won't have a stamp on it,' said Amouan, turning a bar of Kit Kat in her hand.

'But I thought that was what the chocolate companies had promised,' I said.

'It's not a question of a stamp.'

N'Djore picked up a chocolate bar and examined it. 'You will not see any difference to the wrapper,' he said. 'The protocol is an obligation to have a system running, not to have the cocoa certified.'

I wasn't sure what that meant. In fact, everyone I spoke to seemed to have a different interpretation of what had been promised in the protocol. But the text was precise – 'the development of global, industry-wide standards and independent monitoring, reporting and public certification to identify and eliminate any usage of the worst forms of child labor in the growing and processing of cocoa beans'.

I cited that to N'Djore. He dropped the bar of chocolate onto the table and leant back in his chair. 'This is a protocol for your society,' he said. 'Not for us.'

'But you signed it.'

'Yes. We were asked to.'

Ange, who had been leaning silently against a wall, stepped forward and spoke softly in French. His cadence ebbed and flowed, sometimes dropping to a whisper. He was a big man, well over six feet, but he exuded a huge gentleness, mixing humility with favours. In handling the powerful of his societies, Ange knew exactly how to move. He was asking them to suggest somewhere we might go to see how the protocol was being implemented.

'Oumé,' he declared N'Djore. 'This is our pilot project. If you go to Oumé, they will show you everything.'

We went to Oumé and found just the mud-hut school built by villagers just one month earlier and we heard from Thomas Lasme that the money had dried up.

So why isn't it working? Why did the chocolate companies and the Ivorian government sign an agreement with Western democratically elected politicians that they have no will or ability to keep? The whole scenario was littered with paradoxes. The chocolate companies carry out practices that deeply worry their consumers, while the government's policies do little to help their citizens.

One reason is the way the money works. The multinationals are primarily responsible to their shareholders and not to the moral values of the consumer. As long as the consumer keeps buying the product the multinationals believe they are doing their jobs.

In a similar way, the Ivorian government is responsible to those who pay their taxes and bring in revenue. The cocoa farmer himself is so poor that any tax he pays is negligible. The main revenue comes from the tax paid by the international cocoa buyers. The government's economic relationship, therefore, is not with its citizens but with foreign companies. As long as the government keeps the cocoa supply routes open, the revenue will continue to roll in.

The penniless cocoa farmer can only plead for decent roads, schools and hospitals from the position of a victim, not as a revenue-contributing citizen. The only recourse he has is one of protest, which invariably is put down by police or military.

For the society to work, the axis between government, citizen and multinational has to change. The cocoa farmer has to make enough money for his tax payments to be a significant slice of the government's revenue. And in the West, consumers have to stop buying morally suspect products to such an extent that the company's shareholders feel threatened. This has been happening over the years with some success in the Fair Trade industry where multinationals pay farmers a set price that allows them to build clinics and schools and educate their children to a level where they have a choice of career beyond cocoa farming.

Their products carry the stamp of certification that the Ivory Coast government said would not be on the chocolate bars.

From Thomas Lasme's dusty office in Oumé, we headed to Yamassoukro where the war had brought a leaden oppression. We pulled up at the President Hotel just before dark. The police and army were everywhere. Their brand-new vehicles overflowed from the car park and they hung around in the lobby, cigarette smoke blending with the smell of rotting mould from the velvet armchairs. The garden lights were broken. The swimming pool was empty, and prostitutes were at the bar. In my room, little had changed, except that the pink telephone didn't work.

The prime minister was in town, which is why we were there – to doorstep him outside a banquet. Charles Konan Banny, a banker by trade, was a transitional prime minister in a post-war deal hatched by the United Nations, the French and the Organization of African Unity. He walked out of the double doors of the hotel ballroom with an entourage of staff and security guards, a rotund, barrel-chested man in an expensively tailored suit and with an avuncular, shiny face that broke into a huge smile when I asked him about child slavery.

'It doesn't exist,' he said, his eyes flitting toward an aide who nodded. 'Believe me, it is a hundred per cent clean. It has always been a hundred per cent clean. Of course, it's a matter of culture, you know. We don't have slavery children in the field. The first right of a child is to go to school, but going to school does not mean that you should not help your parents if they are working the cocoa plantation. But they should not do hard work. So I'm convinced a hundred per cent that we will be able to certify the cocoa.'

The prime minister swept off down the hallway toward the entrance. He must have had fifty people with him, all with their expensive vehicles supplied through that revenue-building relationship between the government and the multinational.

I had hoped to retrace our steps back to Sinfra and the village where we had found the child slave-gang before. But, the next day, as we filmed general shots around Yamassoukro, we kept getting stopped by police – outside the hotel, near the Basilica, on high ground near an overpass – until Ange advised us to get away from the city altogether. We would go to Soufre, he said, where he knew people and then we'd head down to the big cocoa port at San Pédro.

Once clear of Yamassoukro, we turned off the main road toward the cocoa farms. We passed a sign warning against child trafficking. It was the first indication that anyone was taking any action. It was on a post by the side of the road like an advertisement for a village fete. Keith asked if we should stop and film it. No need, I said, there were bound to be more. But I was wrong. Over the next three days, that was the only one we saw.

We drove deeper into the cocoa belt, heading west toward the border with Liberia. We had to keep stopping to heave wooden planks onto broken bridges so that we could pass. At best the road was peppered with huge, lurching holes. At worst we were driving along a fast-running riverbed. Eventually we even had to abandon our four-wheel-drive and rent a flat-bed truck – the only vehicle that could deal with such appalling conditions.

In the early afternoon, we met Sangone Lamine, a tall, elegant man, dressed in a freshly laundered cotton smock and grey trousers. He had been farming cocoa since 1975 and he lived with his extended family in a cluster of mud huts. Although neatly kept, it was primitive beyond imagination.

When he started out more than thirty years ago, Sangone Lamine said he was being paid 30 pence (US$0.60) a kilo for his cocoa, exactly the same price as he was being paid now. Over the same thirty-year period, the chocolate industry's income had increased more than fourfold and was worth more than US$70 billion a year.

'How much do you need?' I asked, 'to make ends meet?'

We were sitting on low stools in his immaculately brushed earthen front yard. He closed his eyes, thinking deeply, before he answered.

'We need three to four times what we are getting now,' he said, which pretty much matched the inflation rate between then and when he began farming more than thirty years ago. It was also in line with the Fair Trade rate.

His small family settlement was spotless. It reminded me of Moumino Syllo's village in Mali. The ground was swept and the pots washed and smoke rose vertically in the still air from a fire of dried cocoa husks.

A cocoa buyer had been there a couple of days earlier and there didn't seem much work to do. A girl dozed lying on the ground using a pair of blue plastic sandals as a pillow. One of his sons and wife sat on stools, leaning back against the mud wall of the house. Children ran here and there. Sangone's other children had headed off to the cities to find work and bring in money. The family didn't even have a small motorbike. There was no telephone or electricity, of course. They lived in a rhythm of rural Africa, cut off (not least by the appalling condition of the road) from what the think tanks so fashionably call 'civil society'.

Sangone picked up his machete that was leaning against a tree trunk and led us a few yards to where his plantation started. The ground was covered with leaves. Sunlight speckled through. The cocoa pods were light green and hung in clusters like small rugby balls. He plucked one off, held it in the palm of his left hand and made two slices on the pod, one across and one along. Then he flipped off the skin with his thumb.

'Try one,' he said.

The beans were covered in a sticky white milk. I took one out and put it in my mouth. It was very bitter, almost inedible, then slowly that seductive taste that makes a chocolate bar what it is came through. To reciprocate, I asked if he wanted to try some chocolate we had brought.

'Yes,' he said enthusiastically. He had never even seen it.

Tentatively, he pulled a chocolate biscuit out of a packet. He first nibbled, rather as I had done the cocoa bean. Then, as the taste took, he munched it keenly and I gave him the whole packet.

'It's good,' he said. 'Really good.'

'Show him how much it cost,' I asked Kone who was translating.

Kone pointed out the price label. Sangone couldn't read.

So Kone told him. Momentarily, Sangone stopped eating, his mouth filled with chocolate biscuit. His eyes bulged and he asked Kone to repeat.

'Why so much?' he said.

As we walked back, I recalled the complaint of Dr Francis Appiah of NEPAD that export tariffs made it too expensive to produce chocolate here. If that is how the system had been set up, no wonder Sangone had never tasted chocolate. No wonder, also that the system had left Sangone so poor and uneducated. It was as if globalization deliberately did not include those who made the raw products because the extra cost involved would skew – as the chocolate industry's advocate Bob Eagle so delicately put it – that sacrosanct 'world market price'.

We drove deeper into the cocoa belt, bumping through the lush, reeling landscape that was filled with smells of truck diesel and fresh rain. The red-brown dirt of the road had been softened and often collapsed into cavernous flooded potholes.

The further we went the more we saw children with machetes, many with wounds that were untreated because we were far from medical help. At one village, we cleaned wounds and put on antiseptic cream from our basic first aid kit. Then, a few miles on, we found two boys, standing by the side of the road on the edge of a cocoa plantation – and we stopped.

Their names were Marc and Fabrice Kwame. As Kone started talking to them they offered to take us into the plantation. They led us to the farmer, who was talkative and uptight. His name was Kanga John Kwame. The two boys were his sons, he said. They were both aged twelve, but from different mothers, both of whom lived far away.

Kone translated, but added: 'He's hiding things. Anyone can tell. These boys are working cocoa.'

'Ask him why they're not at school,' I said. 'Shouldn't they be at school today?'

'Absolutely. It's Tuesday. Today's a school day.'

Kone fell back into conversation. We were walking through the plantation, moving from sunlight to shade between clumps of cocoa trees. Kwame was bare-chested. Marc and Fabrice had on sandals and ragged sports shorts, so worn that it was impossible to tell the logo.

'He says he is a farmer and he is teaching the boys to be farmers so he is educating them,' said Kone, breaking off from his translation to listen more to Kwame, who was angrily tapping his fingers against his chest.

'He says life is very poor in the Ivory Coast,' translated Kone. 'This is how we live. We make no money.'

We tried to talk to Marc and Fabrice, but Kwame kept interrupting. We left them and pressed on.

The further we went, the worse it became. In village after village, plantation after plantation, we saw children's wounds running septic and covered with flies. Many had dripping noses and protruding stomachs, symptoms of malnourishment. These were the child workers of the chocolate industry, thousands and thousands of them, their illegal work delivering a luxury into Western shops.

We wanted to keep going, but we also needed to get back to the main road before dark. Ange had warned that in the late afternoon checkpoints were set up, some military, some by an agricultural union – all demanding money, all carrying guns, and some of the gunmen drunk.

We turned round and on the way back, standing alone by the side of the road, looking a little lost as if he were waiting for us, was Marc Kwame. From the look on his face, it was clear he wanted to say something, but he didn't seem to know how. He was a child with raw human emotion, but denied everything a child naturally yearns for – a mother, an education, a sense of play and expression. As he spoke, his lip trembled and his eyes filled with sadness.

'He used to go to school,' said Kone, 'but this man who calls himself their father said there was no one to work the farm, so he took him out of school.'

Marc fell silent, his eyes dropping to the ground, then he looked nervously back at the line of trees that marked the start of the plantation.

'And your mother?' I asked.

Marc spoke softly, his fingers pawing his filthy, torn shirt.

'He doesn't know,' said Kone. 'She is far away. He doesn't remember her face and it makes him unhappy.'

We asked Marc where we could buy some cocoa. He pointed to a stall a couple of hundred yards away. We parked the truck and bought a sack.

I wanted to see how the supply chain worked, where the provenance of the bean became obscured, and why the chocolate companies insisted that it was impossible for them to know where their raw product came from – hence disclaiming responsibility. Fifty per cent of the world's cocoa was grown in this country, yet Mars, Nestlé, Hershey and the rest of them said they couldn't source it.

If you buy even a cheap bottle of wine from the supermarket, the chances are it'll tell you exactly where the grape is grown, often with a drawing of the vineyard. But look at most chocolate bars, and you will have no idea where the cocoa bean is grown.

As mentioned a little earlier, the road conditions were appalling partly because the people living here paid no taxes therefore could make no economic demands on the government. Given that the road outside my own house in London is constantly being dug up and resurfaced, it would not have taken much to fix the road along which Sangone Lamine lived. Aid organizations have estimated that whole issue could have been solved, including the building of basic infrastructure, with less than 1 per cent of the chocolate industry's annual revenue.

Because that doesn't happen, the farmers have no choice over whom they sell their cocoa to. The much advocated 'free market' is for the farmer to be given a price dictated by a buyer turning up unannounced in a truck – like we did.

We weighed the sack on a pair of scales, didn't haggle and probably paid way over the odds. We heaved it onto the back of the truck and headed off. As we were waving goodbye to the farmers, I caught sight of Marc Kwame again, half hidden on the edge of the undergrowth, his hand hesitantly raised in a goodbye, but his face was crushed, it seemed, in disappointment that we were leaving.

On the journey back, we paid bribes at more than a dozen checkpoints, each with its own spiked nails embedded in a plank of wood on wheels; each run by a different group of armed men; each putting up the price of the cocoa before it reached the wholesaler. Once off the dirt tracks, we headed down to San Pédro. Darkness fell just outside of town, cooking fires lit the road, their smoke drifting across the windscreen, creating clouded images of headlights. We drove through clusters of people and the encroaching smells of a big city. San Pédro was the cocoa shipping capital of the world.

Like the Hotel President in Yamassoukro, our hotel by the port had been designed as a vision and stopped some decades ago. The rooms had no telephone or Internet. It was a low-rise resort-style complex with rooms wrapped around a swimming pool. The sea was just beyond a line of trees. As the waves broke, the moon lit up fluorescence in the water and just beyond a container ship steamed off heading for Europe or

America with a cargo of cocoa beans. Three French cocoa buyers ate in a desultory restaurant while prostitutes waited at the bar for them to finish.

Ange arranged for us to sell our cocoa through a Lebanese businessman. They were often the middlemen of the cocoa trade, and Ali M. Lakiss of SAF-Cacao was one of the cocoa kings of San Pédro. Multinational brand names also operated here, but they had not replied to our requests to visit them,

Lakiss was refreshingly open. Untainted by spin-doctors, he rose above the chocolate companies' double-speak as he opened up the huge metal doors to his warehouse and trucking centre. Outside the doors were the edgy, tense streets and bush land. Inside was Lakiss's slick, efficient, fast-moving operation, a corner of Africa that had to keep pace with the commodity markets of London and New York.

Lakiss was in his late forties and worked from a raised office that overlooked a vast yard of trucks and pallets piled with cocoa sacks. Lines of workers heaved sack after sack onto their shoulders and loaded them onto trucks. Beyond that was an equally large warehouse with cocoa stacked up, row after row amid the constant whir of forklift trucks. We weren't that far from Sangone Lamine's small settlement. But it wasn't until the cocoa reached here that the real money started being made.

'So you have become the *pisteur*?' said Lakiss, laughing, referring to the name given to the traders who buy cocoa from the farms, then sell to Lakiss. His office was air-conditioned with an array of telephones on his desk, mobile phones and broadband Internet connection directly linked to London Life, one of the main commodity markets. On the screen, the cocoa price changes kept flashing up in red as speculators did their business. Lakiss's eyes kept darting back to the screen. As he talked, he jabbed a button and laughed. 'Ah, you bring me luck,' he said. 'I have just sold. I have become a millionaire today.'

At his desk sat two of the French businessmen we'd seen in the hotel the night before. They didn't say a word, even when Lakiss introduced us.

'This system,' I asked Lakiss. 'Is it fair, because many of the farmers are so poor?'

He shrugged, most of his thoughts on the changing prices far away in London. 'Yes, it's fair,' he said. 'It's this market which arbitrates between us and the farmer and us and the international chocolate traders. It tells us how to trade.' He pushed a button on his cellphone and began talking. The light on another phone flashed on his desk. 'Go with Nabil,' said Lakiss. 'Before the price changes again. Or you will get less for your cocoa.'

Nabil was Lakiss's brother, a quieter more reflective man. Kone and I heaved the sack off the back of our truck and carried it into a covered area, the floor slippery with spilt cocoa beans. Nabil plunged a knife into the sack and drew out a handful of beans. He took them to table, put them under a lamp, sliced each one in half. He inspected the inside through a magnifying glass and brought each bean up to his nose to smell it. He pushed back his chair, shook his head and talked to Ange.

'He says they have been out in the sun for too long,' translated Ange. 'He cannot give you the full market price.' The price he offered gave us about a 20 per cent mark up on what we paid.

'What about the roadblocks?' I asked. 'Would they have been the same if the truck had been loaded?'

'Maybe the same,' he said thoughtfully. 'But only for the farmer's union. With the military and the police, it is impossible to say.'

'So what went wrong with these beans?'

'The farmers were saying that the last *pisteur*'s truck was full and he could take no more. So they had to wait for the next truck.' That was us, except by the time we came, the beans were going rotten.

Nabil insisted on paying us. Two workers carried our beans outside and threw them onto a truck already loaded with others' sacks. It was here that the exact source of the cocoa became lost. The truck drove off to the port, from where our sack would be loaded on container ships that sailed usually either to Europe or the United States where the beans would be processed into chocolate.

In Europe, I tried talking to politicians about child slavery in the cocoa trade, but they were not interested. They steered the conversations into circular quagmires about millennium goals and global poverty. So I headed to Washington to see what the Democratic Congressman Eliot Engel thought about the impact his protocol was having on the ground in West Africa.

Engel had become involved in the issue in 2001 after seeing a news report about the MV *Etireno* and then a follow-up Knight Ridder investigation exposing the slavery. He was raised in a low-income housing project in the Bronx and familiar with the obstacles of dragging people out of poverty.

With photographs from our Ivory Coast trip spread across the coffee table in his congressional office, Engel, fifty-nine, was visibly angered. 'They're not going to fool me twice,' he said quietly. 'Six years is enough.'

He stared at the pictures of the mud-hut school and Marc and Fabrice Kwame. 'When I first went to the chocolate industry, they were in a state of denial and said I didn't know what I was talking about. But I'm not going to accept any more of their excuses. It's quite one thing for someone to say "Well we're trying our best to meet these standards but it's impossible to do it because of this reason or that reason" – which is essentially what they said in 2005. But, frankly, now I would be in favour of implementing some sanctions.'

'Encapsulate for me, then, what the law would say,' I asked.

'One approach would mandate that every chocolate bar sold in the US would have to have a label that clearly states that this chocolate was processed without any kind of slave labour or child slave labour whatsoever. It would be slave labour free.'

The Chocolate Manufacturers Association (CMA) happened to be holding a lavish reception the same day in the Canon Building at the US Congress. Outside the room were brochures of smiling workers on the plantations. Inside, was the clink of wine glasses. On the guest list was the name of Susan Smith, the spokesperson for the CMA with whom I had been in contact. She had actually sent me an eight-page email about what the industry was doing to help the West African cocoa farmer. Although she mentioned the Harkin–Engel Protocol she did not specify any of its deadlines. Nor did she mention the fly-blown town of Oumé.

I passed my card to a waiter, asking for Susan Smith to come out. Meanwhile, as the door to the room open and closed we filmed snatches of the celebrations inside. One of the guests who emerged was Donald Payne, the recently appointed chairman of the House Foreign Affairs' Subcommittee on Africa and Global Health. He was laughing, and gave a handshake with the grip of an elbow to a besuited man. He stepped away still smiling. I intercepted him and showed him a photograph of Marc and Fabrice Kwame. It was a cheap trick, perhaps, but Payne, the politician, exchanged his smile for an expression of gravity.

He pointed back toward the reception: 'We're going to continue to do all we can to get the industry to stop these abuses,' he said. 'They know that they can no longer do business the way they did business before.'

'And what's your message to these two boys?'

'My message is that the West has to stop exploiting Africa.'

Susan Smith didn't come out of the reception, but she agreed to meet me with her British counterpart Alison Ward on a Friday at the offices of the BCCCA in central London. I was to interview them separately. I talked to Smith first and asked her why the pilot project at Oumé had run out of funds.

'It's a long-term problem,' she replied.

'But they don't have the money they were promised.'

'Actually, you know, I think I've learned that they're moving forward on pilots. It will take a while.'

'Given that your industry has been using cocoa from West Africa for decades, why did it take you so long to get involved? Why did Harkin and Engel have to push you?'

'We've been involved since the 1940s and we've been involved with helping children and families since 2000, since the protocol.'

'Engel told me that your industry was hostile, that it accused him of exaggeration and getting his facts wrong.'

'The industry has been concerned with children and the cocoa farming community for a long time. What we know is that children work with their families on the cocoa farms, just like I did. I grew up on a farm and I helped my parents on a farm. That's the kind of things that children do.'

'Is there abusive labour in the Ivory Coast?'

'Children are on farms all over the world—'

'No. My question is: Is there in the Ivory Coast cocoa industry?'

'With regard to children in West Africa—'

'Is there or isn't there?'

'There are issues with children. But progress is being made to help those children and that's really the question you're asking – what kind of progress is being made? And it takes a long time because it's a change in the way people think but there are definitely solutions in progress.'

'The prime minister, Charles Banny, told us in the Ivory Coast that there wasn't a problem, that it was a hundred per cent clean.'

'I don't know what the prime minister told you. I was at a meeting yesterday when Ghana—'

'We're talking about the Ivory Coast.'

'As you know there's a civil war in the Ivory Coast and there are pilots moving forward in the Ivory Coast also. The important thing is that Ghana is serving as a model. There are changes that need to be made and they need to be made in the whole of Ivory Coast and West Africa.'

I asked her whether the new target of July 2008 would be adhered to.

'A lot of progress is being made and we're on track to deal with that and Ghana and the Ivory Coast are very involved with that effort.'

'What is the target?'

'We will try to have a goal of 50 per cent of the cocoa communities covered in those countries. Ghana has already done a pilot. The Ivory Coast is behind.'

'Will you meet the target?'

'We are on track.'

I showed her the photograph of the mud-hut school near

Oumé. 'This is the pilot project in Oumé. This is a school. It's a mud hut. You signed the protocol in 2001. This hut in the pilot project in the Ivory Coast was built in November 2006. What has been happening in the intervening five years?'

'There's much has been happening.'

'In the pilot project, what has been happening?'

'What we've learned is the more that we are on the ground the more we're looking at the issues of the cocoa community and families and the more we're looking at . . .'

'Why wasn't that hut built within a month or so of the protocol being signed?'

'I was in the Ivory Coast when there was military action. There are a lot of issues in the Ivory Coast but they're moving forward. Ghana is a great example. We're frustrated when things don't happen as fast as we would like.'

I showed her the eight-page statement she had sent me about the industry's work in West Africa. I asked why, not once in the email had she mentioned the specific targets of July 2005, later delayed until July 2008, agreed in the Harkin–Engel Protocol.

'We are definitely on track. It takes time.'

'But why didn't you mention them?'

'Well I'm mentioning them now.'

'Why not in this document?'

'We are concerned about cocoa communities and where cocoa is grown and we're working towards solutions. It takes a lot of people to do that. It takes a lot of effort to do that.'

'Who's actually in charge?'

'This is something that takes an overall effort. There's not one company in charge.'

'But who takes responsibility?'

'It's an issue that everybody in the entire industry is working on and that's partly what makes it work.'

I moved on to talk about Sangone Lamine who said he was getting the same amount for his cocoa now that he was getting thirty years ago. 'In the US, the inflation rate – presumably your chocolate bars – has gone up 325 per cent in that time. Under that system how can any community develop?'

'One of the programmes we're doing is to help farmers increase their incomes so that they can feed their families,' said Smith. 'That is part of what we have to do. There are field schools where communities are working together.'

'What I don't understand is that we drove two, three days out into the bush in the main cocoa belt of the Ivory Coast and we met nobody who had come into contact with anybody involved with any of these organizations whatsoever.'

'I don't know who you met. I know I have been there and know how much the programmes have going.'

'We were just unlucky, were we?'

'There are programmes going on I can tell you that I know. There are plenty of people working with these farmers. They have seen increases of 20 to 30 per cent and that's to feed their families and take care of their families.'

'Mr Lamine told me he needed three times that price in order to feed his family. Would you be happy to pay that?'

'The important thing is helping farmers increase their income.'

'But not paying a higher price. Supposing there's a glut in the market and the price goes down.'

'What we can help with is helping farmers make more money.'

I showed her the pictures of Marc and Fabrice Kwame with their machetes. 'You're probably familiar with these kinds of pictures. They are a familiar sight in the Ivory Coast.'

'I want to make one thing very clear. Children should

not be subject to inhumane treatment whether it is at home—'

'How long does it take?'

'Progress has been made.'

'How long?'

'There are lots of things going on. The question is, what are the solutions? There are roles to play for lots of organizations and people. We don't have all the answers and we're working to—'

'Mr Lamine has an answer. He says could you please pay him three times what he's getting for his cocoa.'

'One of the things we've done is to figure out how to make more from their cocoa.'

'What labour conditions would you not buy cocoa from? How bad does it have to get?'

'Whenever we know about children in danger we are working with organizations to help children get out of the situation.'

'If I give you the address will you go and get those children out of there?'

'This takes an effort.'

'Who should I contact on this issue?'

'I'll give you the name of—'

'But you won't pass it on?'

'There are organizations, NGOs and government organizations in Ghana now. There's a rescue centre. The important thing is to make progress . . .'

I gave Susan Smith the address – Allanbakro, near Soufre in the Ivory Coast. I gave it to her colleague Alison Ward too. Both had a difficult job because, in just about any other business, I would have been interviewing not the public relations staff of a trade organization, but an accountable executive from one of the companies involved.

'What have you done in the Ivory Coast in the last six years?' I asked Alison Ward.

'In the Ivory Coast one of the programmes is the farmer field schools.'

'Where?'

'I can give you the names of the villages.'

'OK, then.'

'I don't have the names. But I will give you the names.'

But it was too late. I had already been. I had been in touch with both Susan Smith and Alison Ward long before leaving. No names had been given.

Some months after getting back from the Ivory Coast, I was contacted by Mark Charman, a teacher at the Gallions Primary School in east London. One of his pupils had seen the report on Marc Kwame and wanted to put on a school play about him. We went to the school to film the rehearsals. It was in one of London's poorer areas and the children were from a rainbow of religions and races. Yet, they shared a common, unequivocal view about Marc Kwame. To them, what was happening to Marc fell beneath a benchmark expected of the society in which they themselves were being brought up. They were all under ten years old, but they had an instinctive sense of decency.

'If I was in his shoes I'd probably want to kill myself,' said Babu Chowdry.

'They're making millions of pounds and they can't even give out any money to them who are making them rich,' said Jahid Ahmed.

'If they [the farmers] got fair money, they should be quite rich,' said Amy Morgan. 'But it's because of these companies that they're not. The companies are very greedy.'

'At the beginning of this project I just thought slavery

50

was one of those things like what happened years and years ago,' said Spencer Forte. 'But it's still going on today for these poor African children just like what happened years ago.'

Their sentiments matched my own instincts when the chocolate company press officer had first yelled at me for lying. They also matched those of the NEPAD delegates I had met at the Hotel President all those years ago, and of Congressman Eliot Engel over in Washington.

As for the chocolate industry, I eventually got a response about them finding Marc and Fabrice Kwame, through Peter McAllister at the International Cocoa Initiative. He emailed me on 28 June 2006 – four months after we got back.

'We struggled to identify the village at first,' he wrote. 'But your colleague at Reuters was contacted this week by our local contact [who] has now given us precise details.'

Why did it take four months to call Ange Amboa in Abidjan? Why did it take five years to build a mud-hut school near Oumé? Why does it take twenty-five years to find a different way to deal with Africa?

Over the past twenty or thirty years, there have been many examples of elections being held in Africa that have often ended up with catastrophic consequences. The causes are varied. There are also many common strands but, too often, we fail to find ways of preventing problems repeating themselves.

In the late 1970s, after years of civil war, it became clear that the continuation of white rule in what was then Rhodesia was untenable. Britain brokered a peace agreement in December 1979 to arrange elections and a transfer of power. But it allowed no time for training the black population to take control of the previously white-run institutions. In March 1980, barely two months after the agreement was signed, Robert Mugabe and his guerrilla fighters swept into office.

Rhodesia became Zimbabwe. It was one of the wealthiest countries in Africa and the West hailed the elections a success. But now, Zimbabweans have one of the world's lowest life expectancy levels and rely on aid to survive. Mugabe exploited weak institutions and ran Zimbabwe into the ground.

In the Ivory Coast, Houphouët-Boigny began a transition to democracy by holding direct presidential elections in 1990 – which he won. But in 1995 after his death, the opposition boycotted elections with street protests and anger that eventually turned into war. The Democratic Republic of Congo held elections in July 2006 that were hailed as a first step toward democracy. By October there was full-blown war.

It took decades to mend Europe after the Second World War, which had far more of a civil society and an educated and wealthy population. Within the overarching European rescue package was the plan, still in place today, to subsidize farmers so that they had enough to live on. Within it also were long periods of time before full elections were held so that the institutions could be strengthened.

This begs the question as to why, if such mechanisms were needed for Europe's development, they were not seen to be needed for Africa's. But then, as we find later on, many of the mechanisms that have made Europe successful have been denied to Africa, as if basic human longings and behaviour were different in the two continents.

Tens of millions of Africans put their trust in the West's administrative and economic systems and now feel let down. They see themselves at the bottom of an international supply chain that refuses to allow wealth to spread to the poorest and the weakest. It is only natural that they seek alternatives. Similar feelings were prevalent in 1940s China, 1930s Germany and early twentieth-century Russia. The alternative systems that took control then shook the world.

But this thinking isn't confined to Africa. After 9/11, the Middle East became the target for the West's democratic vision. For some reason, our political leaders believed that, as if by magic, the Middle East could be suddenly transformed into what Europe and America had shed much blood to become over hundreds of years.

THE MIDDLE EAST AND THE ISLAMIC WORLD

IRAQ – Democracy's Precipice

We drove through the gates of the Palestinian embassy in Baghdad where a barbed-wire pen had been set up in the garden. A day earlier, American troops kept Palestinian diplomats hooded and cuffed inside the pen for several hours while trashing the embassy. No one at the Embassy knew where the diplomats were now. Inside the building a shattered glass-framed photograph of Yasser Arafat, the late Palestinian leader, lay on the ground, with a boot imprint on the picture. Books and files had been pulled from cabinets. A copy of the Koran, a centrepiece of the ambassador's desk, had been ripped, its pages strewn on the floor.

It was May 2003, just a few weeks after the invasion and before Iraq's civil war had begun. The sight of the Palestinian embassy that day encapsulated the repetitive problems of the Middle East into which Iraq was being drawn. The contempt shown by US troops for the Koran seemed to symbolize a cultural derision that over the next few years would play out from Gaza to Islamabad to London and beyond. The soldiers could have been instructed, as they were five years later, to act with dignity and honour. But those orders had yet to be issued.

A few days later, I was in an upmarket Baghdad suburb built for military families, interviewing a group of officers from the Iraqi army. There were half a dozen, ranging from a retired general to a young tank commander in his late twenties who had fought the invasion. Over coffee we discussed Saddam Hussein and what the Americans now planned to do. In the middle of our talk came news that the Iraqi military was to be disbanded immediately. The room fell quiet. Everyone exchanged glances. Then a colonel expressed a thought uppermost in everyone's mind. 'What about our pensions?'

The general glanced around the room. 'And my house,' he asked. 'Will they take that?'

The tank commander was visibly furious. His wife was expecting a baby. He had been waiting for a call back to barracks. Instead, he'd been fired. 'We will have to fight them,' he said.

Washington had decided to transform an Arab society with weak institutions using a post-Second World War manual designed for a European society with strong institutions. The de-Nazification of Germany in the late 1940s became the de-Baathification of Iraq in the early twenty-first century. Those who had made the country function, whether tank commanders, power-plant electricians or university professors, were cast out because they had been members of Saddam Hussein's Baath Party. Under a dictatorship, largely decent people often have to make what to us might seem unacceptable compromises just in order to exist. There is a blur of morality with each person setting the line they will not cross. Many Iraqis might have joined the Baath Party, not because they yearned for the opportunity to use chemical weapons, but because they wanted a promotion at work, or needed a pay rise to pay for medicine or schooling. These people were the bedrock of Iraq's institutions. However fragile, they were the foundations of a new civil society. Now their livelihoods were being destroyed.

The reaction in the general's living room that morning was to think of pensions, homes and children. It was human and instinctive.

That weekend, I headed north to the oil-rich city of Kirkuk, which was holding post-invasion municipal elections. It was barely a month since America had taken control. Huge murals depicting Saddam had been defaced. Statues of him had been pulled down. After years of the portrait of an absolute ruler staring out everywhere, there was a vacuum. Nothing, not even a logo symbolizing the new US-run government, had replaced it. Iraq had no civilian authority, only men with guns. At the magnificent art deco railway station, once a terminal for the Orient Express, staff rebelled because they hadn't been paid. Outside the fashionable Sheraton Hotel on the banks of the Tigris river, Iraqis who lived locally were getting pushed to the ground by nervous American soldiers, with a boot on their shoulders and a gun to their head, simply because they had looked the wrong way. Civil society had collapsed, as shown by the widespread looting that saw incubators stolen from hospitals and offices stripped down to light-fittings. It was at its basest, a society too suddenly freed from repression. On the drive from Kuwait to Baghdad we had not been stopped once by any agency from any government. The border town of Safwan had been abandoned to stray dogs. There was no immigration control. Military convoys filled the huge six-lane highway north, but there were no checkpoints. Anybody could have got into Iraq then, and they did. Al-Qaeda fighters and bombers from Afghanistan, Yemen, Saudi Arabia, Jordan and elsewhere were driving across Iraq's borders with plans to unleash the coming storm.

Kirkuk's municipal elections were held in a lecture theatre, with benches rising steeply up to the back wall. Floorboards on the wooden platform below resounded with the sharp steps of military boots. American officers, in light beige camouflage uniforms, filled the front bench. Behind them were delegates for the election, fanning themselves against the still, hot air. They had been chosen as a caucus who would vote for members of a city council. Taped up along the aisle were signs marking out the seating area for what were meant to be different political parties, although there weren't any. Therefore voters were asked to choose between tribal and religious groups. The signs said Arab delegation, Assyrian, Kurdish, Christian, and so on, showing up the very loyalties that would define the factions of the civil war.

Kirkuk itself was one of the more fragile communities in Iraq. It bordered the northern Kurdish area that, because of Western protection, had enjoyed a large degree of autonomy – even under Saddam. Because it had reserves of oil, Saddam had forced Kurdish families from their homes, replacing them with more loyal Sunni Arabs. The Kurds now wanted their homes back. Everyone sought a slice of the oil. No one knew where government power now lay. In the lecture theatre, as we were waiting for an American general to arrive, a Christian delegate came up to me, shaking his head. 'Why are they arranging it in ethnic groups like this?' he asked.

'I don't know,' I replied. 'Let's find out.' I spoke to a lieutenant who was taping up the signs.

'That's how they say they want it,' he answered, looking straight at me, but ignoring the delegate.

'No,' said the delegate with a frown. 'For us, this is very dangerous. How would you like it if someone took over the BBC and made you work according to your religion?'

There was no time to answer as the hall fell quiet, and General Raymond Odierno strode in. A tall, charismatic man with a military buzz-cut, he later became famous for capturing Saddam Hussein and eventually was promoted to be commander of US forces in Iraq.

But today he was a military election commissioner. 'This is an historic occasion for the region and for all of Iraq,' he said. 'And it marks the beginning of the process of democratization within your country.'

When the results came in, arguments spread like wildfire. Delegates stood up hurling abuse at each other with accusations of cheating and fraud. The mayhem reached such a level that Odierno returned to the microphone to restore peace.

'You have just experienced how democracy works,' he said through his interpreter. 'There are winners and losers, and you had better learn to accept it.'

Yet democracy was never designed to share out power on grounds of birthright. In fact, its aim was precisely to stop that happening, so that voters could choose between different policies laid out by competing political parties. Tribal and religious voting did not achieve that.

What Odierno also failed to mention was the general Western etiquette of showing magnanimity in victory. In much of the developing world, far from there being a conceding conciliatory phone call between political rivals, the routine practice was often a winner-takes-all scenario – homes, jobs, freedoms and sometimes lives with the losers being bundled off and shot. This was not a phobia that could be shed overnight.

That May, I was in Iraq for only a month, and the day before leaving, we drove to the Iranian border. As the disenfranchised Sunnis headed off to start the war, and America began the road to democracy with municipal elections, another influence – Iran – was placing itself to get the maximum leverage out of Iraq's chaos. The journey only took a couple of hours, although a few months later it would be impossible because the expressway cut through the insurgent heartland of Diyala.

American troops commanded a hilltop about a mile from the border itself. But, not wanting to be eyeball to eyeball with the Iranians, they had given control to a Kurdish militia, known as the Peshmerga, US allies who had opposed Saddam Hussein. At the crossing itself, minibus after minibus came through filled with Iranian pilgrims heading for the holy Iraqi cities of Najaf and Karbala. On the Iranian side, travellers, the women covered in black burqas, milled around waiting to go through customs and immigration.

The deserted Iraqi border buildings had been put up just over ten years earlier as an act of reconciliation after the Iran–Iraq War, and they included a travellers' mosque. The windows were smashed. Glass littered the floor inside, together with copies of the Koran. The lectern had been pulled down. Posters of a revered Shia cleric, Ayatollah Mohammed Baqir al-Hakim, had been torn up and scattered about the floor.

'Who would have done this?' I said to my interpreter. He asked a couple of people watching us from outside. 'The Americans,' he said. As we left for the drive back to Baghdad, I wondered what the point had been of trashing the mosque. But then what was the point of wrecking the Palestinian embassy?

Three months later, Ayatollah Mohammed Baqir al-Hakim was killed in car bomb in Najaf. In Baghdad, al-Qaeda blew up the United Nations offices, murdering the UN representative Sérgio Vieira de Mello. And in November, I headed back to take a journey through Iraq and test the progress of America's democratic experiment.

Except we couldn't get in. Flights had been cancelled because a ground-to-air missile had almost shot down a DHL courier plane flying into Baghdad. The land border, which since my last visit had reinstalled immigration and customs, was closed because of the festival of Eid-ul-Fitr that marked the end of Ramadan. No one seemed to know when it would open again. Then we discovered that a ferry was still running between Dubai and the southern Iraqi port of Umm Qasr near Basra. We booked ourselves cabins.

She was an amiable old car ferry called the *Meredith II*, with an empty, dilapidated swimming pool, and signs in Greek left over from the days she used to ply the Aegan islands. The captain and crew were from India; the cooks from Bangladesh; the waitresses and bar staff from the Ukraine. Alcohol was banned. The restaurant was decorated with a Christmas tree and electronic bells chimed Christmas carols.

The ship buzzed with optimism. Gleaming new cars and trucks filled the vehicle decks. Passengers rented multiple cabins, some just to fill with televisions, fridges, air conditioners and generators. These were Iraqi merchants who worked where money feels safe and they were heading off to test Iraq. The destructive tribalism that was peeling away Iraq's veneer of nationhood hadn't yet reached these men. Even before casting off, Sunni, Shia, Kurds and others were striking business deals in smoke-filled corridors for the next trip and the next one after that. During the Saddam years Dubai had been a sanctuary. That era had ended and there were opportunities for the taking. Iraq might have been tilting toward war, but on the *Meredith II* there was a sense of a new nation in the making.

Among the passengers were three Iraqis going back for the first time since the war. The first day out to sea, sitting on old plastic swimming-pool chairs, we talked for hours about what they hoped to find when they got there. Clear sunshine warmed the winter chill. To our left was the hazy landfall of the Gulf – Qatar, Bahrain – none of us were sure how far up we were.

Somewhere across to the east was Iran. And far to the north, still several days away, was the southern landfall of Iraq.

With us was Saleem Maihar, who worked as a supervisor in a paint factory in Dubai. He was from Basra, the big southern city near where we were to dock. He was going back for the Eid festival – his first trip back for four years. Saleem was in his thirties, with restless eyes, wearing a long black Arab robe with a carefully trimmed moustache and haircut. He was excitable, apprehensive and impatient. He was a Shia, the community that had been oppressed by Saddam.

Zaid Mugheer, an electrician by trade, came from Babylon, south of Baghdad. His face was stubbled and he looked tired like a man drawing on the last reserves of energy. He had been away from Iraq for more than two years and on his mind was the health of his daughter, Fatima, who needed a bone-marrow transplant because of a blood disorder. When I asked his religion, Zaid said his mother was Shia and his father Sunni. 'We pray together in the same house,' he said. 'We are all Islam.'

My question brought an immediate objection from Firaz al-Binook, a Sunni from Baghdad. 'Why do you ask this?' he demanded. 'In your own country would you ask people if they are Protestant, Catholic or Jew before speaking to them?'

Firaz, a computer engineer working in Dubai, was highly educated and his English was fluent. He was dressed in a black fleece and rimless glasses and explained how he was going back to his family in Baghdad to see if he could get back property confiscated by Saddam's cronies.

'Are you upset by the question?' I asked.

'Yes, and I tell you why,' he said. 'When I was small in school in Iraq, a friend asked me if I was a Sunni or a Shia. I didn't know because I was a small child at the time, so I went back to my father and I asked him. He said who asked you that question and I said a friend at school. He said: "That guy is not a friend of yours." So basically I am a Muslim and we are all Muslims. There is no hatred between Sunni and Shia and no hatred between Kurds and Arabs and no hatred between Christians and Muslims. There was only one kind of hatred. Everybody hated Saddam Hussein and that hatred has gone. But human people, when the pressure has gone, it is like being hit by a big baseball bat. They don't know what to do.'

No one objected to Firaz's eloquent response, and I felt chastened. Yet the divisions did exist. In the months since the Kirkuk elections, war had broken out. Sunni and Shia were fighting, and my question could have been transferred to Yugoslavia, Sri Lanka, Northern Ireland or Rwanda. Firaz's reaction encompassed the often-cited accusation of the West's tendency to exploit communal differences in policies of divide and rule. Yet that would only be possible if there was something within those societies that was divisible. Clearly, in Iraq there was. Similar Western intervention in Japan, Korea, Panama, Haiti and so on had not resulted in such immediate home-grown bloodshed.

'The Americans,' said Zaid in the silence that followed. 'They came and removed Saddam Hussein. I would like to thank them.'

'But what have they done in the past eight months?' countered Saleem. 'I want to see something with my own eyes. I want to feel something. The Americans, why did they come to Iraq? To give freedom, right? OK. So give it.'

Firaz nodded thoughtfully. 'Even if they tried, the Americans cannot rule Iraq. It is a different society. People think differently.'

On the paint-peeling ferry deck, we talked long into the evening. We touched on Iraq's history as the 'cradle of civilization', and Zaid told of his home near the Hanging Gardens of Babylon, one of the Seven Wonders of the World that date back to 600 BC. Saleem spoke about picnics with his family on the Shatt al-Arab waterway which looked towards Iran and formed the confluence of the Tigris and Euphrates rivers. Firaz spoke knowledgeably about influences from previous invasions by the Mongols, the Ottomans and, after the First World War, by the British who had found themselves fighting Arab and Kurdish insurgencies and then left. They spoke randomly, without order, but their enthusiasm for Iraqi nationhood was infectious, appealing to my own imagination for the exotic. I allowed to flitter through my mind that we had all been wrong and President George W. Bush had been right. His democratic vision would take root here and spread throughout the Middle East.

Yet, I couldn't shake off the thought that America's experiment had become a crapshoot with everyone trying to load the dice in his favour. Hopes were running unchecked, but enmeshed with contradictions. On the ferry, we heard how Iraqis were thanking America for ousting Saddam, yet demanding that American troops now leave the country. There was optimism for the future but no details of how it might work.

'Iraq. My country is a rich country. We don't need any help from another country,' said Saleem.

'Iraq is like a pregnant mother,' said Zaid. 'The successful delivery will take a very special operation. But I have a simple dream that when I enter Iraq I will not see any picture of Saddam.'

'I feel scared,' said Firaz. 'We used to dream of waking up to an Iraq without Saddam. But to wake up without Saddam and with everything burning is not something we dreamed about.'

We spent three more days, stopping and starting, until we reached the first checkpoint. It was run not by Americans, but by the Australian navy. They grouped us in the main dining room, ticking off our names from the manifest. It took less than two hours. But Saleem became immediately edgy and broke away from his table to confront the officer.

'Why are you taking so long?' he remonstrated. 'Today is the Eid. Everyone here wants to be with their family. Every minute we lose here is a minute we lose from being with our family.'

'We need seven more names from the manifest,' said the officer. 'As soon as we've got them, you'll be on your way.'

'But this is what we expect under a dictatorship,' continued Saleem. 'We were promised freedom.' He suddenly stopped, his face masked with confusion, then breaking into a huge smile. 'But, yes. Thank you. I am wrong,' he conceded. 'With Saddam's government, we cannot talk like this or we get killed.'

Saleem put his hand on the officer's shoulder and pointed at Nick Woolley, the cameraman who was filming. 'You must tell everyone that these are very nice people.'

The Australians handed out War on Terror leaflets offering up to US$25 million for information about al-Qaeda and the Taliban. This policy had impacted on millions of lives around the world and was now allowing these ferry passengers to come home. The leaflets stayed on the tables unread, until the Australians left. Then children grabbed them to make paper darts to fly around the canteen.

We were at sea for another day and half before docking. The captain grumbled that it had worked more smoothly before the invasion. Zaid found me in a quiet moment to explain his worry. His daughter, Fatima, had thalassaemia, a genetic disorder that reduces the haemoglobin levels in red blood cells, causing severe anaemia. She was fifteen and under Western sanctions had had trouble getting the drugs she needed. Ultimately, she would need a bone-marrow transplant that was not possible in Iraq.

Zaid was a worried man. 'She's young, and I need to save her,' he said in a moment when we were alone looking out over Iraq's arid southern coastline. 'Can you help her, Humphrey? I need someone to help her.' He pointed towards the shore where there was a huge warehouse with the United Nations logo in huge letters on the side. 'I am not sure if she will be safe here any more. When they have that sign in your country, you know that something is wrong.'

With no working telephones and the war getting worse by the day, it was a precarious promise to make, but I said I would try to meet Fatima and see what we could do. The BBC Baghdad bureau sent down two vehicles for our journey. Wisam Panndit had come, too, as our interpreter, carrying a list of telephone numbers of government officials and aid agencies should we need them.

I took Zaid's and Firaz's addresses, hoping to find them again in Babylon and Baghdad. Firaz asked if I knew anyone at Lloyds Bank in Britain. Since Iraq's invasion of Kuwait in 1990, they had frozen his family's bank accounts.

All three drove brand-new cars off the ferry. Zaid was met by his brother. Firaz by friends, and Saleem had an entourage to greet him. He only lived twenty minutes away and we planned to go with him to meet his family.

This time entering Iraq my passport was stamped and on the other side of immigration we bumped into Firaz, who had dressed up for his arrival with a stylish headdress.

'You know in Saddam's time, when you got off the boat it took you about five, six hours and you had to give out money,' he said, slapping the bonnet of his BMW that he had just got through customs. 'This took half an hour and I haven't been asked for anything.'

Saleem, at the wheel of his new Mercedes, headed home. The motorway stretched through a yellow-brown sun-cracked desert. This was a Shia heartland, huge, desolate, empty. The people had never supported Saddam here. Saleem looked expectantly left and right. 'I don't know,' he said. 'I feel something is changed. Really now, I feel that I am not afraid of anything. I can really feel my freedom now.'

Up ahead was a checkpoint. Saleem slowed, his face beaming as he spotted Iraqi police in brand-new uniforms. 'Those Australian soldiers came to our ship and made the passengers wait,' he said. 'But this is normal. They want to make everything safe.'

The litmus test for many military-based societies is the checkpoint. From the Balkan wars to Israel and the Palestinian territories and beyond, it is here that one group openly controls another, where dignity is lost and the guards have a choice between treating people with courtesy or humiliation.

Saleem snapped open the boot and got out of the car. Two policemen carried out a quick search. Saleem closed the boot and embraced them both. 'You see. Everything is good now. They make it quickly for me. This is the Iraqi police now. They don't make any problem.'

We left the motorway for a residential area of large houses protected in high-walled compounds. 'Everything is so quick,' said Saleem, his conversation still racing. 'We're all done and home in maybe an hour. Very, very fast. These are very nice things. The Americans should stay in Iraq longer. We need them. Yes, we need them.'

He drew up honking the horn outside the compound. The elaborately decorated gates opened and a woman walked out with outstretched arms. 'This is my mother. This is my mother!' shouted Saleem, getting out of the car, leaving the door open and rushing over to embrace her.

They went inside, and a little boy ran up. Saleem scooped him into his arms. Then another younger boy. 'This is my little baby,' said Saleem. 'I have not seen him since he was a baby.' He put the child down and turned away, tears streaming down his cheeks. 'You know, I want to cry but I can't because I am a man. If I was a woman I could because I want to cry so much. I'm sorry I cannot talk any more.'

He stepped inside the house. 'My mother! I can't believe I am seeing my mother.' He turned towards an elderly man and held out his arms. 'This is my father. This is the best of the world. We have freedom now and we can say what we want.'

Not long ago, the Basra Sheraton hotel had been a magnet for the rich and carefree of the Middle East with cocktail-mixing barmen and cabaret acts from Europe. Those glory days ended in 1990 with Saddam's invasion of Kuwait and sanctions. But even then, the hotel limped along, its waiters in frayed jackets with an air that perhaps the good times would come back again.

Now the hotel was a wreck. For some reason someone had decided to destroy it. Its long, flat modern facade, windows shaped like squat Islamic arches, looked out over the Shatt al-Arab waterway that – if America's experiment worked – would soon resemble the bustle of the Creek in Dubai. Inside, scattered among the rubble, were 'Do Not Disturb' signs, room service menus, a copy of someone's bill and coasters from the coffee shop.

Saleem had a point. It had been eight months, and no one had put as much as a warning sign or a tape across the Sheraton that it would be dangerous to go inside. It was a theme that stayed with me during the days of our journey. Iraq was a land of ruin. Nothing was being rebuilt, nor was there, any-where, a sign that it would be. The mindset was not on nation-building, but on protecting the family and the tribe, a mindset of knuckling down for war.

We stayed in a small hotel and ate upstairs in my room with a bottle of wine we had bought in Dubai. We couldn't be seen drinking, and if anyone sold us alcohol, they risked being shot by Shia militia. After dinner, we walked down the road to an Internet cafe to check email – one of many that had sprouted up since the invasion. Almost all the computers were logged on to porn sites.

Wisam arranged for us to meet in the morning Dr Haj Abbass al-Shawi, the Basra head of one of Iraq's most powerful political movements, the Islamic Dawa Party. Like many Iraqi leaders, al-Shawi had just returned from exile. He had spent twenty years in Sweden so I had expected him to know a thing or two about how a Western-style democracy worked.

I was upbeat that we would get a sensible blueprint of how things would move forward. On the way to his office we stopped by the market where last time I had bought Saddam memorabilia, including a carpet that showed him as a warrior leader of the whole Arab world. His posters and trinkets had now been replaced by those of Islamic clerics whose legends were becoming interwoven with Iraq's politics.

On offer were portraits of Ayatollah Al Sayeed Mohammed Sadiq al-Sadr, who was killed under Saddam in 1999; of his son Muqtada al-Sadr who later led the Mehdi Army into pitched battles with the British and Americans; of Ayatollah Mohammed Baqir al-Hakim, the cleric whose posters I had found littered around the mosque on the Iran–Iraq border and who also had been killed in August in a car bombing in the holy city of Najaf; of Ayatollah Mohammed Baqir al-Sadr, who was murdered under Saddam in 1981; and of Imam Hussein ibn Ali, who was killed in the Battle of Karbala in 680. None had died peacefully in their beds. Each was a story about violence, often used hundreds of years later to justify revenge.

The only poster of a living cleric seemed to be of Ayatollah Ali al-Sistani, who from his modest office in Najaf was keeping a low but commanding profile. During those years of war, al-Sistani remained a crucial influence.

The Dawa Party's compound was guarded by young men with AK-47s wearing laminated ID cards issued under the British occupation. There were a lot of them, sitting around with nothing to do. They didn't know where al-Shawi was, and drew chairs up in the shade of a tree for us to wait – which is a bad move in many countries if you actually want to get something done. Never sit until you are with the person you want to be with.

Al-Shawi was in another part of town. He didn't even work at the compound, but from a makeshift office near the city centre. His bodyguard came out to greet us, while pushing a pistol into his belt. But he dropped the weapon instead and it made such a clatter on the floor that al-Shawi poked his head around the door to see what was happening. He was forty-seven with a shining bald head, dressed in a beige suit and open-necked cream shirt. I was hoping his Swedish exile would have left him speaking some English. But he didn't. Instead of sitting down to explain his party's manifesto he insisted on taking us out to show us his old family house. His brother had been murdered there.

We walked off the main road onto a dirt track piled high on both sides with uncollected rubbish. Above us, electrical wires sprouted off each other and, on the ground, we stepped over puddles of fetid water. Everywhere was the stench of rotting food. The house lay at the end of the track and nailed to the wall was a large black cloth with white Arabic text, telling how Saddam's regime had killed al-Shawi's father and brother.

As he told how his house was raided and his relatives mur-dered, it dawned on me that he saw this as the manifesto that would get him elected to office. It wasn't about schools, roads and hospitals as in the West, but about the degree of personal suffering from the wrongs of history.

Did he think the Islamic Dawa Party would win elections and come to power in Iraq? I asked.

'We hope to win power by democratic means and not by force,' he answered. I shot a glance at Wisam Pandit, my inter-preter. 'Are you sure you got that right?' I said. 'Ask him what he means – "not by force".'

Wisam and al-Shawi fell into conversation, then Wisam said: 'Yes. That's what he means. He said that there are many possible ways to win power. One is democracy, but he said all means were available to them, including force.' (I was so worried about the translation that I rechecked it after leaving Iraq. Wisam was right. That was exactly what al-Shawi had said.)

'What about the rubbish?' I asked. 'What are you doing about clearing that up?'

'When we win power the rubbish will be cleared.'

'Not before?'

He didn't answer. Uncollected rubbish is a sign of a soci-ety's broken morale, a tendency to blame history for all ills. It was a symptom of Kosovo, before NATO intervention. It was all over India. It was in Dharamsala, the capital of the Tibetan government in exile, and in the Palestinian territories. But you would be hard-pressed to find rotting rubbish on the streets in Taiwan, South Korea or Singapore, whose people could have claimed equal cause for historical grievance. For some reason, they picked themselves up, brushed themselves down and moved on.

Having determined that the Islamic Dawa Party planned to

take office regardless, I asked what its policies were towards stereotypical repression within Muslim culture as seen by the West, such as the treatment of women and drinking of alcohol.

'The Koran forbids the drinking of alcohol,' he said, 'and, in the West, you use women to advertise merchandise, but in our country women are more respected. No one is ordering women what to wear. They choose to dress respectfully with the hijab. You have to understand that after so many years of tyranny, they feel that Islam is the best way for them.'

Not so, I thought, but said nothing. Our freelance reporter in Basra had been staying with a family since the invasion. She had watched one of the daughters change from being an outgoing young woman, dressing in jeans and T-shirts, to becoming subdued, silent and fully covered in black because her husband had ordered it.

'What about other policies?' I said. 'Road-building, for example? Or schools? That sort of thing.'

'The holy cities of Karbala and Najaf are very important and Shia take their decisions from there. They are the sources of all power and original ideas.'

'I'm sorry,' I pressed, pointing to the street around us and clutching once again at the straw that this man had lived for a generation in democratic and modern Europe. 'I meant more practical things such as in Sweden, like health care, urban renewal, employment.'

'Democracy is for the West,' he answered. 'Islam is a religion of freedom.'

Had Dr Haj Abbass al-Shawi been profiled by the United States as an electoral candidate for Iraq's democratic experiment, he would no doubt have scored highly. But in Basra and with alarming honesty he came out with statements that would have horrified ideologues back in Washington. He had no manifesto. He was happy to fight his way to power. And his Islamic Dawa Party had strong roots and funding that stretched all the way back to America's sworn enemy in Tehran.

Iraqis had seamlessly swapped their repression by the Baath Party to that of religious parties and by defeating Saddam, far from ushering in freedom and democracy, the Americans had opened the flood gates to Islamic fundamentalism.

We headed north toward those sacred cities of Najaf and Karbala that al-Shawi insisted were the source of new Iraqi power. Najaf was 250 miles from Basra and it was another 50 on from there to Karbala, which was close to Babylon, where we hoped to find Zaid and his sick daughter Fatima.

The two cities represented the schism within Islam that had created the Sunni and Shia sects and now in the early twenty-first century were bolstering up for a civil war.

In AD 632, on the death of Mohammed, there was argument over who should succeed him that led to bloodshed. Karbala is dominated by the tombs of Imam Abbas and Imam Hussein ibn Ali, stepbrothers and grandsons of the Prophet Mohammed, who were killed in AD 680 in the now legendary Battle of Karbala. Hussein's 'martyrdom' is celebrated every year in a ceremony of mourning and sacrifice on what is known as the Day of Ashura.

Nineteen years earlier, in AD 661, their father, Imam Ali, a cousin and son-in-law of the Prophet whom Shia believed should have been the successor, was killed while praying in the mosque in the small town of Kufa near Najaf. His tomb is now the centrepiece of Najaf.

The bloodshed in these two cities was not only historical. They were the focus of the Shia uprisings against Saddam after the 1991 Gulf War and it's widely believed that chemical weapons were used in an attack on Najaf's Imam Ali Mosque where many of the rebels were hiding out.[1] Najaf had also been the home of Iran's revolutionary leader, Ayatollah Khomeini, who had lived there in exile from 1965 to 1978. It was presently the headquarters of the influential Ayatollah Sistani and a focus for much of Iraq's violence.

In April 2003, days after Saddam's downfall, Abdul Majid al-Khoei, a leading cleric just back from London, was knifed to death inside the shrine of Imam Ali. In August, Grand Ayatollah al-Hakim was blown up by a car bomb as he left the same mosque after delivering a Friday sermon. Both Karbala and Najaf were frequently attacked in car and suicide bombings.

On our journey north, mile after mile and town after town, we passed through the same depressing, grey-brown ruined landscape; the wrecks of burned-out vehicles; the rubble of destroyed buildings; hanging cables; blotched murals of Saddam; rusting signs, all interspersed by interruptions from American military convoys forming the supply chain to the war machine.

It was as if it hadn't yet crossed anyone's mind that people needed to see Iraq on the mend, as if the land had lost its energy. To take part in democracy you had to feel you were a stakeholder which was near impossible when surrounded by ruined buildings, overflowing drains and rotting rubbish. Of course, you can blame Saddam. But for how long? Where were the billions that were meant to be spent on reconstruction? What were all those unemployed doing? Instead of rolling up their sleeves to clean up, they were learning how to

---

1 General Wafiq al-Samarae (the former director of the Iraqi Intelligence Service) admitted in his book (*Eastern Gate Ruins*) that Saddam's regime used chemical weapons against Iraqi people in the holy cities of Najaf and Karbala to crush the popular uprising of March 1991 that followed Saddam's defeat after invading Kuwait – www.globalsecurity.org.

kill with AK-47s, rocket-propelled grenades and roadside bombs.

On our clumsy satellite telephones, Wisam and I began calling the list of numbers we had of key Iraqi politicians. The US Coalitional Provisional Authority (CPA) had appointed them to the twenty-five-member Iraqi Governing Council that was due to take over the reins of government in June next year – six months away. But we could barely get anyone to pick up, and when we did, the people we needed to talk to were not in. No one would take a message.

Four years earlier, I had listened to a fairly precise prediction of Iraq's slide and that was without any American invasion. It was about education. On a 1999 trip to Basra, we slipped our minders and went round to the city's university. It was a Sunday evening and we found the vice chancellor and a scientist who headed the botany department. He had just come there from church. I don't have a record of their names, but the vice chancellor had graduated from Edinburgh University and the botanist from Reading. We talked openly about the UN sanctions and inspections for weapons of mass destruction that were then going on and the botanist explained how his department at the university had been raided twice.

'I don't understand what they are doing by sanctioning education,' said the botanist.

'Looking for biological and nuclear weapons?' I suggested. 'You do run a science department.'

'No,' he said. 'I don't mean that.' He showed me tokens from the British Library. 'In the old days we would send these tokens to the British Library and they would send back new academic papers that we used to teach with. But now the British Library refuses to send them because of sanctions. It means that our students are cut off from new scientific research. It is not just science. If I wanted a new critique of Shakespeare, I couldn't get it. Or a biography of Margaret Thatcher would be banned.

'If the West wants to encourage dissatisfaction at the current government, then it should look at traditional centres of unrest which are the universities. If they helped educate the young, then we can create a generation of modern thinkers. But by blocking education, what do we get? Teenagers chant: "Saddam, Saddam and down with the West."'

He picked up the British Library token again. 'We need to be able to persuade them about their careers and teach them how to think things through, and be inspired and motivated, but your government is stopping us from doing that.'

I discovered that not only were scientific papers sanctioned, but also everything else. Iraqi students couldn't get copies of Stephen Hawking's *A Brief History of Time*, Nigella Lawson's *How to Eat: Pleasures and Principles of Good Food*, Michael Palin's latest travel adventure or John le Carré's novels. In short, they had no world to look to for inspiration except the one around them.

It was brave of him to speak out, and I have never received an acceptable answer from anyone in Britain or America on his points. But reflecting back on that evening, the botanist had openly been to church; he had given thinly veiled guidance on how to carry out peaceful regime change; he had warned against the Iraq we were witnessing now; and he had walked from his home to church then to the university and back home again without any fear of being attacked. As a Christian, he probably had more freedom in 1999 than he did in 2003. And both he and the vice chancellor engaged in the type of mature debate I had been hoping for from the Dawa leader al-Shawi in Basra.

*

We couldn't get to Najaf. American tanks were parked across the road. Apparently a minivan carrying Italian and South Korean contractors had been attacked and several of them killed. It was getting dark, and we needed to get off the road to a secure area, so we headed straight for Karbala. After the desolate landscape of our journey, arriving in Karbala was like driving into another world. On both sides of the road were shops and hotels bustling with people. Strung over the road were portraits of Shia clerics. Pedestrians criss-crossed in front of us, many clad in black holding up the Iranian flag, and up ahead, glittering in an amazing aura of light, were the minarets and dome of the tomb of Imam Abbas.

Iraqis might be unsure about mapping out the future, but they embraced their history with great style. The central square of Karbala around the two tombs was clear of rubbish and stinking drains. Someone was keeping it as spotless as Switzerland.

The hotels had been block-booked for months by Iranian tour groups, but Nick Woolley, who had been here before, managed to get us rooms. We ate lamb kebabs grilled on charcoal on the street. Wisam fixed up for us to meet a senior Karbala politician the next day. We also needed to track down Zaid, who was not far away in Babylon. We gave his address to a taxi driver with a note that we would be there in the morning to meet Fatima.

In the morning, the taxi guided us in and we got there just after eight. Zaid's house stood in a wasteland of mud and weeds. But the electric bell at his gate worked. Inside the doorway was draped a huge American flag and inside the living room one wall was decorated with a poster of the footballer David Beckham. Zaid greeted us like old friends. He introduced us to his wife, Nihad, explaining that she was dressed in black because twelve years earlier her brother had been killed by Saddam's regime.

Then we met Fatima. She was a slight teenager, frail and small, looking more around eleven or twelve than fifteen. She was shy, expressive and when we talked about her illness, thalassaemia, she was frightened. But above all she was thrilled to have her father back home.

'She's very happy,' said Zaid as he ushered us to sit down on a carpet in his living room. 'She can't believe I have returned from Dubai. There has been so much crying, tears and laughter.'

Nihad collected medicines and doctors' notes and explained what they were for. 'The drugs are very painful,' translated Zaid. 'She lives by having regular blood transfusions and only then does she become lively again.'

Fatima chipped in. 'She says, like now,' translated Zaid. 'She only feels really strong after she's had a blood transfusion. If she doesn't have one, she becomes tired. She can't go to school. Sometimes she can't walk. But she says she doesn't tell her friends because she doesn't want to be boring about her illness.'

Fatima told it all with a huge smile, her eyes gazing across to her father. After a day of depressing conversations in Basra and a drive through the decay of occupied but unreconstructed Iraq, Fatima's enthusiasm was like gold. It took a moment to pinpoint exactly, but I sensed a young person as yet unaffected by the culture of victimhood. She carried no blame or self-pity, no quest for vengeance. She was bubbly, enthusiastic and curious.

'What do you want to do when you grow up?' I asked her.

'A teacher,' she said bashfully.

'What sort of teacher?'

'*Islameeya*,' she said, looking across to Zaid. 'An Islamic teacher,' he said. 'She wants to teach Islam.'

Why? I wanted to ask, but held back because she spoke it like a fantasy, like a child saying they wanted to be a postman or an astronaut. Except, in Fatima's world her vision was all around her, tagged to car bombs, legends of sacrifice, and martyrs' tombs just a few miles down the road. Just as my own modern society created heroes from footballers and celebrities, something in Fatima's society had coaxed her toward the idea of being a teacher of Islam. Did it, I wondered, reflect the prediction from the botanist at Basra University? If Fatima's teachers had not been constricted by dictatorship and Western sanctions might they have given her a wider spectrum from which to choose? A nurse? An architect? A cook? Or perhaps it was simpler than that, and religion gave her comfort against her disease.

Zaid asked if he could use our vehicles to take Fatima to hospital for an appointment. Of course, we agreed, also suggesting that, as she wanted to be an Islamic teacher, we might visit Karbala afterwards. Fatima's eyes shone.

We piled into our two vehicles and headed off to Babylon's main hospital. Fatima's eyes soaked in everything around. When we passed an American convoy, she waved furiously. 'Hello, Americans!' she shouted. 'Welcome, Americans.'

Zaid explained that before Saddam invaded Kuwait, Iraqi hospitals were the envy of the Middle East. Built on oil money and staffed by highly trained doctors, Iraqi health care, even at the grass roots, was superb. But after Western sanctions, they fell into disrepair. It was impossible to replace equipment and very difficult to get drugs. Many of the doctors fled into exile. Baath Party officials took their place and ran the hospitals as their own fiefdoms, charging bribes for medical care. 'They were so dirty,' said Zaid. 'No one smiled, and now you'll see everyone there is smiling and happy.'

The hospital was purpose-built and relatively modern, except nothing had been maintained. The Baath Party officials had gone, and it was now being run by doctors and nurses who were knuckling down and getting on with the job.

Thalassaemia is a fairly common condition in the Middle East, and Fatima joined a queue of other patients, all of them children. It can lead to deformity, fatigue and early death. She didn't have to wait long, perhaps because we were there, and her check-up went well.

'She will need a bone-marrow transplant,' said Dr Riyadh K. Mezeil, the hospital director. 'And we can't do that in Iraq. We hope soon to build a centre for it in Baghdad. But the main treatment for thalassaemia is the blood transfusion, so as long as we have the blood and it is tested properly she will be well looked after. And now that the sanctions are over, we have no problem getting the drugs.'

'And before,' I asked.

'It was dreadful,' he said, shaking his head. 'Truly dreadful.'

The issue of medicine distribution under Iraq's international sanctions had become a scandal. The estimated number of children who died because of lack of medicine runs between 100,000 and well over 1 million. Infant mortality rates more than doubled during the thirteen years of sanctions.[2]

Sanctions didn't work. Instead, they left a generation of school and university students without the education they would need to build democratic institutions that would supersede Saddam. And they had left children, like Fatima, without

---

2 In 1995, the British Medical Society journal, the *Lancet*, published a report based on a Food and Agricultural Organization (FAO) survey estimating that Western sanctions were responsible for the deaths of 567,000 Iraqi children. The report was widely disputed. But further studies, such as by researchers from Columbia University and the World Health Organization, came up with corroborative findings – that a substantial number of children had died. In early 1999 a UN study found that child mortality rates in south-central Iraq rose from 56 per 1,000 births for the period 1984–89 to 131 per 1,000 for the period 1994–99. This compares to figures in the autonomous Kurdish region in the north, where child mortality rates actually fell during the same period, from 80 per 1,000 births to 72 per 1,000.

basic health care. The argument, put forward by Western politicians that it wasn't their fault because Saddam's cronies were selling off or failing to distribute medicine was both self-serving and spurious. The sanctions were in place precisely because Saddam was a bad guy. So they should have worked around it to make sure that children got the medicines and education they needed. But they didn't.

In Karbala, we left Zaid, Nihad and Fatima filming with Nick Woolley in the main square. Wisam and I found ourselves in a dingy office sitting across a desk from Abdul Murtafie, the head of the Islamic Dawa Party in Karbala. He was the direct counterpart to al-Shawi in Basra, but from a different world. Murtafie was small, stocky man in an ill-fitting suit. His face was seamed and pockmarked with little scars, his eyes flat and unafraid of direct contact. He had the look of a man who had been through a lot, both physically and emotionally.

I asked Murtafie if, instead of interviewing him in his dark office, he would come to the square. No problem, he said. And, I added, we had with us a girl who needed medical treatment and, for the purposes of our programme, could I ask him there how the Islamic Dawa Party would improve Iraqi health care and therefore help sick people like her. No problem, he said again, getting up from his chair and instructing his staff to organize a car.

We found Fatima outside the tomb of Imam Abbas. Wisam introduced Murtafie to Zaid, Nihad and then Fatima. Zaid was wearing a dark fleece jacket with a blue checked shirt. Nihad was in a full-length black niqab, but with her face uncovered. Fatima wore a loose, light green woollen jersey and a pale headscarf. In the busy area around us, with pilgrims, tourists and hawkers selling kebabs and trinkets, the family blended in as did Murtafie in his grey suit and open-necked pale shirt. Wisam explained how Nick Woolley would film us. Nick manoeuvred round with the camera on his shoulder. A crowd of pilgrims and sightseers began to form around us. I asked the same question that I had asked al-Shawi outside his home in Basra, but using Fatima's health, not rotting rubbish, as the issue.

'I wonder, what your party can do in improving the life of people like Fatima here,' I asked.

Murtafie began answering and I waited for Wisam to translate. Except he didn't. He fell into conversation with Murtafie who stepped back, his face darkening.

'He says the agreement was just to meet, not with a woman and child,' explained Wisam.

'OK,' I said softly. 'Is it a problem?'

'Definitely. He says that in the Islamic religion it is not possible for men to speak on issues like this with women present.'

'Why?' I said.

'Don't ask,' whispered Wisam. 'He says the filming was not agreed.'

'But it was.'

'I'm just translating, OK?' retorted Wisam, sharply.

Murtafie jabbed his finger at Wisam, then at Zaid. Nihad took Fatima's hand. Zaid put his hand on her shoulder and guided the family back into the crowd.

'He says they should have come directly to him. They should not have asked through a journalist.'

'All right. I'm sorry,' I said. 'That was my fault. Could he then give me a general answer about the Islamic Dawa Party's policy on health care?'

Murtafie's gaze darted over to check that Fatima was no longer there.

'He says there's a lot of disease in Iraq,' translated Wisam.

'He says that you come from a rich country. Why don't you offer help?'

'Yes, but it's you, not Britain, that is about to govern Iraq.'

'I'm not translating that,' snapped Wisam. 'He's very angry. Just walk away.'

Wisam stayed to calm Murtafie. Nick and I found Zaid at the edge of the square. He was visibly taken aback. 'I don't know about the future of Iraq, Mr Humphrey,' he said. 'Iraqis, they never help each other. He kept saying in the future, in the future, his party will do something. But they are so powerful now. Why can't they do something now? And what will they do? He didn't know. Has he thought about the future? Where is the future for Fatima? After ten years? When she becomes old? When she dies? Now, she is young and I need to save her. I am looking for anyone to help her.'

He leant forward, remonstrating with his hands. Then over my shoulder, he spotted Murtafie moving toward us. 'We should go,' he said quietly, his expression shifting to apprehension. Zaid knew what Iraq could be like when its people angered its rulers. The family melted into the crowd, and I never saw them again.

'Just say sorry,' Wisam said as he approached with Murtafie. 'Just keep apologizing and don't argue with anything he says.'

Murtafie pushed his way through to stand directly in front of me. He was carrying a two way radio. He pointed his finger and started yelling. 'He wants proof that you are reporter,' said Wisam. 'He says that the way you work makes him think you are not a reporter, but a spy.'

I showed him my ID card. 'I'm sorry,' I said. 'We didn't mean to cause any offence.'

Murtafie spoke sharply to Wisam. 'He says you might be lying to him. You have to wait while he contacts his superiors.

He says your cars are parked illegally. He is in charge of security. This is a sensitive area, and the cars will be taken away.'

I guessed we had a few minutes before real muscle arrived. So far it was just Murtafie and a couple of his staff. Our drivers from Baghdad had already gauged the atmosphere, had started engines and were backing out, doors unlocked ready for us to get in. I offered Murtafie a handshake which he reluctantly took. I held the grip for a long time, speaking apologetically in English, while Nick got in the vehicle, followed by Wisam. Murtafie didn't react. A minute later it was clear why. I said goodbye, climbed in and, with a wave, we drove away.

The police stopped the vehicles at the entrance of the square with instructions to arrest us.

'On whose orders?' I said.

'The Dawa Party,' translated Wisam. 'He says they have no choice but to obey. I've told him a political party can't do that, but he's not listening.'

'Let's just go,' I said.

The policeman shouted. The drivers didn't need any translation. None of us wanted to experience the inside of a Karbala jail. They gunned the engines and pulled away. A policeman raised his pistol, but didn't shoot. Soon we were lost amid the melee of traffic heading north toward Baghdad.

What on earth had America unleashed? Six months from now people like Murtafie and al-Shawi would be governing Iraq. But they didn't seem to have a single policy between them, except to threaten violence if they didn't get their way.

As we drove north through the afternoon, Wisam and I tried phoning the numbers of the Iraqi politicians in Baghdad again. There were twenty-five appointed members of the Iraqi Governing Council, made up of thirteen Shia, five Sunni, five Kurds, one Turkoman and one Assyrian. The people to find were the Shia because it was this community that would be running the government. The Sunni politicians, still bruised from losing power, were boycotting the process and waiting out the results of the insurgency. With al-Qaeda infiltration, they also faced high personal risk by getting involved.

On our list were men like the urbane, English-speaking Ahmed Chalabi, whom many in America wanted to be the new leader in Iraq; Ibrahim al-Jaafari, head of the Dawa Party and a doctor, with links to Iran, who spent his years of exile in Britain; and Jalal Talabani, the Kurdish leader who, through skilful political pragmatism, had won near-autonomy for his people in the north. There were others, too, and we had satellite, office and home phone numbers for them. Al-Jaafari's office picked up, but told us to call back later. When we did there was no reply.

We reached Baghdad before dark, crawling through the suburbs of low-lying squat buildings, telegraph poles rising stick-like out of the landscape and American military vehicles with young soldiers turning their machine guns in arcs of fire to protect their own.

Huge concrete blast walls sealed off the street where the BBC Bureau was. We had to snake round them to get to the front door. I could barely recognize the area from my visit earlier in the year.

Protection had become Baghdad's boom industry. Massive armoured vehicles, both civilian and military, bullied their way through the local Iraqi traffic of dilapidated cars. Blast walls were everywhere, together with razor wire and checkpoints where you could get shot if you misread the guards' signals.

Everyone was protecting themselves and damning the consequences to others. In Karbala, Murtafie's instinct of self-preservation was to lash out against the moral choice posed by Fatima. Al-Shawi threatened force if his party lost the election. Self-protection of the family, tribe or religion offered up a cause and narrowed choice away from the complicated process of creating civil society.

I checked into the Al Hamra, a small and once boutique hotel, now sad, empty and ringed by twelve-foot high concrete. They gave me a room on a lower floor to avoid rocket fire. Wisam went home to his family. Nick lodged at the BBC Bureau. I had an indifferent dinner in the hotel restaurant, empty except for an Australian general who had broken out of the heavily fortified Green Zone just to eat somewhere else.

Within the hotel's protected area was an Internet cafe. After closing the porn pages, I searched for websites of Iraq's political leaders. There were none, at least none the search engines could find. Why had they not bothered? What an easy way to reach out to the electorate, given that the war made it too dangerous for them to go out and campaign for any length of time. So how would voters know who they were and what they stood for? But then, as I was learning, it wasn't about the electorate. Power was seized and used, not earned and accounted for.

Before turning in, there was one success. The phone of Firaz al-Binook, our ferry friend, was working and he answered. We were invited round for coffee the next morning.

We found Firaz's house because in the entrance was the brand-new white BMW he had driven off the ferry a few days earlier. Then through a gap in the fence, we heard the hum of the generator he had also brought up from Dubai. The noise of generators in Iraq was a continuing indication that basic services remained far from functional.

Firaz, dressed in a casual shirt and jeans, opened the gates so we could drive our vehicle in. He walked us across the small garden into the house. He introduced us to his mother, his sister and brother, all of whom were doctors and seemed to have the same concerns as I had about Iraq's new leaders.

We sat around a table in the living room where it took me a moment to realize there were no pictures of Islamic clerics, but instead family heirlooms, antique furniture, and dust particles dancing on the light streaming in the front window. Nor was Firaz interested in lecturing us about Islamic values. He produced a letter headed by the logo of a Lloyds Bank branch in Northfield, Birmingham that said it was unable to transfer money to him because of international sanctions. The sanctions had been lifted back in May, but perhaps the news had taken some time to drip down to the bank tellers at the Birmingham office.

He also showed us a map of the land stolen from his family by the Baath Party. He had a roughly sketched drawing of the River Tigris winding its way through Baghdad with an area on the northern bank marked up as the family land. It was riverside and prime location real estate and he was determined to get it back.

'But you'll have to wait,' said his brother, dressed like Firaz in a casual shirt and jeans. 'There are no courts to verify your claim, and whoever's using it now is not just going to give up good land.'

'I guess you're right,' said Firaz, shaking his head.

'People here don't know how people in democratic countries actually live,' continued his brother. 'They have no idea what freedom and civil society actually is.'

'They will soon,' said Firaz. 'I think democracy will work for us eventually. Not for the first two or three years, but for the next ten, fifteen, twenty years.'

'Maybe,' said his mother. 'But a lot of people don't understand what democracy is. After you've lived under a very harsh regime like Saddam's, it is difficult to understand.'

'I want to say something,' said his sister, lifting back her headscarf that was falling down her shoulder. 'I don't know any of the political leaders because during Saddam's leadership he didn't allow anyone to be against him.'

'Anyone who rules Iraq must be better than Saddam,' said Firaz, 'even a foreigner.'

'Iraqi people have difficulty with foreigners,' interjected his mother. 'We say we don't like any foreigners. We say we don't like Americans. But we needed foreigners to get rid of Saddam, but we don't want to thank them for it. Even I can see there is something crazy about that.'

I brought out the list of phone numbers and flattened it out on the table. The paper was now dirtied and dog-eared from its journey up from Basra. 'What about these?' I said. 'Which names on this would you vote for?'

'Al-Jaafari,' said Firaz. 'He's Dawa Party.'

'Yes. He's Shia,' said his brother. 'He's a good leader. He's a moderate. He's open-minded.'

'No,' interjected his sister. 'The point is: who are they all? What have they done? How will they govern? We don't know anything about them. We know who is Bush, Cheney, Blair, but really who is this al-Jaafari? Who is this Talabani? Who is this Chalabi? We haven't seen them. They haven't worked here. We want to know more about these people.'

I had turned down an offer from the BBC Bureau to use contacts to find the politicians we wanted to speak to. I intended to access them through similar mechanisms available to Firaz's family. Even the list of phone numbers was cheating a bit. But given our failure so far, I decided that we would seek them out as we did back home, by going to their offices, waiting outside and – as we say in the trade – doorstepping them. The offices, though, were in the Green Zone, which was ringed by fortification. Firaz would never be able to get in. But we could.

Before leaving, we did pull one string for Firaz. Since his request on the ferry, I had found the number of the Lloyds Bank press office. We called, got through and then put Firaz on the line. Then the satellite phone connection fell down before he could speak. We left Firaz the number, wished him luck and headed off to the seat of Iraq's government in waiting.

The Green Zone covered about four square miles of Baghdad on a bend of the Tigris river along whose banks was a former presidential palace of Saddam's that became the American embassy. Other landmarks included a massive sculpture of swords that arced over a parade ground used to display military power. Giant copper fists holding them were meant to be modelled on Saddam's own hands. A main gathering point was a convention centre that would end up doubling as the Iraqi parliament, its walls decorated with murals showing faces of all cultures against a backdrop of modern roads and buildings. At the edge of the Green Zone was the Al Rasheed, the best hotel in town; the entrance floor was once tiled with a mosaic of President George H. Bush who was in office during the 1991 Gulf War. Guests had to walk over the former president's face in order to get inside, thus sullying him with the soles of their shoes, an act seen as an extreme insult in Arab culture. Two later ironies were that Iraqis slapped Saddam's statue with their shoes when it was pulled down in 2003 and an Iraqi journalist hurled his shoes at George W. Bush during the president's last visit in 2008.

The Green Zone was bordered to the south and east by the Tigris river and the rest was protected by coils of razor wire, chain-link fences and concrete barricades. At the entrances were tanks, armoured cars and heavy calibre machine guns in watchtowers. We couldn't take our vehicle in, so Nick Woolley, Wisam and I went in on foot through so many checkpoints that I honestly lost count. There seemed to be perimeters within perimeters and then more checks to each separate compound. Once inside the chaos and danger, the noise of traffic and the tang of the polluting diesel particles in the throat dissipated into an ordered tranquillity enforced by American law.

SUVs cruised the wide roads adhering to the 35 miles an hour speed limit. Bodyguards unclipped ammunition magazines from their weapons. This was place where you could jog by the river while listening to Freedom Radio, buy a bottle of wine and dance the night away at the Al Rasheed. It was perfectly designed for an occupying power because it had been Saddam's gated compound created to protect his inner circle from the pressures of dealing with the masses outside.

The palaces were opulent and spacious; the villas numerous and well appointed; the roads maintained and built to take military vehicles. It was easy to see how Iraqis believed one dictator had simply replaced another.

The Iraqi Governing Council was housed in a large building in landscaped gardens that used to be a section of the defence ministry. I had expected a foyer and reception area where I could hand over my business card and hope that someone might come out and talk to us. But I must have been nuts. We walked down the driveway to be met by a former Gurkha soldier manning yet another checkpoint. This one was impassable. The guard had been told to give out a phone number, which turned out to be the American military press office.

'I'm sorry, sir,' said the soldier who answered. 'They keep giving out our number, but they run their own show.'

'Do you have any way of getting a message to them?'

'We won't have any better luck than you.'

'But six months from now, they're going to be governing Iraq,' I said, unable to hide my irritation.

'Tell me about it,' he said. 'Welcome to democracy in the Middle East.'

Wisam unfolded our list of numbers. We dialled them all again. Two were just a few yards away inside the building beyond the concrete barriers. It was early afternoon on a weekday, but there were no answers.

Our Gurkha's supervisor came out and we used his phone to try some numbers. That didn't work either. Then, the anti-terror barriers slid to one side as a convoy of three SUVs flying the American flag drove out, the windows so darkened it was impossible to see who was inside.

The supervisor tried again. He used his two-way radio to ask if the Islamic Dawa Party leader, Ibrahim al-Jaafari, was in his office.

'I am sorry, sir. He says he is not allowed to confirm or deny Mr al-Jaafari's presence.'

A group of men walked out from a garden path, speaking loudly in Arabic. They were smartly dressed in dark suits and carried briefcases and document files.

'That's Jaafari,' said Wisam. 'I'm sure of it.'

'Excuse me!' I shouted. They slowed and one of them glanced over his shoulder toward us. Wisam spoke to them clearly in Arabic. The man looked away and they kept walking.

'Excuse me. Do you have just a minute?' I yelled. And then they were gone, melting back into the safety of their palace.

I didn't know what to think. I was more sad than angry, not so much about our story, but the whole charade that so many of us had reported on, argued about, voted on for so many years, that had caused so much death and misery, and this was how it was, not a bang but a whimper, a kind of Orwellian *Animal Farm* where the victims move into the palaces of their tormentors and then begin business as usual. For the past few days, we had been trying to prove that the country would be getting some form of responsible Iraqi-run government, some vision, some leadership, some sense of accountability. But we had failed. The end of the road in our journey was not a big, revealing conversation with a founding father of a new democracy but a disjointed language-hampered exchange with a Nepali security guard working for an American private company.

The next day we drove south to Kuwait, bypassing Basra and speeding through the ransacked border town of Safwan, which had become a magnet for armed gangs – or Islamic freedom fighters, depending whose side you were on. There was no immigration or customs there, just the same derelict buildings I saw in May, an empty road and silence in the vehicle as we flashed past at close to 100 miles an hour.

I lost contact with Firaz from Baghdad and Saleem from Basra. But years later in December 2008, out of the blue I got an email from Zaid. He had been working as an interpreter for the US military. He had seen constant action and had been wounded in both legs. The US had now given him a visa to settle in America, and he had just arrived in Chicago, but without Fatima. She was still living on blood transfusions and medication. Once Zaid had a Green Card, he hoped to take her to the United States, although the recession was biting and money was tight. Fatima had given up her ambition to be an Islamic teacher. She was at university in Babylon, studying English.

The journey through Iraq was only a snapshot, but it left

me troubled because those who had opposed the invasion and predicted that it would lead to catastrophe had been proved right. While I was one, I was more a reporter than a campaigner, and I had set off from Dubai with a yearning for the naysayers to be proved wrong. I had hoped that our leaders in London and Washington had known what they were doing and that our public servants, although working in secrecy, had drawn up plans on how to bring democracy to Iraq successfully.

But they hadn't. It seemed they had barely thought about it. Like many of us, I felt a fool.

After leaving Iraq on that revealing journey, I kept track of America's vision for a democratized Middle East with trips to Morocco, Egypt, Lebanon, Turkey, Israel and often back to Iraq. While Iraq held elections in 2006 in the midst of its civil war, Moroccan bombers attacked Casablanca in 2003 and again in 2007, and Madrid in 2004; Lebanon went to the brink of civil war; Israel fought a war with the Hezbollah Lebanese militia in 2006; Palestinian elections in 2006 gave a resounding victory in Gaza to the banned terror group Hamas; the Taliban began an offensive to take back Afghanistan; Pakistan veered towards terror and extremism and the electorate in democratic Turkey hovered on the cusp of voting in an Islamic government with policies that could have prompted military intervention.

In Washington, after the failure to find Iraq's weapons of mass destruction and the growing criticism of the war, policies on what America actually wanted to achieve and why were drafted and re-drafted until in 2005 the then Secretary of State Condoleezza Rice, speaking in the Middle East, announced a new ambition.

'For sixty years, my country, the United States, pursued

stability at the expense of democracy in this region, here in the Middle East, and we achieved neither,' she said. 'Now we are taking a different course. We are supporting the democratic aspirations of all the people.'

Rice's statement brought into the open a debate, much of it being conducted within the then ruling Republican Party, as to how to deal with autocratic regimes, with the administration now arguing that dictatorships caused terror, therefore democracy would end it.

She was referring to the Cold War policies that created dictators like Augusto Pinochet in Chile, Ferdinand Marcos in the Philippines and Mobotu Sese Seko of what was then Zaire and is now Congo.

The policy was new but the argument was based on a false premise. True, the 9/11 attackers were mainly from Saudi Arabia – a dictatorship. But the bombers who struck Madrid in 2004 came from Morocco, which could be regarded as a reforming autocracy. Its parliament is elected, but power lies with the king. The 2001 and 2008 attacks on the Indian parliament and Mumbai, and many others in between, originated in Pakistan, which swung between equally dismal military and elected leaders. The 2002 Bali bombers came from Indonesia, a new democracy emerging from generations of dictatorship and colonialism. And the 2005 London bombings were carried out by young men who had full access to everything Western democracy has to offer. Terrorism had been spawned throughout the full spectrum of political choices.

'There is no evidence in the past that democracy is related to the reduction of terrorism,' argued Republican academic Gregory Gause. 'There's really no evidence that any form of government is related positively or negatively to rates of terrorism. So my first impulse on this is leave it alone. We can't even control politics in Iraq when we have 140,000 troops on the ground and effectively put the government in power. How can we stage-manage politics in Egypt, or Syria, or Saudi Arabia?'

A key point that was emerging in Iraq, the Palestinian territories, Lebanon and elsewhere is that if free and fair elections were to be held throughout the Middle East, Islamic extremist movements would become politically powerful and naturally hostile to American interests thus increasing the risk of conflict.

The American Enterprise Institute (AEI), the natural home for neo-conservatism, provided the intellectual base for much of the administration's policy, and when I discussed it with one of its vice presidents, Danielle Pletka, she spelled out the consequences of democratic change with raw honesty.

'There are places where, yes, there's going to be violence,' she said. 'In a region where bloodshed has been the main means of governance and the main means of problem solving, it should be no surprise to us that there will be bloodshed. You will see more violence in some places and less in others. But what democracy does, is it provides alternatives to the ideology of terrorism. Democracy is an ideal and if you don't stand up for something and don't push for something you will never get there. I suppose you could say we're all stupid and say "I give up. Let's just give up." Those beaches are really steep. Let's not go into Normandy. But that's not how things work. You have ideals, you strive for ideals and you use power and influence to reach them. We've done a terrible disservice to hundreds of millions of peoples over the years. The foreign policy of the United States has changed for good and we will never ever revert back to the idea that we will pick the dictator over the oppressed.'

Danielle Pletka's argument was solidly based in the American psyche and went far beyond the invasion of Iraq or even the

9/11 attacks. While President George W. Bush was demonized throughout much of the world for ordering the Iraq invasion, his underlying thinking reflected the founding values of his country – which is why he won a second term in office. Three years after the Iraq invasion, President Bush stated that it was 'the policy of the United States to seek and support democratic movements and institutions in every nation and culture, with the ultimate goal of ending tyranny in our world'. But as far back as 1780, Thomas Jefferson spoke of America as the Empire of Liberty. Almost 200 years later in his 1961 presidential inaugural speech, John F. Kennedy said, 'We shall pay any price, bear any burden, meet any hardship, support any friend, oppose any foe, to assure the survival and success of liberty.' And with that, Kennedy began to embroil America in Vietnam.

It is worth looking at the broad issues of Vietnam, communism, and South East Asia, to understand American thinking over Iraq, Islam and the Middle East. Once again, we come across that democracy dilemma of what happens when voters choose the wrong type of government.

Colonial France was defeated in Vietnam in 1954, after which the North Vietnamese leader Ho Chi Minh planned to hold elections. But, as President Eisenhower pointed out at the time, the overwhelming majority of voters were expected to support Ho, a communist who would ally himself naturally to the Soviet Union.[3] Therefore, every effort was made to bolster the far more corrupt and inefficient regime in South Vietnam.

Ho wanted America to see his country not through the prism of international communism, but of Vietnamese nation-

---

3 Dwight D. Eisenhower, *Mandate for Change, 1953–1956* (Doubleday, 1963).

alism. But he also wanted Vietnam reunited and therefore set himself on an inevitable collision course. For its part, America wanted to draw a line against the communist threat and chose to do it in Vietnam.

In 1964, the US navy picked a fight with North Vietnamese patrol boats that came to be known as the Gulf of Tonkin incident. Congress reacted by giving approval to do whatever necessary to stop the spread of 'communist aggression' in South East Asia.

The equivalent in Iraq's case was the weapons of mass destruction claim, culminating in Secretary of State Colin Powell's presentation of evidence, much of it wrong, to the United Nations Security Council in February 2003.

With both Iraq and Vietnam, the more pragmatic, early goal was to make a point to an enemy and eradicate a threat. The longer worthy ambition was to create democratic societies that would be friendly to the United States. Vietnam was a Cold War frontier to stop Soviet communism. Iraq became one against Islamic extremism, although neither Saddam Hussein nor Ho Chi Minh started out as natural ideologues to the wider causes.

Soviet communism failed not through US military power, but because the idea didn't work. Soviet achievements in technology, infrastructure and building civil society were light years ahead of those of extreme Islam, whose people even have to import the batteries and explosives for their suicide bombs. Therefore aggressive Islam is also almost certain to fail because it, too, would prove to be an unworkable system of government.

Attempts at political reform in the Middle East have been cautious, the results mixed. Elections held by some governments fall far short of the exacting standards of democracy as defined by the West. Those that actually hand power to a new government often deliver a result deeply hostile to Western values, as the United States faced in Vietnam in the 1950s. Examples are the victory of Hamas in the Palestinian territories and inroads made by Hezbollah in Lebanon. These more productive elections are also played for higher stakes, thus increasing the risk of violence. The view in much of the Middle East, therefore, is that full Western-style democracy is too dangerous an experiment upon which to embark.

Kuwait has one of the most active parliaments in the region, dating back to 1963. But its powers remain limited. The emir routinely dissolves parliament because of deadlock[4] and recent elections have seen gains for the Salafists, who follow the fundamentalist Sunni ideology, a strand used by al-Qaeda. The fifty members have also been locked in disagreements, holding up key economic projects such as foreign investment in the oil sector.

Other Gulf states have eyed Kuwait's track record with scepticism. Instead of following suit with limited democracy of their own, they have mostly retained the status quo with none at all, while accepting the need to pay lip service to Western ideological interests.

Qatar passed new constitutional measures for a partially elected parliament in 2003, but one that would only have advisory power. In 2003, Oman held elections to a consultative council and again in 2007. Three years later, the United Arab Emirates allowed voting for a similar council but, again, one

---

4 In a recent case, in March 2009, the emir of Kuwait Sheik Sabah al-Ahmad al-Sabah dissolved the National Assembly that had only been sitting for ten months, saying he was taking the action to 'safeguard the security and stability of the nation'. New elections were held on 17 May 2009. Fundamentalists lost badly and reformists won, including – for the first time – four women.

that only advises and with only half the members elected from a small caucus of the population.

The Omani government actually invited me to cover the 2003 elections and provided a translator and a vehicle. Oman has a population of about 3.5 million and runs between the United Arab Emirates to the north, Saudi Arabia to the west and Yemen to the south. Its oil reserves are modest, so it has been developing agriculture, fishing and tourism as alternative sources of income.

Men and women were segregated into separate voting booths to choose members of the Consultative Council. There was already a Majlis al-Dawla or upper chamber of seventy-one seats with all members appointed by the monarch. These elections were for the lower chamber, the Majlis al-Shura, with eighty-four seats. Both chambers, as the name suggests, were strictly consultative. The Sultan Qaboos bin Said al-Said, who was also prime minister, could do what he wanted.

Once there, I found that I was banned from interviewing any of the candidates and it was near impossible to find out who they were. The newspapers published nothing about them and election law barred them from broadcasting on television or radio.

I complained to a local government leader, Sheikh Sulaiman bin Saad al-Aljabii, just outside the capital Muscat. This was undemocratic, I protested.

'No,' he said. 'Islam is democracy. There is a verse in the Koran which says leaders must consult. It is what the Prophet Mohammed did and this is how the Shura works.'

He cut a rather magnificent figure, in the evening light standing on flat, arid land where children were playing football, in a striking white robe with a curved dagger sheathed into his belt.

'But I do need to interview some candidates,' I insisted.

'It is not necessary,' he said with a courteous smile. 'We are a small society. Everyone knows each other.'

'So what are the election issues?'

'My aim is to provide good services for the people, give them a better life, things like getting them good street lights – things that immediately touch their lives.'

His succinct mission statement was far removed from those of the election candidates in Basra and Karbala a few months later. With the wind so politely taken out of my sails, I tried putting my case to the Omani information minister, Hamad bin Mohammed Rashdi. But he dismissed it out of hand.

'I don't think we want that in the near future,' he said. 'It is not our way to say we have democracy just by shouting at each other in public. Nothing beneficial will come of it.'

Even the American ambassador gave me short shrift. 'I think what they're doing here is admirable,' said Richard Baltimore. 'We must support the wisdom of the Sultan. These elections are an incredible development within the preserves of Omani culture and history.'

So with political parties banned, no public campaigning allowed and with the winners having no power to change government, America praised this as a model. It was all very Alice in Wonderland, but it was also a phenomenon being repeated throughout the world.

In Iran, for example, elections can actually send presidents from office, but in the West's view they are the wrong kind of elections. Africa is awash with countries that have held elections fuelled by corruption and vote-buying and have delivered nothing but blight. Yet these countries are listed as being democratic, unless they throw up a hostile threat, in which case they become a rogue state. When, for example, did

Robert Mugabe slip from being democratically elected leader to dictator?

China, so routinely condemned for its oppression and lack of democracy, is now the key ally in fighting the economic crisis. But because that goes against the grain of our own value system, I wouldn't be surprised if soon China is being praised for a semblance of political reform, so that in one sweep apparent oppression will become apparent freedom.

Numerous initiatives have accompanied the push for democracy in the Islamic world, just as they have in drives against poverty in Africa. The Middle East Initiative, originally created at Harvard in 1998, was now calling on Turkey to become a democratic model that other Islamic countries would follow. Morocco was negotiating for increased status with the European Union. The Cedar Revolution was gripping the imagination of Lebanon. And each of those three countries reacted in a different way.

Morocco lies on the edges of the Atlantic Ocean and Mediterranean where its coastline is only twelve miles from British-run Gibraltar and southern Spain. Its 35 million people are ruled by the young-ish King Mohammed VI, who can dissolve parliament and dismiss ministers, holds all power but has been pushing through reforms, although nothing like the shock democracy that unfolded in Iraq. Morocco's slums were home to Islamic bombers who struck Casablanca and Madrid. Its beaches and mountain resorts are playgrounds to the international jet set and package tourists, and its politicians are a fascinating example of shifting sands, of how the friendly ideology of one generation becomes the hostile one of the next.

'I feel for the Islamists,' Mohammed Guessous, a veteran of Morocco's Socialist Party, told me. 'In the seventies and eighties we were all being beaten up and jailed and the Islamic movements were being encouraged because the government thought they represented the best protection against communism. Now, it's us who offer the protection against Islamism, and they who are being beaten up and jailed. And what do we have in common? We both represent the interests of the poor.'

During the Cold War years, some 10,000 people in Morocco are believed to have been killed, jailed or forced into exile. In the War on Terror, Morocco has put hundreds under arrest and Moroccan jails have allegedly been used to torture al-Qaeda suspects under instructions from Western intelligence agencies. For this and similar work, Morocco was rewarded with the status of being a non-NATO ally. It also has a particularly close historical relationship with Washington because in 1776 it was the first country in the world to recognize newly independent America.

A few months after the 2003 Casablanca bombings, I found myself in the offices of the royal palace in Rabat, asking André Azoulay, the king's special adviser, what impact the attack would have on the reforms taking place.

'Nothing will undermine the democratic process,' he said. 'We want to improve day after day the democratic rules of our political game. I don't see any threat of having our process slowing down. On the contrary, the majority of Moroccans want to speed up the process to make it bigger and stronger to make clear that democracy is the right answer to terror.'

But further into the conversation in his opulent office, the clarity blurred somewhat, and Azoulay made an astute observation. 'As a Moroccan, I know about your history, your philosophy, your literature. It is more than the West will ever know about us. This gap in knowledge is a big problem when you and I are talking about democracy because it creates misunderstanding.'

I wasn't quite clear what he was saying, so I asked him to

repeat the point. He shifted in his chair and pointed his finger directly at himself and then at me. 'I know about you. But you do not know about me. I know about the West, but you do not know about Islam. That is why we have misunderstanding.'

That evening, I went down to Casablanca's seafront, where the young were dressed in tank tops, T-shirts, jeans and shorts, hanging around a huge multiplex cinema. Not one of the many theatres was showing a Moroccan, Arab or Middle Eastern film. They carried the same diet of Hollywood and European films that were on at my local cinema in London. What about local culture? I asked the manager. 'No one wants to see those movies,' he said. 'We tried a Palestinian film last week and barely sold a ticket.'

On the same shoreline was the magnificent Casablanca Hassan II mosque, one of the biggest in the world, where waves from the Atlantic Ocean crashed onto rocks below, creating a dramatic image of man, nature and God. Juxtaposed against the nearby Hollywood-driven cinema, the scene threw up a common contradiction about how the developing world views the West. It craves the technology, science, medicine, music and movies. Yet it rejects the system that produces them, and the power and influence that the system projects.

In late 2005, I was back in Morocco again, this time to look specifically at elections and democracy. At that time, the social-ists were the strongest movement, but the main Islamic group, the Islamic Justice and Development Party, was becoming a powerful opposition force.

I wanted to see how the stakeholding elements of democ-racy had percolated down to the grass roots. In other words, did the electorate feel that their vote would change anything? Or, as was argued in much of the developing world, did they believe the electoral process could be detrimental to their living standards?

We headed out of Rabat to the shanty slum village of Akrash. It was a few miles inland on raised rolling ground of arid yellow-brown caked earth, peppered with dull green under-growth all laid out under a clear blue sky. Within seconds of getting out of the vehicle, I counted half a dozen basic things that contravened the rules of the European Union that Morocco was so keen to join – open drains, rotting rubbish, unsafe electrical wires, children exposed to fetid water and so on. It would not have required rocket science to fix these things and begged the question that if Malaysia can deliver basic services to its most remote islands, why can't Morocco clean up a village twenty minutes' drive from its capital city?

It also raised another question of human needs and aspira-tions. Time and time again, we in the West are lectured that Islamic societies are different from ours in their customs, culture and the core view of how people think – which is what André Azoulay, the king's adviser, had alluded to. Yet, walking around Akrash, it soon became resoundingly clear that the families there were on the same thought pattern as me. The place was a dump. What they wanted was pretty basic, but their experience of elections had left them totally disillu-sioned.

The only government presence we found in the village was run from a roadside shack that served as the office for the Interior Ministry – the apparatus that kept a check on what people were doing. We were about to cross the road to talk to the two men inside, when a young mother, dressed in bright blue and carrying a baby, stormed up to us. She had heard that we were asking about democracy and elections and insisted we look at a brand-new water standpipe, built into a concrete enclave with a drain running into the ground.

'See this tap,' she said, 'try turning it on.' I did and nothing came out. 'The politician came here with builders and a concrete mixer and said we must vote for him because he would give us running water.' She handed her baby to a friend so she could show me how the standpipe was connected to nothing at all, and the drain just vanished into gully of stinking water. 'The day after the election, the builders disappeared,' she said.

She led us further up the street. 'You see that street lamp. Another politician put it up and for a week before the election we had light. Then afterward, zap, the power was cut off again.'

'Who did you vote for?' I asked.

'Does it matter?' she said angrily, taking back her baby. People in the crowd that had gathered round were nodding. This was a community far away from making the link between elections, democracy and government actually having anything to do with their day-to-day problems.

That was when I met Souffian Baghari. He stood out in the cluster of children gaping at us. Eleven years old and wearing the filthiest yellow shirt, he had a puck nose, dimples in his cheeks and scarecrow dark hair. Souffian was alone and homeless. His parents had split up and abandoned him, it seemed. His father was in Marrakesh, he thought, and his mother in Tangiers. Souffian had no home, no money and no schooling. But he was bright and charismatic, such that the other children deferred to him when they spoke.

'Where do you live?' I asked.

'Up there,' he said, pointing to a hillside about a mile back from the village.

We drove up, turned the final corner of the road to his home and came face to face with a scene out of a biblical apocalypse. It was huge rubbish tip. Seagulls and crows swooped down. The birds landed on the backs of goats and sheep and pecked at their wool soiled and dangling with rubbish. Birds, animals and people foraged for food. Many were children, rags hanging, heads down, hacking with pitch-forks or their bare hands.

'This is where I sleep,' said Souffian, walking over to a huge old tractor tyre, lying among weeds. Inside the rim were a few possessions, a twig with a red cloth on it, a pair of sandals and a toy racing car.

'Here, watch,' he said. 'This is how I sleep.' He climbed inside the tyre, curling round inside where the inner tube would have been. He put his head on two clasped hands, closed his eyes and pretended to sleep. But when he opened his eyes, some-thing had changed in his mood. All the way up from the village he had joked and laughed. He had put on a front of how much he enjoyed his life and his friends. But for an eleven-year-old boy, whatever his culture or religion, being abandoned by your parents is a loss that is only ever thinly beneath the surface. He pulled himself out of the tyre, brushed his hands over his shirt and looked straight up at my interpreter, Hassan. As he spoke, tears welled up in his eyes.

'He says he does whatever he can to eat,' translated Hassan. 'He works on the dump all day and sleeps in the tyre. His friends help him out and bring him clothes, but he's asking if you think this is a normal life. He says what he really wants is for some new parents to adopt him so that he can have a normal life.'

'Does the government help him at all?' I asked.

'He says he's never seen them.'

We took Souffian back down to the village to see if Morocco was so poor it could not look after its abandoned children, or whether it was just badly run. I believed Souffian, but the truth of his story didn't really matter. He was a child who needed the protection of the state. Hassan had seen a local school, a low-rise, whitewashed building, with a large playground shaded by trees. We headed there and, as we walked in, Souffian's head turned left and right, his expression becoming excited as he saw other children, then a matronly teacher, Kalada Elghalia, wearing a crisp, white tunic.

'Can this boy enrol in your school?' I asked her.

'Yes, of course,' she said, putting her hand on Souffian's shoulder.

'Does he have to pay money?'

'No. No money at all. He can come any time.'

Souffian reached up to take her hand, his face breaking into a smile.

'All right,' I said. 'That's great.'

'But he must first register and see the headmaster,' said Kalada.

'Then, can we do that now?'

'The headmaster is not here today.'

'When will he be back?'

'Maybe next week.'

Hassan shot me a glance. It wasn't going to happen. Souffian knew, too. He lowered his eyes and turned away. Possibly he had been through this process before. Maybe, he lived in the tyre on the rubbish tip because no one would take him in. We walked back to the village and headed for the Interior Ministry shack. Here, at least, was an arm of government bound by international law on looking after children. Two wiry men emerged.

'Let me tell you something,' said one of them, peering at us through dark glasses. 'A delinquent child like this represents a big danger to society. We have a list of people like him which we forward to our head office. His parents aren't here, so what can we do?'

'Hold on,' I said, 'you're saying that because he has no parents, you can't help him?'

'The problem is with the child,' said the other, pushing a dirty white baseball cap back on his head. 'It's pointless to talk about it.'

'But why isn't he in school?'

'He doesn't want to go to school.'

'But there's a law.'

'The problem with this kid is that he's from Marrakesh. His father has abandoned him completely and now he has to fend for himself. It really is his problem, not ours.'

Hassan took their number. We drove Souffian back up to the rubbish tip and left him there. That evening, I tracked down the education minister, Habib Al Malki, a suave French-speaking politician with perfect manners dressed in an immaculate cream suit.

I asked him why Souffian, an eleven-year-old boy, was living on a rubbish tip and was not being given an education. I cited the United Nations convention of the rights of the child to which Morocco was a signatory. Article 20 stated that a child deprived of family environment should be entitled to special protection and assistance provided by the state. Article 28 recognized the right of the child to education, and at a primary level it should be compulsory and free.

'Yes, I am aware of that,' said Mr Al Malki. 'There is social marginalization, it's true, but the policy we've put in place is to set up strongly representative local committees which we help to find solutions to put back all the children who've fallen through the education net.'

We talked for some time, but never once did he ask where he – or his staff for that matter – could actually find Souffian. Eventually, I got fed up with his *blah blah* and told him. We also gave Souffian's details to a local charity that notified the government through its own channels.

But two weeks later, when they went to check, Souffian was

still sleeping in the tyre. No one had been to help him. Eventually, a Moroccan organization based in the United States took up his case and the last I heard Souffian was in Rabat, at school and learning the hotel trade.

Souffian's story was unconnected with democratic reform. Neither the autocratic government of King Mohammed VI nor the politicians vying for election had penetrated far enough into the Akrash slum to lift its medieval standard of living. The woman who showed us the fake standpipe was spot on. What did it matter whether the politicians were conservative, socialist or Islamic? The point is they hadn't delivered. In fact, they had lied in order to win votes.

Does that sound familiar?

There was no unshakeable doctrine embedded within the people of Akrash. Those were being written in the mosques of the Middle East and the think tanks of the Washington beltway. They had yet to reach such dismal places. So far, none had proved it could do a better job than the other because Akrash was not about religion, democracy or freedom. It was about infrastructure and good governance.

That Harvard brainchild known as the Middle East Initiative had now been taken up by America, which wanted Turkey to take a lead in a democracy drive throughout the region. Unlike Morocco, Turkey was already a reasonably fully-fledged secular democracy that was a member of NATO and had ambitions to join the European Union. It understood, therefore, the concept of good governance and it was possible to hold a discussion that went beyond Islam, uncollected rubbish and open drains.

Its territory strategically straddles both Asia and Europe and the Bosporus waterway runs between the two continents, therefore controlling the entrance to the Black Sea and its energy supplies. For six hundred years from fourteenth to the twentieth century, Turkey's Ottoman Empire covered much of Eastern Europe, the Middle East and north Africa. It was at its height in the sixteenth and seventeenth centuries and ended in the early 1920s after the First World War. But after its collapse, Turkey did not linger. Under the nationalist leader Kemal Atatürk, it tried to mould itself into a forward-looking secular republic. Atatürk banned sharia law and Islamic schools and marriage. He switched the weekly holiday from Friday to Sunday. He adopted the Western calendar, and gave women the right to vote. It took him just thirteen years – the same period that Iraq stagnated between the first Gulf War and the US-led invasion.

Turkey held its first elections in 1950. Since then, the military often stepped in when it believed democratic inclinations would steer the nation away from its secular constitution. The War on Terror brought the issues to the forefront with the army keeping a tense vigil on an increasingly Islamic-minded government. After being a solid anti-Soviet Cold War ally, Turkey's 75 million people were beginning to shift allegiances. A pivotal example of the functioning executive parliament was the 2003 vote banning American troops from crossing Turkish soil to invade Iraq from the north.

We were heading to a coalmining town called Beypazari just outside of the capital, Ankara – the equivalent of an American heartland community, a good place to gauge grass-roots opinion on key issues. A small community with a main road flanked by narrow winding streets, it had cash machines, cellphone shops and metal workshops with glowing forges. The cafe we went into was thick with cigarette smoke, a place of gloomy colours, dark winter clothing and hardwood tables where men played cards amid smells of tobacco and rich Turkish tea.

When I opened a conversation by suggesting that Turkey could take a lead in democratizing the Islamic world, disdain spread around the half-dozen tables coupled with a shaking of heads.

'What America wants to do is divide us into small weak countries so that we can be controlled from the Pentagon,' said Huseyin Yulmaz, a retired coalminer.

Another card player, Yinasi Ertugal, agreed. 'America's trying to set a trap for us, wanting us to think that we, too, will become like Iraq if we don't do what it says.' He cupped his huge hands to light a cigarette. 'I wish America was not the only policeman in the world now. It's doing whatever it wants, like a naughty child breaking things when it doesn't get its way.'

'He's right,' said Huseyin. 'The American behaviour in Iraq when they smash up mosques and kill people is not good. Condoleezza Rice was recently in our region and she said that all countries from Tunisia to Kazakhstan will change to become democratic. But what America really wants to do is make those countries weak.'

'So you don't trust America?' I asked.

'America cannot be trusted.'

Their views echoed those in many parts of the Islamic world. But the nuance was interesting, particularly when I asked whether Turkey should lessen its alliance with America.

'There's no point in that,' said Yinasi Ertugal nonchalantly. 'But I do wish the Soviet Union was still around to keep them in line.'

They were not speaking from the viewpoint of the oppressed or the victim. These were men whose grandparents and great grandparents had run the Ottoman Empire. Their culture was one of controlling and deciding destiny, the mindset of a colonizer over the colonized.

The political views and confident sense of self was not confined to coalmining community of Beypazari. They were also mirrored in one of the fashionable coffee shop areas of cosmopolitan Istanbul.

'Most empires screw up after about 250 years,' said a college professor with a buzz cut wearing a red T-shirt with Che Guevara emblazoned on the front. 'But America seems to have started earlier. So where Turkey is now, the great United States will soon be.'

'America should learn about democracy itself,' said a designer, clad totally in black, taking off his shades to make sure I got the point.

'America is now a threat to the whole world,' agreed a television presenter, walking two huge but finely behaved and coiffured dogs. And it went on like that – one after the other.

While sentiment came from the streets, specific answers about Turkey's role in the Middle East Initiative came from parliament and academia. 'Before we do anything, America has to solve the problem of Iraq,' explained Dr Cagri Erhan, a political scientist at Ankara University. 'Without shaping Iraq, they have no hope in making further inroads into these Middle Eastern societies.'

'But they are looking for Turkey to take the lead in proving democracy can work in an Islamic society.'

He laughed. 'You have to understand that the nation-state building in the Middle East has been mainly based on anti-Turkish sentiment. As the Ottomans, we stand accused of keeping their societies poor and underdeveloped for five centuries. In their eyes we have no legitimacy to give a lead in anything.'

Then we spoke to a senior parliamentarian who had also been Turkey's ambassador to Washington. Dr Sukru Elekdag invited us into his elegant wood-lined office and picked up in detail from where Dr Erhan had left off.

'Yes,' he said. 'We, too, want to see a Middle East which is democratized and stable and at peace. This would be wonderful because it would create a large market for trade and we would be surrounded by prosperous neighbours who would not be a threat. But many governments in the Middle East look at this American initiative as a new colonialism, as subterfuge, as a threat that America wants to lavish itself on this area in order to control the petroleum and intervene in their internal affairs.'

'Is this how Turkey looks at it?'

'That is irrelevant. We cannot lead an initiative when many of the countries do not accept its premise. Yes, this part of the world needs modernization. We all agree with this. But, unfortunately, the present circumstances do not allow America to implement this project successfully.'

'But Turkey,' I pressed again. 'If you involved yourself more, America could take a lower profile.'

Dr Elekdag spread his arms expressively in the air and his face broke out into a smile. 'Our own empire is too recently broken up to take on that mantle again,' he said. 'But perhaps if America can solve its own problems then we could be more willing.'

'Like what?' I said, half knowing the answer.

'The occupation of Iraq and of the Palestinian territories.'

The Israeli–Palestinian conflict peppered my conversations through Iraq, Morocco, Turkey and elsewhere. I have never known any issue to have had such a resonance among so many people for so many years. Often it was mentioned tangentially, thrown in to underline a point. It was like a stovepipe, an insoluble fact that would take you to a dead end with nowhere left to move. But if the West really wanted stability in the Middle East, this problem had to be resolved, although it was by no means certain that elections would be the mechanism by which to do it.

One day, while covering the 2006 Hezbollah–Israel war, I headed off to the village of Ilaniyya in southern Galilee that was supposedly the oldest Jewish settlement in what was then Palestine. Land title documents go back to the mid-nineteenth century, with the village itself first titled in 1898 – long before the Holocaust and the creation of Israel that followed. Ilaniyya was one of the first places Jews, escaping European anti-Semitism, came to live.

The village was a cluster of rugged single-storey homes, flowers in front gardens and grit-coated four-by-four vehicles in back yards with other machinery needed to tame land and stay self-sufficient. It was built on high ground that commanded views eastwards to the now disputed area of the Golan Heights and Syria.

A local historian, Dr Estie Yankelevitch, took me to a point where we could see the Israeli flag flying above an army camp.

'Over there,' she said. 'That's where the first-ever militia was trained up to protect Jewish settlers. Now we call it the Israeli Defense Force.

'When the Jews first came here, they bought the land from Arab owners. They paid for everything. But local people were used to walking through it and the settlers needed it for cultivation. There was trouble, but it was only petty crime.

'It became more serious in 1908 with the Ottoman revolution in Turkey and nationalism started emerging. Then came the great Arab uprising 1936–39, then Independence in 1948, then . . .' She paused, to flick away dirt which had blown into her face. 'Well, it hasn't stopped, has it?'

'Did they know,' I asked, 'that there'd be so much violence?'

She shook her head. 'Nobody anticipated that the cost would be so heavy. You see, it's a clash of ideas. It's Europe in the Middle East. The Jews didn't realize the Arabs would become their enemy and be so strong. They thought they could live side by side and, with their Western technology, help them advance. But a hundred years of conflict and we are still having to fight for this land.'

'What happened to the Arabs who lived here?'

Dr Yankelevitch pointed north-west. 'Just over there,' she said. 'They went to Turon.'

She was referring to the ethnic cleansing that took place during Israel's independence in 1948, known by the Palestinians as *al Nakba* or the *Catastrophe*. We left Ilaniyya and headed down to a crossroads of Highways 77 and 65, known as the Golani Junction. It looked like a modern American country intersection with a service station, McDonald's and huge road signs to Haifa, Tel Aviv and Tiberias. We turned left, drove for about a mile, then went off up a small road to Turon – where the minarets of a mosque rose above houses built up a hillside.

Immediately, we were in a different world of winding alleys, minibuses filled with families, children running around, laughing, men talking in groups and workmen repairing buildings.

Along the street, which curved round to the mosque, Ibrahim Salaymeh, a teacher, heard us speaking English, asking about Ilaniyya, and he came up to correct us. He was a thoughtful, diffident man, keen to put us right, but nervous about giving offence. As he talked, he kept cuddling his daughter to stop her running off to play with other children.

'Are you talking about Segera?' he said. 'The Arab village destroyed by Jewish fighters in 1948. In Arabic, it's Segera. In Hebrew it's Ilaniyya. It means tree. My parents, my uncles and aunts all lived in Segera. Here in Turon we're called the Segera people. My parents used to go back again and again just to see their destroyed houses and their land.'

'But now, surely, you could go back and live if you wanted,' I said.

He laughed. 'I could. But this isn't Britain. It wouldn't work. No Jews here. No Arabs there. I've accepted the reality. I enjoy being an Israeli citizen and the higher standard of living.'

'Then, why all the fighting still?'

'Search me,' he said lightly. 'I think politicians are making it tough. That's all.'

A flicker of hesitation crossed his face. His smile vanished. Distracted for a second his daughter wriggled free and ran off to play. 'But we cannot ever forget it,' he said softly. 'Nobody can forget their homeland.'

Israel is a vibrant European-style democracy created on territories of competing homelands in the middle of a swathe of mainly non-democratic communities. Its very existence is disputed by its neighbours. Its ancient monuments look back to a troubled past while sweeping highways and hi-tech companies speak to the dream of building a nation out of its calamitous history. The Holocaust is the tragedy from which Israel came into being. But it is as if the Vatican and California had merged to be suddenly reincarnated in the Middle East where it was unwelcome. It has made Israel an edgy place unable to rid itself of the spectre of persecution and war.

Both Israel and the Palestinian territories are technically democracies. Israel's is more mature. It delivers to its people, but fails its neighbours – and most significantly the Palestinians. The Palestinian democracy is embryonic, not yet delivering the fundamentals that accountable government should be all about. In 2006, Palestinian parliamentary elections threw out a lethal conundrum that Western democracies have yet to come to grips with. It is essentially the same issue by which Mao Zedong won China in 1949, Ho Chi Minh's North Vietnamese communists took Vietnam in 1975, and Salvador Allende swept to power in Chile in 1970.

In all those places, people looked to a more disciplined and visionary leadership than the one in place, but one that was hostile to Western interests. In China, the pro-American nationalists became complacent and corrupt. In Vietnam, the south was propped up by the United States, but with no real idea of what the society should become. In Chile, the people were persuaded by policies of education, health care and land reform. In the Palestinian territories, the lead organization for many years had been Fatah, regarded by many as becoming self-satisfied and inefficient.

Mao Zedong never stood for elections and took power by force. Ho Chi Minh was widely expected to have won a land-slide in elections due in 1956, but the United States arranged for them to be cancelled. In Chile, Salvadore Allende was overthrown in a US-backed military coup. In the Palestinian territories in 2006, Hamas won elections using the destruction of Israel as a cornerstone of its policy. In the eyes of Western democracies, Hamas was an illegal terrorist organization. Palestinian voters had delivered them an unpalatable lesson, disproving a much-cited maxim that elections are the best way to deliver peace. In this case, it led to difficult moral choices and war.

Flushed with electoral success, Hamas used military force to expel its rival Fatah from Gaza – a narrow twenty-five-mile-long strip of coastal Palestinian territory. Israel blockaded Gaza, and the West imposed sanctions. Hamas attacked Israel with rockets, and Israel responded with the early 2009 Gaza war. Shortly afterwards, Israelis voted in a more hard-line government.

The main issues in both the Palestinian and Israeli elections were far more about security than development, which is a common voter reaction for communities that see themselves under threat. In 1983, Margaret Thatcher was swept back into office after victory in the Falklands War. In 2004, George W. Bush won a second presidential term because of the War on Terror. Short electoral cycles of only three or four years rarely give leaders enough time to push through peace policies. But they do provide plenty of scope to reap the benefits of war.

The conundrum was not confined to Hamas. Six months after its electoral victory, Hezbollah, another banned Islamic organization based in Lebanon, fought a short war with Israel, even though Hezbollah was a prominent political party in democratic Lebanon.

Had Israel and its enemies been fighting it out in a hidden corner of central Asia or Africa, this might have become a forgotten issue. But they were not and their hostilities have defined relationship between the powers since Israel's creation in 1948. From Morocco to Malaysia, the unresolved Israel–Palestinian conflict continually spills out when discussion turns to the United States and Western democracy. Why, when so many other disputes with similar origins do get resolved, does this issue continue to linger, and would democratizing the Middle East help solve it?

In Haifa, during the 2006 Hezbollah war, I went to see Dr Eli Somer, a clinical psychologist who had been counselling people traumatized by the rocket attacks. He was in his mid-fifties with a full head of unkempt grey hair and I spoke to him in his living room lined with books, decorated with tapestries and paintings, and with a small piano in the corner.

'To understand Israel you must consider the lesson of the Holocaust,' he said. 'Most Israelis do not take for granted their independence, their statehood, the legitimacy by which they are seen from the outside world. People feel that, given the history of the Jewish people, we have no one to rely on but ourselves and that the world will forsake us.'

'If Israel were your patient,' I asked, 'how would you psychoanalyse her?'

Somer laughed quietly at the challenge and thought for a moment. 'I would describe her as a persecuted person, somewhat paranoid, but being paranoid does not mean you are not being persecuted. I would see this patient as having a lot of difficulty relying on the benevolence of others. She would not be in a healthy state because if a person is not trusting and feels threatened she can lash out.'

'And how would you treat that patient?' I asked.

'It's an interesting anthropological summation of a nation you are asking of me,' he chuckled, shaking his head. 'I would need to convince that client of mine that the threat is not there any more, that it's safe out there, that she can take a risk and trust her neighbours and bring down the guard and relax her general state of alert. But with such a history, the slightest sense that the threat and the danger is out there will immediately reinstate a psycho-pathological state of hypervigilance and suspicion.'

His analysis was along the lines of what I had heard from professionals working in similar traumatic situations. Kosovo and Serbia immediately come to mind, together with the Sinhalese and Tamils in Sri Lanka. In professional jargon it is often referred to as an interface breakdown, when trust is so low that compromise is not possible. Israel is a special case because of the Holocaust and its impact on regional and global policy.

If elections on both sides were creating even more hard-line governments, then there was another momentum that was proven to move a fragile peace to a permanent one – trade. Yet neither the Palestinians nor the Israelis nor their Arab neighbours have brought trade levels anywhere near a tipping point that makes war unthinkable, as have for example China and Taiwan.

Ninety-two per cent of Israel's trade is with Europe, North America and Asia. Its trade with Jordan and Egypt combined, the two Arab countries with which Israel has formal peace agreements, is just 0.6 per cent of the total.[5] Israel's products are hi-tech. Its Arab neighbours are low-tech. Efforts so far, to find more common trading ground have failed.

'Israel is very anxious to establish these links,' economist Michael Ben-Gad from the University of Haifa told me. 'But the Arabs are very reluctant because they are genuinely unpopular with their own people.'

In comparison, 40 per cent of Taiwan's trade is with China, its historical enemy. So despite there being many ingredients for hostilities to break out the prospect of war has moved off the agenda.

In recent years, figures have begun to emerge of how much wealth individuals need in order to feel they are stakeholders in their societies, which is a different concept from being stakeholder in a cause. This is the level at which it's thought democracy can begin to take hold, a point when the individual feels something is worth protecting rather than sacrificing violently for a greater ideal.

---

5 Central Bureau of Statistics, Israel.

Dr Paul Collier, in his book *Wars, Guns and Votes*,[6] estimates that a perception of about US$2,700 a year is the balance point. If democratic reform is attempted beneath this level, societies are more prone to violence. But if reform is not started after income levels exceed US$2,700 then those societies are at risk of violence breaking out. In 1985, when Taiwan's per capita reached US$5,000, the government judged the society was becoming cohesive enough to loosen the reins and began to test democratic rights.[7]

While Collier's was an academic study, the government of Taiwan was on the cutting edge of the calculation. It may have been more cautious than necessary, but, like Collier, it identified the balance point.

For the Palestinian territories average per capita income is about US$600 in Gaza and US$2,500 on the West Bank. By both Collier's and Taiwan's benchmarks, it is too low for democracy to take root safely. Therefore, in the Israeli–Palestinian issue there is a lethal cocktail of hostile neighbours, clashing cultures, negligible trade and elections that produce extremism. It is a formula for war, and that's even before we get to the blame-game details of rocket attacks, settlements, and historical grievances. And the conflicts surrounding Israel spill over elsewhere and one of the countries most affected has been Lebanon.

In the Chouf Mountains inland from Beirut lies the castle of Walid Jumblatt, the hereditary leader of the Druze, a warrior Muslim sect whose men have been deployed as fighters from as far back as the thirteenth century when they protected Lebanon from Christian Crusaders from Europe.

---

6 *Wars, Guns and Votes: Democracy in Dangerous Places* (Bodley Head, 2009).
7 More details on this are in the final chapter.

Jumblatt became famous in the 1980s during the Lebanese civil war as a stylish young heir on a motorcycle. In 2005 he had become a debonair elder statesman. When I met him, there was talk of the outbreak of another war, and he was impatient and frustrated on the question of the West and democracy in the Middle East.

'They have an idea of regime change in Syria and we oppose that,' he said. 'They shouldn't push too far. We don't want that kind of democracy. We don't want the same experience in Syria as in Iraq.'

Lebanon's civil war ran from 1975 to 1990. It was partly fuelled by the Palestinian diaspora from Israel, partly by tension between Christians and Muslims and partly, as Jumblatt was about to show me, by superpower rivalry. America, Britain and France tried to bring peace, but instead came under attack by Islamic fighters who later went on to found Hezbollah. The West then handed the mantle of forging peace to non-democratic Syria – the power that had controlled Lebanon on and off for centuries.

Together with successive Lebanese governments, Syria provided an imperfect stability and allowed Lebanon to rebuild into a far freer society than Syria itself was. Lebanon's parliament and other institutions began to put down new roots.

In 2005, while these institutions were still vulnerable, the West pushed through a UN Security Council resolution insisting that Syria withdraw. Lebanon was at a dangerous and sensitive transition point where the Lebanese wish for self-determination was rubbing up against Syria's continuing will to keep control. While its heavy hand was causing much resentment, little outside thought appeared to have been given to how Syria, or its rogue agencies, would react to a sudden and forced withdrawal.

In February 2005, the charismatic former prime minister,

Rafik Hariri, an advocate of Syria's withdrawal, was killed in a bomb attack on the Beirut seafront. His death was blamed on Syrian agents. Lebanon's ubiquitous cedar tree, emblazoned on the national flag, became the symbol for anti-Syrian protests, which were hailed by Washington as evidence of democratic winds sweeping through the Middle East.

Syria had a large constituency of support that included the Hezbollah. Its public expulsion had the result of instilling a natural fear in one community that comes with sudden lost influence. The result was assassinations, car bombings, scraps between militia, an ineffective, divided government and – arguably – Hezbollah's 2006 war with Israel. Once again, Lebanon became a dangerous place. Compare that to the staged, negotiated withdrawal that took place over many years between Britain and China on Hong Kong's handover in 1997.

Jumblatt, however, was convinced there would be no return to civil war. Despite the pressures and regional power politics, one ingredient was lacking. 'For war you need money,' he said, 'and money comes from rich patrons. If there are no patrons, there will be no war.' He stood up and spoke to one of his staff in Arabic, then said, 'Here. Come and see my office.'

From a small entrance hall meeting room, we walked up stone stairs into his spacious office. It was a museum to Soviet memorabilia. A wall-size portrait of Lenin stared down. There were rows of Soviet medals, a military uniform on a tailor's dummy, a huge oil painting of a Soviet battle victory against Hitler. A centrepiece of the living room next door was a Soviet artillery range-finder, now a polished ornament standing by the window with sweeping mountain views.

'Were you a communist, then?'

'No, never,' he says. 'But during the civil war, the Soviets gave us weapons to defend ourselves against the Christians. They also gave us scholarships to educate our poor. They were very good to us.' On his desk was a model of a Harley-Davidson motorcycle. He picked it up and thoughtfully turned it in his hand. 'Yes, the Christians had Israel and the Americans and we had the Soviets. But it wasn't as simple as that. I was friendly with some Christian militia and afraid of some Muslim ones. Civil war is horrible. We do not want it to happen again.'

In Beirut itself, I spoke to an influential Christian member of parliament, Nassib Lahoud, who was in the running for the presidency. 'Christians and Muslims alike won't allow factions to reintroduce violence,' he said. 'The Lebanese have put war firmly behind them and are looking for peace, prosperity and harmony in the Arab world. But there is a very large vacuum now because the Syrians have practically run the country for the past twenty years. The Lebanese have been yearning to fill that vacuum themselves. We want to go back to what we've done successfully for tens of years – to run our own affairs in a democratic climate.'

'How then does Hezbollah fit into that scenario?' I asked.

'Hezbollah liberated southern Lebanon from Israel,' he said. 'They created in us a conscious feeling of Lebanese national unity. What we're hoping is that there will soon be a dialogue with Hezbollah to decide on its future as a military faction.'

Lahoud represented a widely held view in Lebanon that cut straight across the Western view that Hezbollah was a terror organization that had to be destroyed. It raised again that spectre of how the West would react if Hezbollah ended up winning power through the ballot box in Lebanon.

One of the Hezbollah strongholds is in Baalbek in the Bekaa Valley, a city famous for magnificent Roman columns that soar skyward, dwarfing the minaret of a nearby mosque. The columns are dedicated to Bacchus, Jupiter and Venus, and are evidence of the ebb and flow of Middle Eastern civilization, built in the second and third centuries before either Christianity or Islam had taken grip.

Driving down through the Bekaa Valley into Baalbek itself we passed a set of billboards showing a scantily clad woman advertising shampoo, then another promoting Islamic religious leaders, stern, bearded, turbaned with authoritarian expressions, similar to those I saw in Iraq. Closer to town we passed dog-eared posters of candidates for recent local elections.

Hezbollah candidates had won by a landslide and now controlled the municipal council. The voting had been far from a rubber stamp. In the previous election, Hezbollah had been trounced, not on weighty issues of Islam and America, but on how the market was arranged and how water flowed through the drains.

I was shown around by Dr Haj Hassan Hussein, the local Hezbollah MP, an earnest, tired man with huge spectacles, a crumpled suit and a few days of stubble. He gave me lunch in a Hezbollah restaurant, washed down by non-alcoholic Iranian beer, and we went through a detailed and stringent exchange about Hezbollah's involvement or not in the world of terror. This, after all, was the issue that was threatening Lebanon. It was Washington's reason for wanting Syria out of the country and for proscribing Hezbollah as a terror group.

'We're not involved in the Iraq insurgency,' he said.

'Do you give money to it?'

'No.'

'Advice?'

'No.'

'Are you sending any people there?'

'No.'

'Nothing?'

'Nothing.'

'Do you have any links to al-Qaeda?'

'Al-Qaeda are as much our enemy as America and Israel. We condemn their violence. It is terrorism. It is against Islam.'

The West disagreed, and I have had since classified-cleared intelligence briefings in Iraq that cited evidence of direct Hezbollah links to anti-American Shia militia there.

Back from Baalbek, I went to see the American ambassador, Vincent Battle. The US embassy had a memorial to the sixty-three people who died in a 1983 suicide bombing against the embassy. An organization called Islamic Jihad claimed responsibility, which the CIA describes as the forerunner to Hezbollah.

When I asked Battle, twenty years later, how the US viewed Hezbollah, he answered bluntly: 'We consider the Hezbollah to be a terrorist organization with a worldwide reach.'

'Still?' I asked.

'Yes. Still.' Then, he paused. 'Having said that, they do have members in parliament. They are part of the political process.'

I sought out my Baalbek host Dr Hussein in Lebanon's parliament and found him in a corridor, in deep conversation with Dr Bahia Hariri, sister of the then prime minister, who would later be assassinated. Even though she was from a party deeply opposed to Hezbollah's policies, they were discussing agricultural policy.

'I've just come from the American embassy,' I said, 'and the ambassador believes the Hezbollah are a terrorist organization.'

'Terrorists?' countered Hariri with a withering look. 'No. They are great national movement. Why ask such a question?'

'Well that's what the Americans say.'

'The Americans,' she said, walking off and rolling her eyes.[8]

I decided to write this book during visits to Iraq in 2008, close to five years after the Kirkuk municipal elections, five years after President Bush declared an end to 'major combat operations' and five years after my ferry journey with Firaz, Zaid and Saleem.

But Iraq's parliament was still barely functioning. Members of the 275-seat assembly faced constant threats. No substantive legislation such as on oil revenue or institution-building had been passed, although apparently there had been a successful debate on olive farming.

Iraq's Ministry of Defence had taken the original parliament building, so MPs were confined to meeting in the convention centre inside the Green Zone. They had no idea what the schedule would be until they arrived following a journey that often involved high personal risk. In April 2007, a suicide bomber infiltrated far enough to blow himself up in the cafe next to the chamber, killing several people.

The political groupings remained based on ethnicity and religious birthright. The Sadrist bloc of elected members, for example, was loyal to the Shia cleric Muqtada al-Sadr who ran the Mehdi Army militia that the West says was funded and trained by Iran.

One afternoon, a debate on the crucial issue of oil revenue was postponed and the floor was instead given to a Sadrist

---

8 On 7 June 2009, Lebanon held a closely fought election between a pro-Western Sunni-led alliance, and a pro-Syrian and Iranian Hizbollah-led alliance. Hizbollah lost, conceded defeat and remained a powerful political movement.

MP. Dressed head-to-toe in black, she read out a letter from al-Sadr, lambasting President Bush as the one-eyed Antichrist who had planted hatred, rancour and conflict throughout the world. At the time, al-Sadr had a price on his head and was wanted for murder. His militia was killing British troops in Iraq.

The members themselves were unconvinced as to whether Western-style democracy would eventually work. One positive sign was that, as with Hezbollah, the Sadrists were actually fielding their own politicians who, despite the unorthodox approach, were using parliament to voice their opinions.

'To build a democratic regime means changing the minds of people,' explained Dr Alla'a Makki, a Sunni MP. 'If they have lived under a dictatorship like ours, that takes a long time. The thinking that was kept locked inside the minds of the people has broken out to the surface and we need to concentrate a lot of time and effort into calming those thoughts and ideas.'

Makki was a medical doctor whose clinic had been in a predominantly Shia neighbourhood of Baghdad. It had been ransacked by Shia militia and shut down. He had fled from his home nearby. He cut an authoritative figure in his dark worsted suit and silk tie, but like some 4 million other Iraqis he was a displaced person, ethnically cleansed from his home.

'In getting rid of Saddam,' I asked, 'was violence inevitable?'

'Iraq may have been able to pass through this stage without violence, but we also have to deal with interference from neighbouring countries and the US occupation. These are the causes of the real violence.'

His argument brought me back to the Chouf Mountains with Walid Jumblatt and his maxim that if there are no foreign patrons there will be no civil war.

'Even in America, there was much sacrifice for democracy,' said Layla J. Alkhafaji, a Shia member of parliament from the SCIRI group. Its loyalty was to the followers of the cleric Mohammed Baqir al-Hakim, who was killed by a Najaf car bomb in 2003, and whose portrait I found defaced by US troops in the mosque near the Iran–Iraq border.

The Shia SCIRI had a militia known as the Badr Brigade that was viciously opposed to the Sadrists' Mehdi Army – an example of how Iraqi factionalism broke down into a smaller and smaller feuds. Layla had been jailed for ten years by Saddam for refusing to join the Baath Party. She had managed to escape to Canada in 1993 and came back after the invasion.

'Iraqis made up their minds that after three decades of the dictatorship, they want a democratic state. Let me remind you of the elections when Iraq amazed the whole world, and even with the threat of al-Qaeda you saw them lining up from six in the morning to take up their right to vote. Even with all these killings going on we are not going to give up that process. Everybody talks about democracy and stability, but they have to know it has a price.'

Unlike in 2003, I now had the working cellphone number of the national security minister, and when I rang it he answered. One thing, at least, had improved. Dr Mowaffak al-Rubaie was a neurologist who lived in Britain before returning to Iraq after the invasion. I had interviewed him before, and as before an American adviser sat in on the filming.

'Give me a blueprint of how you can remove a dictator and bring democracy into the Islamic world,' I asked.

'It's very difficult and there is no one formula,' he said. 'But I believe that overthrowing a dictatorship is worth the world. Overthrowing dictatorship means we regain our freedom and freedom is priceless. It's well worth spending your treasure, blood and tears to get your freedom and to maintain and sustain this freedom. Freedom is part of a human being, and dictatorship and tyranny takes that part away from you.'

This was the view of Danielle Pletka from the neo-conservative American Enterprise Institute – one often heard in Washington and inside the well-guarded areas of the Green Zone.

But talking to people outside, there was a clear distinction between having freedom and what elected politicians could deliver. 'I don't trust them,' said a man fixing an air-conditioner. Electronic equipment from his store spilled out onto the street and our conversation was drowned out by two American helicopters flying loud and low overhead.

'Democracy has given us this,' said another technician, pointing skywards. He paused to watch a military convoy pass carrying huge concrete blocks to make anti-blast walls. The soldier in the leading armoured vehicle swung his machine gun towards us and kept us in his line of fire until the convoy was clear. 'Democracy means military occupation and politicians who steal money and support terrorism,' he said.

Whatever trust they might have had in the system was now being eroded because it wasn't delivering. It seemed impossible in Iraq to imagine a path between the two brutalities of dictatorship and the new democracy under which the people had to live.

Furad Ahmed, a father of three, had lost a leg in a car bombing round the corner from his home. He had just popped out to get a loaf of bread when he was blown up and became one of the million or more who have been wounded or killed in the Iraq war.

The stump of Furad's leg had healed and he was learning

to manage on crutches. He was fixing the generator and doing odd jobs around the house. Furad put on a tough exterior, but he was a traumatized man. His lips quivered when he told the story of the bombing, sitting on the floor in his small living room under portraits of Islamic clerics. His discoloured leg stump rested on a rag on the deep-red, patterned carpet. His crutch lay by his side and he angrily held up doctors' notes about the injury with stains of his own blood soaked into the paper. He was angry at the police for not stopping the attack and at the hospital doctors for not treating him more quickly. As for the bombers, he drew on a deep reserve of self-control, went quiet, and lowered his head. 'I will never forgive them,' he whispered. 'How can I forgive them after they make me like this? What can I say? Why do people make these blasts?'

'You are a lion, Father,' said his nine-year-old son, Mustafa, who was sitting on the arm of the sofa. 'You survived the terrorists.'

Furad's three-year-old daughter, Daniah, nestled up to him, holding a doll in her right hand. She then did something utterly natural to her, yet appalling to me, something that explained how a single brutal act of war can colour the human spirit for generations to come. Daniah tore the right leg off the doll, reached up and offered it to her father. Embarrassed, Furad took it. Under the doll's dress, there was just a torso. Every limb was missing.

'She does this now,' explained Furad, touching the edge of his eyes to hide a tear. 'When I ask her what happened to the hands and legs of the doll, she says they are like mine – lost in an explosion.'

In London, at the height of the Iraq insurgency, I found myself sitting next to a conservative American who was about to start work on John McCain's 2008 presidential election campaign. As we discussed Iraq, our conversation became brittle.

'Iraq is now eighty per cent peaceful,' he said. 'The only problem lies in the Sunni triangle and we'll be tackling that soon, then all Iraqis will have their freedom.'

I told him that wasn't the case and he cited Washington intelligence reports back at me. I told him he was confusing peace with the absence of US military deaths and freedom with lack of violence. He cited the elections to me and the working parliament. I was aware that, while my trips to Iraq were mainly confined to Baghdad for security reasons, he might have access to material that painted a different picture.

But the next time I was in Baghdad, I asked our security advisers: 'Could you tell me one place, anywhere in Iraq, apart from the northern Kurdish area, that I could walk down the street, talk to people and have a cup of coffee for any length of time.'

They looked at me as if I were crazy.

Usama Rehda was an Iraqi technology graduate who scraped a living as a wedding photographer. We were walking through a park that had been opened on the banks of the Tigris river, a place that was considered to be relatively safe. We strolled through an area where children were playing soccer and others were hanging around watching. Rehda had taken three taxis to get here, because they had crossed between rival Sunni and Shia neighbourhoods. Taking a wrong turn with the wrong driver could get you killed. Usama tensed and turned, and we saw that two children had taken a snapshot of us with cellphones. He spoke to them in Arabic. They waved the phones at him like weapons.

'They say they will send my photograph to al-Qaeda to kill me because I am talking to a Westerner.'

'Should we leave?' I asked.

'No. They're just kids,' he said.

We found a bench, smelling of fresh paint in the govern-ment's effort to beautify at least one spot in Baghdad, and I asked him what he understood democracy to be.

'Democracy is meant to give you the ability to change things,' said Rehda. 'No one here has that ability.'

'This is how the new Iraq works,' he said. 'You get a threat or someone close to you gets kidnapped. You pay the ransom. You give your house keys to your neighbour and you leave.'

He brought out photographs of his family and university friends, students in group pictures with their professors and family gatherings.

'I lost two cousins. No sorry, three cousins. This cousin here,' he said, pointing to an attractive student with a beam of a smile, 'she was killed by a suicide bomber. She was twenty-two, studying economics at university. The second one – this is her – she was killed by death squads and another one – he's not in the picture – he was followed by terrorists. He was living in a Sunni area and they saw him enter a Shia neigh-bourhood. They drilled his knees with an electric drill and then they killed him.

'All of us were very excited about having democracy in Iraq. We began by opposing the terrorists, whichever side they were on, but when the heat got turned up there was no one to protect us. So, most of us preferred to save our lives and the lives of our families. Now I have relatives in Jordan, Egypt, Sweden, Australia and, I think, one reached Canada last week.'

'And you?' I asked as his eyes lingered on the photographs. 'I am too late,' he said. 'They are not letting us into Jordan any more, even if it's to go to another country. And I don't have enough money to bribe. I rely on my neighbourhood militia for protection.'

I had to keep reminding myself that it was really five years since the invasion and my ferry journey. This was one hell of a long time to not sort things out. Apart from this small park, I had seen little else that showed any progress. Karrada, the fashionable shopping area nearby, would one day be busy with signs of a bustling economy starting up again, then a car bomb would go off and everyone would leave.

'I would really like it if I could go to the police or the army or the government to help with things,' said Usama. 'But if you have a problem, the last people you think about are the police.' He shook his head, slipped the photographs back into their envelope, then looked up sharply, managing a sad laugh. 'You know what they say – "Be nice to the Americans or they'll punish you with democracy."'

'So Iraq is not a democracy?'

'I am sorry. It is not. Democracy is when you choose someone and this someone is a good man and this man will protect you and do good for the country. It means that you as a voter can also make a difference to the country. But in our system you vote and a bunch of people get into parliament according to some list. We don't know most of the people on the list.'

'OK,' I said. 'If someone said you are not allowed to vote or criticize the government but you could travel, go to school, make money and live a safe life – would you prefer that?'

'Yes.'

'Why?'

'As long as I have a good job and good services and have freedom to travel, why would I not give up my right to criticize the people in power. I am happy to give up this right.'

'Would that be a better way?'

'Of course,' he answered, his eyes lighting up as that might soon be a new option. 'Outside Iraq they talk about democracy and blah, blah, blah. But Iraqis don't have very big thoughts. They just have three wishes – security, electricity and water, and it is impossible to make them happen. This is all Iraqis are thinking about. Now you ask about my right to criticize the government. For years we have been asking for these three very simple things and it seems impossible to make them happen. If this is criticism, what good has it done? Sure, now I have the right to criticize but will my criticism change things? No. It's like criticizing someone and this person says I don't care, you can go and smash you head against a wall. This is democracy for them.'

Shortly before leaving Iraq at the beginning of 2008, a car bomb went off in Karrada. It was an arbitrary attack that killed a dozen people who were trying to go about their daily lives. It was the equivalent of a bomb going off in Regent Street or Fifth Avenue, with lines of cars torn apart, the wailing of sirens, the blackened road strewn with bodies, the wounded and the traumatized, a high street transformed into panic, fear, loathing, an urge to help and a need to find a reason.

The attacker was a Muslim suicide bomber. His victims were Muslims. Under Saddam Hussein, there might have been immense brutality, but it was not random like this, nor carried out with such intensity in the deceptive names of religion and democracy.

The carnage around me brought to mind the seventeenth-century English philosopher Thomas Hobbes. Reacting to the bloodshed of the English Civil War, he argued that the best way forward was to govern societies through a strong consti-tutional state that guaranteed the rule of law and protected its citizens, preferably through a monarchy. It probably wasn't a good comparison, nor a particularly accurate one, but Hobbes interested me because I was heading for Dubai that was run by precisely the type of government he recommended.

A few days later, I stood amazed in Dubai's Mall of the Emirates, an enormous, jumping complex of shops, cinemas, food halls, and a place where the young congregated to see and be seen. Some were in sloppy and loose clothing. Some were dressed up to the nines in designer jeans or the men wore flowing white robes and the women body-clinging chadors with matching coloured cellphones. In a bookshop next to the multiplex cinema the Dubai police chief was attending the launch of a Middle Eastern cookery book. Across the hall, riding up the escalator, was a celebrity with her new boyfriend, and I was fresh in from Baghdad, staring at it all like an awestruck kid.

The cinema, like the one in Casablanca, was showing all Hollywood films, and I went up to a group of youngsters and asked: 'What do you think of this idea to spread democracy around the Middle East?'

'We have democracy,' answered a guy in loose jeans, T-shirt and baseball cap in his late teens.

'But you can't vote,' I challenged.

The guy paused for a moment, curious at my question. 'Oh yeah! That's a point,' he said. 'We can't. But it's not a problem. Nobody's complaining. Nobody cares.'

'Really?' I challenged.

'Yeah, really,' nodded a girl by his side dressed in a tank top and silver studded jeans.

'But don't you want a stake in your future?'

Confusion creased across her face. Her friend pushed his

cap back on his head. 'I don't get your question,' he said. 'If you're asking, do we want what they have in Iraq?' He widened his eyes. 'Please. Give me a break.'

Here I was in Dubai, a pulsating environment of consumerism, fashion and ambition being run not by an elected government but by an absolute monarch who had banned political parties and never held elections.

Wandering through the early evening scenes in the Mall of the Emirates, with Baghdad only a short flight away, it was like being in swinging London while war raged in France. The young were spending money to look beautiful and cool while, in Iraq, they were joining a militia and learning how to kill.

Which one was the heart of the Arab-Muslim world – Iraq or Dubai? Which one represented the values of that world, the Dawa Party leaders I had met in Basra and Karbala who believed women should be covered, alcohol banned and people watched by religious militia, or the avuncular Dubai police chief being photographed with an attractive cookery book author?

Which one was more in tune with our own Western values? And if it was Dubai, why did the West want to change things when they seemed to be working so well? Why are we so attached to our own concept of democracy?

Craig Secker, my Australian cameraman who lived in Dubai, suggested we go for a beer at Après Ski, a bar that turned out to match its name. At one end was a floor-to-very-high-cciling window looking out on a massive indoor ski slope built to replicate an Alpine village, complete with ski-school, beginners' and intermediate slopes.

Inside, people mingled, flirted, drank and enjoyed. In Iraq, where an uncovered woman could be murdered for stepping outside her home, women here were as scantily clad as on a Californian beach. Here, too, was a bar filled with the most adventurous alcoholic cocktails, and people challenging each other with conversation and ideas. It was a simplistic image of the type of freedoms our politicians envisage when they talk about liberating the people of the Middle East from their dictators. But it was real. It was what so many Iraqis craved when they discovered that the ballot box did not automatically bring either basic freedoms or a panoply of good things. In Dubai, with the iron-grip rule of an absolute monarch, people felt safe and secure enough to do pretty much what they wanted – except criticize him. But as Usama Rehda pointed out, he would happily exchange that right for the guarantee of other freedoms.

This tiny, cosmopolitan, Muslim microcosm of glittering utopian autocracy posed a direct question to our Western leaders. Did they really want to export their style of democracy throughout the world? What would be the result if everyone in Dubai was invited to put a cross next to a political leader and drop their decision into a ballot box?

Why was it that Kuwait, Qatar, Oman and other wealthy Gulf states had adamantly refused the West's offer of democratization? Was it about tinpot dictators holding on to power and lining their pockets? Or was it because they believed strongly that it wouldn't work?

Instead of comparing tiny Dubai to tumultuous Iraq, let's instead match it against Iraq's southern province of Basra. Dubai's population is about 1.5 million against Basra's 2 million. Much of Dubai's wealth comes from its port, just as Basra's potential wealth would come from the port of Umm Qasr, Iraq's gateway to the Gulf, where I had entered Iraq on the ferry from Dubai.

Earnings from Dubai's shipping terminals are ultimately regulated by the monarch, who allows wealth to seep down to the population. Earnings from Basra's port used to be regulated and looted by Saddam Hussein. In 2003, when our ferry docked there, the port was briefly run by the British military. Then came the elections that underpinned the country's factional divisions and Basra was up for grabs. The upshot is that under the auspices of the monarch, Dubai's shipping trade is managed by an internationally recognized mechanism, which includes shareholdings on global stock exchanges. In newly democratized Iraq, Basra's shipping trade is run by warlords who use religion to legitimize brutal rackets of organized crime.

So what would happen if Dubai's monarch suddenly announced he was holding full direct elections tomorrow? As in Iraq under Saddam, genuine political debate in Dubai is banned. Schools and universities do not teach the type of cut-and-thrust argument that people in the West accept as part of daily life. The Arab culture more readily takes offence, the giving of which is an intrinsic element of any Western-style election campaign.

Dubai is predominantly Sunni with Shias making up just 16 per cent of the population. I only know this because I looked it up afterwards. Right then at the Après Ski bar, I hadn't a clue, just as I still have no idea what the Protestant/ Catholic/Jewish/Muslim split is in my own country.

Of the people who live in Dubai 85 per cent are foreign workers, very few of whom have citizenship. Those from Pakistan and Bangladesh would be mostly Sunni. Those from the Philippines would be Christian and so on.

Autocratic Dubai is held together by a wealth and security beacon that allows you to knuckle down, work hard and earn money. Elections would unglue that formula, and without a wider understanding on how political parties forge policies, voters would almost certainly opt for their tribal, cultural and religious groupings.

The Shia minority would feel threatened. Foreign workers

would demand citizenship and more rights. Western managers would watch with a plane ticket in their back pocket. Financiers would raise Dubai's risk factor and look for somewhere else to park their money.

Somewhere, lurking beneath Dubai's future-obsessed sparkle, there could be an Islamic cleric, waiting to emerge as a warrior leader and drag people back into historical feuds, tear down its skyscrapers, smash the cocktail bars, cover the women, close the schools and execute all who dare challenge him.

The scenario of power vacuums unleashing destructive horrors is not confined to Iraq, Dubai or the Gulf states or even to Islamic culture. It is the view among many developing societies that have succeeded economically. Singapore's autocratic leader, Lee Kuan Yew, created a global trading centre from a swamp by repressing democracy, just as a series of British colonial governors did in Hong Kong. China is now on a similar path while an awestruck world watches to see what happens. In the 2009 economic crisis, it was not India, the world's biggest democracy, or Russia, the former superpower, that was seen as crucial to a solution, but China, on equal footing with America in a partnership dubbed as the G2.

Supposing the view of the young shoppers in the Mall of the Emirates reflected that of the majority in Dubai: they didn't care about voting and were happy with the style of government. How would we describe the system of government without the stigma usually attached to dictatorship? Is there a word? A phrase? Something catchy that makes sense of what's going on? Something acceptable to our Western values? Is there a more subtle, more nuanced system of government that works for the developing world that hasn't yet been defined?

*

'So what's the plan tomorrow?' asked Craig as we finished our beers. 'Dubai Ports in the afternoon, right?' Dubai Ports World was a huge multinational owner of shipping terminals that we were due to film in order to demonstrate Dubai's role in global trade.

'Right,' I said. 'But tell me, how would you describe what Dubai is? No democracy, but successful?'

'Benign dictatorship?' he suggested.

'Too negative, perhaps.'

'Yeah,' he agreed. 'Like a benign tumour, you'd prefer to be without it.'

'We're only seeing success,' I said. 'Tomorrow, before we go to the port, is there somewhere we can film the underclass, the poor, people who are being exploited.'

The next morning, we headed out to the desert. A light breeze sent sand dancing across the tops of dunes, and the early morning sun soaked the vast landscape in a soft yellow. From a distance Dubai became a hazy, glinting mirage, rising from wasteland, like a city from a science fiction film, a civilization created from a ruler's dream. Towering above the city was the Burj Dubai skyscraper, then the world's tallest building, 162 floors, 818 metres or getting on for a kilometre high at 818 metres.

Architecture must be a factor in determining how advanced a society has become, a kind of cave to skyscraper maturity syndrome. The Khmer Angkor Wat in Cambodia, the Inca monuments at Machu Picchu in Peru and India's Taj Mahal were built to create a sense of recognition and self-esteem. They are expressions of a place in the world. Iraqis often said they wished the new government would build something to make a statement of optimism for the future. Instead, the architectural symbols of their new society were twelve-foot-high concrete anti-bomb walls surrounded by coils of razor wire.

Dubai is one of seven semi-autonomous states, known as emirates, within a nation created as recently as 1971. The overall ruler of the United Arab Emirates is the ruler of Abu Dhabi, the neighbouring emirate, but Dubai is its economic engine – not so much through oil and gas, but by creating a financial and trading centre that serves the Middle East and beyond.

The emirs, or rulers, have few or no checks and balances on their power in the traditional sense. There is no lively press, no freedom of expression, no opposition, or any parliament with muscle. But they set themselves apart from dictators such as Saddam Hussein by using power to bolster instead of to oppress the lives of their people. The judiciary is trusted by international investors, or they wouldn't come there, just as bureaucracy is streamlined in order to attract money and create wealth.

Although run by hereditary monarchs, the emirates are treading a similar path to that of the colonial Hong Kong or authoritarian Singapore. These are small outward-looking societies, using their coastal locations to prosper from trade. They are rigidly opposed to anything that interferes with the making of money. Democracy is high on that list, as is war. Central to their success is the fair treatment of the workforce. If it feels oppressed or that it's being treated unfairly, things will fall apart. It is this benchmark, not the ballot box, that ensures success. The stakes in retaining stability are very high.

In India, poverty greets you at the airport and in Brazil you find it in the crime-ridden slums that cling to the hillsides of Rio de Janeiro. In Iraq, it has mainly been created by war, so it comes with shock and anger. But, in the United Arab Emirates, poverty is not easy to find. Of course it's there, because the UN estimates that almost 20 per cent of people there live below the poverty line. But in the past twenty years or so, the massive construction of office blocks and shopping malls has created jobs, wages and secure employment. From cityscape to desert, you are faced with newness and progress, not the type of squalor and hopelessness seen in many developing societies.

We eventually found a kind of poverty in the village of Alawiya. A worker in a grubby sarong, his shoulders weighed down by a bundle of palm leaves, walked down a dirt track to the edge of the road and dumped his load on a pile of other leaves.

His name was Mohammed Mustafa. Working on a nearby palm plantation he earned just US$3 a day, most of which he sent back to his family in Bangladesh. He was fifty years old. His hard, dark skin was cracked by the sun, and his hands were calloused from years of manual labour. He had been in the UAE for eight years and sometimes job-swapped with his son who was due to join him in a month's time. He went back and forth to Bangladesh as he liked.

As we talked, others from the village gathered round helping to translate and offer explanations. Not one of them was from the UAE. They were from India, Pakistan, Bangladesh and the Philippines. All had made their homes there, but under the UAE's strict immigration laws, as soon as they could no longer work, they had to return to their own countries. They might be raising children and owning businesses and property, but none would ever be able to call Dubai home. This was how the massive port was run and how the Burj Dubai skyscraper was being built. The whole shimmering miracle was created with imported labour working under pay and conditions that would be illegal in many Western democracies.

If any of these men even raised a placard to march down the street campaigning for better conditions, they risked arrest and deportation. But, before my Western democratic tendencies prevailed, I had to accept a basic truth. They didn't have to be here. They had a choice. However unpalatable the working conditions might be to us, it was an issue of advocacy, of pressuring the government and exposing illegal trafficking and employment syndicates. It was not one of mass graves and killing.

'Would you like to have a vote here?' I asked Mohammed Mustafa. He broke into a smile, his brow furrowed, trying to imagine what I was talking about.

'I am poor,' he said. 'I don't have an interest in politics. All I want is to be able to keep working so I can help my family.'

'And your life's dream?'

'Working here is my dream.' He thought for a moment, then added. 'Although I'd like to speak better Arabic.'

Mohammed Mustafa and the 85 per cent of the UAE's population like him were there for the money. US$3 a day is an attractive wage compared with what is available in democratic Bangladesh.

The ballot box was irrelevant to Mohammed Mustafa because in his own country elections had not met his needs. Bangladesh was blessed with debate, that hallmark of Western-style government, but its economy could not provide for his family. Otherwise, why was he here humping palm leaves for a living?

'Did that help?' asked Craig on the way back.

'Sort of,' I said, mulling over the contradictions. 'I'll tell you when we've done the Ports.'

Dubai Ports World (DPW) is huge. It runs more than forty ports in more than thirty-one countries and, in Dubai itself, it loads and unloads dozens of ships a day dealing with thousands of containers. The port shone with fresh paintwork, meticulous organization and state-of-the-art machinery. In our short time there, I saw mainly foreigners: an urbane super-fit Australian in charge of security, a middle-aged Englishman managing a small section, and Indians, mostly, operating the trucks and cranes. It was an image of trade and wealth creation, a massive version of Mohammed Mustafa and his palm leaves. The only food this beast needed was an ability to keep working.

In 2006, DPW got a jolt of Western democratic reality. It had bought the British company P&O, which happened also to own several shipping terminals in the United States. No one thought anything of it until the story was picked up by a local American radio station whose listeners questioned the wisdom of Muslims owning American ports. The scare spread like a prairie fire. Ports were sensitive entry and exit points through which terrorist bombs could be smuggled. Americans were so appalled by the prospect of a company from an Islamic nation owning a port that the US House of Representatives voted 62–2 to block DPW moving ahead.

After years of media demonization of the Arab-Muslim world, DPW was a misconception waiting to happen, not unlike the one peddled by the Bush administration that Iraq was involved in the 9/11 attacks. Just as grass-roots US public opinion found it difficult to separate the politics of Osama bin Laden from those of Saddam Hussein, it also failed to differentiate between the values of Dubai Ports World and those of an al-Qaeda suicide bomber.

The head of DPW worked from a skyscraper in the heart of Dubai's commercial district. Jamal Majid bin Thaniah was a softly spoken, pensive man who spent some time with me at the panoramic window of his office where we looked out over a grey-yellow expanse that disappeared into the curve of the horizon. He explained how Dubai would build out into the desert with expressways, hotels, more port facilities and much else.

He was still smarting from his brush with the United States. It had taught him how popular opinion in America viewed his own society, his culture and his religion. 'It was an image issue,' he explained. 'We have to show the world that whatever it thinks we are is not correct.'

'So what are you exactly?' I asked. 'If Dubai became a democracy, would it help?'

'No,' he answered, using his hands to make his point. 'Democracy is a concept that was brought into the Middle East in the light of 9/11, and I doubt whether it will have any merit. No one would enjoy what we are enjoying here now, from security to standard of living, if we had democracy. Who would want to change this? We have learned a lot from mistakes made in the democratic world.'

'Mistakes? Like what?' I asked.

'Many projects, important for a country, are often debated for months and years and then blocked in parliament. You can visit some of the countries and then go back in ten years' time and you see no changes.'

I understood his point. Recently, I had returned to Mumbai after a ten-year gap, amazed that India hadn't yet even managed to build a decent road from the airport to its biggest financial centre because of wrangling over political and planning issues.

Is this really an issue of democracy, or more one of bureaucracy? Or are the two entwined? Both China and India's bureaucracies can be tortuously slow, but if China wants to build an airport, it'll do so. Whereas India has to go through all the checks and balances that democracy dictates. Every day, we witness this in Britain with debates on building new airports and power stations. But it's different. Our industrial revolution is long over and infrastructure projects are not directly linked to ending poverty and disease.

'With the current structure, we are moving very fast,' Jamal said.

'Then how would you describe this style of government? Is it dictatorship? Does it have another name?'

He cupped his hand around his chin, thinking. 'Smart leadership,' he said. 'Fair leadership with a vision. Then you can move forward very fast.'

Dubai's progress, then, can be compared to that of a successful multinational. It is run by an authoritarian executive that ensures that its workforce and sources of investment remain motivated and rewarded. It is basically a huge service centre, so it did not completely resolve the conundrum of how to move from dictatorship to democracy without bloodshed; how to unglue peacefully that authoritarian formula that keeps passions, hatreds, dreams and jealousies at bay.

It made me wonder if there could possibly be a formula, a set of benchmarks such as literacy and income that would make a society ready for the cut and thrust of full democracy, such as Paul Collier's balancing point of US$2,700.

There was not a template, it seemed. As I began to think it through, I immediately saw the pitfalls, not least because, so often in troubled conflict areas, each group takes solace in their plight by believing that their problem is insoluble and unique.

And it wasn't just about money. One of the first things that struck me covering the Balkan wars in the 1990s was how well off everyone was. We drove through villages of wrecked houses with bulletholes in dishwashers and abandoned designer clothes hanging on washing lines. This was an educated middle class that had lost everything for some undefined cause.

So what is it about?

Francis Fukuyama, the writer who thought Western-style democracy was now a given as the most successful form of government, also wrote about the concept of self-esteem, which apparently comes from a part of the human spirit the Greeks called *emos*. When people are treated badly, they feel anger. When they fail to live up to their own standards, shame kicks in. When they are evaluated at what they believe is the correct level, they feel pride. What it boiled down to was the individual craving for recognition or a place in the story of life.

This is also the theme of a brilliant trilogy about oppression within Islamic societies by the Algerian writer Mohammed Moulessehoul, who had to give himself the female pseudonym of Yasmina Khadra in order to get published. Time and again he highlights the importance of self-esteem.

'When self-esteem has been wounded all tragedies become possible,' he wrote. 'The instance you really learn to hate is when you become aware of your own impotence.'

I had seen those traits of anger and hopelessness in the Baghdad bomb victim, Furad Ahmed and others in democratic Iraq, yet not in Mohammed Mustafa, the poorest worker I had found in Dubai.

In the airport on the way out of Dubai, I bumped into a graceful Emirati I had spoken to briefly when we filmed at the stock exchange and I had tried unsuccessfully to engage him on the issue of democracy. He was in his early forties, in a white ankle-length dishdash, and heading for New York.

'Can you talk more freely about democracy, here?' I asked. He said nothing, but looked at me, his expression etched a mix of curiosity and suspicion. 'We don't talk about that at all,' he said, waving his hand dismissively.

'Do you talk about the Iraq war?'

He shook his head.

'Al-Qaeda?'

He said nothing.

'America?'

Nothing.

'Free and fair elections?'

'Business,' he answered with a smile.

'You talk about business?'

'Yes.'

'Not democracy?'

'Only business.'

'Why?

He leant over, cupped his hand around my ear. 'Because democracy kills,' he whispered forcefully and walked away.

But then, it might not be that black and white because not far away was India, the biggest democracy on earth, where some of the poorest people in the world have been voting governments in and out of office for decades.

SOUTH ASIA

INDIA – Democracy's Contradiction

Alone, on the bend of a long, empty road, the wind blowing up swirls of dust, and the temperature pushing 40 degrees Celsius, a girl dragged a pile of firewood behind her. She was about ten. Her long dress was filthy and torn. Her hands were scarred. She was barefoot and her eyes looked down, concentrating on her task. Like us, she was heading up a hill to a stone quarry, and the journey there and back to get firewood would have taken her the best part of the afternoon. She accepted our offer of a lift without a word, except, when I asked, to say her name was Sita. We turned the corner to the quarry itself, and she pointed to her home – a plastic sheet, strung between poles, where her mother was rinsing a saucepan in filthy water.

This settlement of squalor curved around the quarry's edge. The sheeting of makeshift shanty homes flapped in the wind. Dust let loose from quarry digging blew everywhere. It was a place to where families emigrated because they needed to earn a living and this was all they could find.

Men worked in the quarry with their sons. The daughters kept house with their mothers. The quarry was owned by a private company, and just about everything going on around me from child labour to health and safety was against the law. Weather-worn notices in Hindi and English instructed workers to wear protective footwear and hard hats, but all I saw were open sandals and the sun beating down on hatless heads.

We helped Sita deliver the firewood to her mother, who happened to be with other quarry families talking to a visiting trade union official. She told Sita to put the firewood by a saucepan on the ground. Sita slipped away to join children playing hopscotch nearby. From appearing downtrodden and sullen, her face suddenly lit up and she became a child again. She picked up a stone, threw it on the hopscotch pattern drawn into the dried earth and jumped onto a square.

The trade unionist, Ram Sjaran Yadab, was a former bonded labourer. A person becomes a bonded labourer when their labour is demanded as a means of repayment for a loan, sometimes incurred by parents or relatives. It is against the law, but remains rampant throughout India and much of the developing world.

'By law there should be a proper crèche for these children,' said Yadab, looking over toward Sita. 'But look. There is nothing.'

He turned to Sita's mother: 'Do you come from outside?' he asked, meaning whether or not they were locals. All the women nodded. Their home villages were a long way away.

'Then you should be given housing suitable for a human being,' he said, fingering a flapping piece of plastic that was the roof of the shelter. 'How many of you have been back home recently?'

The women shook their heads. 'We have been here for two months but we've been unable to save a penny,' said one. 'How can we afford to go home?'

'The owner is obliged to give you a loan to make the journey,' explained Yadab. But no eyes lit up with this information.

'We spend more than we earn,' said another. 'How could we pay him back?'

'Has any government official visited here?'

'No,' said one woman, 'and we've been here for more than three months.'

Yadab turned to us to explain: 'The labour law says that the employer must provide the travel expenses both ways for workers who come from outside and living accommodation. But look at this. We don't even keep our animals like this.'

He spoke to the women again: 'Do you have any identity card from the employer?' he asked.

They shook their heads.

'And does he take a thumbprint when you are paid?'

'Sometimes. Not always,' she said.

'Often we don't get paid on time,' added one of the men.

'You see,' Yadab explained to me, 'if he doesn't give them identity cards, he can claim they are squatting and not working here. They have no rights. The law says they must be given safety equipment, clean drinking water, housing . . .'

A woman interrupted. 'The food is filthy, too, because we can't keep the dust out of it,' she said. 'Then when people get sick we have to pay for our own medicines and lose money because they can't work.'

'I have been working twenty years for this quarry,' said Yadab, 'and nothing has changed.'

'At least we know our rights,' said a man who had just joined us, dust covering his face, holding a pickaxe by his side.

'Fat lot of good it's doing us,' chipped in one of the women.

Two more men came over and squatted down, leaning on their pickaxes. 'I've been breaking stones here since 1985,' said one, wiping his face with a filthy cloth. 'If your sandal breaks you have to work in bare feet or you starve.'

'The employer is meant to provide footwear and safety gear, helmets, gloves and goggles,' said Yadab.

'Well, he doesn't,' said the other man. 'And I've broken stones all over this country. It's the same everywhere.'

On the way back, we headed for the local municipal offices in Faridabad, the biggest city in Haryana, the state we were in. We found the employment commissioner whose job it was to police labour law. V. K. Sharma's office was not unlike that of Thomas Lasme, the civil servant in the Ivory Coast's Oumé – piles of paper, telephones that didn't work and a fan blowing everything around. He wasn't expecting us and had his staff move in chairs while he pushed piles of paper around his desk.

'My ministry says I should not meet the press,' Sharma said with complete courtesy as we sat down. He glanced at one of his staff coming in with a tray. 'You will have some tea?'

'I've come to ask you about the working conditions in the quarry at Dhoj,' I said. 'There was no safety equipment and people said they weren't getting paid properly.'

'I have a team of officers,' began Sharma. 'The workers are paid in their presence. The trade unions and government put in a lot of effort. I haven't received any complaints.'

'So everything is fine, up there?' I asked, taking a sip of the sweet thick tea. He lifted a stack of papers and moved them to another part of the desk. 'There may be certain lapses,' he said. 'But as per the labour laws, action is taken and prosecution is filed in the court.'

'Do you prosecute any big fish?'

'Whether he's a big fish or a small fry, action has to be taken. Inspections are carried out. There was a mine when the lessee was a member of parliament. Certainly action was taken then.'

The room fell quiet. A curtain at the back blew with the breeze of a fan. Sharma dropped his eyes to his desk.

'Do you have an easy job?' I said quietly.

'No.'

'Are you happy with your resources?'

'Resources we are lacking because of government policy.'

'Like how?'

'I am having jurisdiction of the whole of Haryana, but I am not even having a vehicle.'

'You don't have a car?' I said incredulously.

'No,' he answered in barely a whisper.

To give an idea, Haryana covers 17,000 square miles with a population of more than 20 million. Yet the man tasked with enforcing labour regulations was not even given a vehicle.

'So how do you get to inspect places?' I asked.

'We are going by bus.'

'But buses don't go to the quarry.'

'That is the point.'

'So you can't just get in a car and go and check out the quarry now?'

'Absolutely not,' he said. Then he paused, as if a thought was crossing his mind. 'I could take a taxi, I suppose.' He rolled a pen back and forth across the surface of the desk. 'But no,' he concluded. 'They would never approve the budget.'

Faridabad, where we were, was a growing industrial city on a national highway about fifteen miles south of the capital, Delhi. We were not in some far-flung forgotten place in India's interior. Yet, the whole country seethes with the sort of poverty and infuriating complacency that we saw at the quarry. Some months later, in Mumbai, the huge financial capital, we were in a slum with rubbish piled high right along the pathway. A community group showed me a pamphlet in which the municipal council promised to solve such problems within twenty-four hours of notification. It didn't, of course, and when we checked it turned out that, like Sharma in Faridabad, it had no resources in the form of a rubbish truck. Nearby, a vast warehouse complex sat crumbling and deserted. The owner had been waiting twenty years for planning permission to turn it into a textile mill that would give hundreds of jobs to local people.

India and its society has many of the conditions that lead to the type of political violence that destroys other countries. India is buffeted. Riots break out over religion, land and other issues. But the centre always holds.

India's politics are corrupt and infiltrated by crime. In the 2004 general election, one in five politicians elected to parliament had criminal cases pending against them – according to an Indian campaigning organization called No Criminals in Politics. About half were for murder, violent robbery or rape. The figures included 48 per cent of the MPs in Maharashtra, the richest state in India, with Mumbai as its capital, and 35 per cent in Bihar, one of the poorest.

Religion spills over into politics, too. One of the biggest parties, the Bharatiya Janata Party (BJP), roots itself firmly in India's identity as a Hindu nation, despite the fact that India's 150 million Muslims comprise the third biggest Muslim country in the world. The Muslim community is roughly 30 per cent worse off than the rest of India with generally lower scores on health, education and jobs.[1] In poorer neighbourhoods, clashes between Muslims and Hindus are frequent, and in Gujarat in 2002 they erupted into full-scale riots in which more than a thousand people died. It is not unusual for the violence to be tracked back to the ambitions and rivalries of local politicians.

India is constantly fighting low-level ethnic and political insurgencies and the threat of more wars with Pakistan has clouded South Asia since independence in 1947. Independence movements such as those in the north-eastern states of Assam and Nagaland flare up from time to time. In the 1980s, India

---

1 Sachar Committee report, 2006.

fought a full-scale Sikh insurgency in Punjab, much of it fuelled by Pakistan. In the 1990s, the focus switched to the Muslim insurgency in Kashmir, the northern state over which Pakistan and India have fought many times.

The country's development is at least a generation behind that of non-democratic China, a neighbouring country of comparable size and population and which began its modern journey two years later, in 1949. In India, 80 per cent of the people live on less than US$2 a day, whereas in China it's under 40 per cent. India's life expectancy is sixty-nine against seventy-three in China; infant mortality is 30 per 1,000 against China's 20; GDP per capita in 2008 was US$2,800; in China it was US$6,000. China scores higher on all counts except individual freedom, the rule-of-law (corrupt as it is in India) and media freedom.

India knows it and it knows why. But unlike some societies that tried democracy and slipped back into authoritarianism, India did things the other way round. It flirted with dictatorship and didn't like it.

In 1975, the prime minister, Indira Gandhi, having been accused of rigging elections, declared a state of emergency. Citing threats to national security, she rounded up hundreds of politicians and activists, shut down the media and curbed political dissent. Surrounding herself with loyal advisers, she set about implementing birth control and housing programmes of the type later carried out in China. When details of the forcible sterilization and the bulldozing of slum areas became known, Indians were appalled. Poverty and inefficiency was acceptable. Institutional cruelty was not.

The pressure against Indira Gandhi became so acute that, less than two years later, she ended the emergency and held elections which expelled her from office. Sixty per cent voted against her. The Congress Party that had forged India's path from British colonialism lost power for the first time.

But, in a twist that could perhaps only happen in India, they voted her back in again in 1980. Indira Gandhi was part of a founding dynasty that endures today. The voters had given her a rap over the knuckles and another chance.

India is an example of how strongly built institutions, even when fractured and inefficient, can prevent dictatorship and to some extent stop the type of war or ethnic violence that can take a society to the brink of destruction. The system embedded by the British during more than 150 years of colonial rule is seen to work and has, therefore, survived. The courts, the police, the military, and others loyally guard their rights and survive. There has never been the hint of a military takeover. Elections, however chaotic and manipulated, are held regularly. Generals and cabinet ministers slip naturally into retirement. Civil society is deeply rooted, not only in the government but also in citizen groups, such as we saw with the trade unionist Yadab at the quarry. Non-governmental organizations and charities are part and parcel of Indian life. Groups that in many democracies would be considered a threat are allowed to flourish. Teenagers, in smart militaristic uniforms, parade in city parks as part of militant Hindu organizations. Maoists, known as Naxalites, threaten to overthrow the government and influence vast swathes in remote areas of central and eastern India.

Even its elections are deeply flawed. During the election of 2009, a colleague, John Elliott, had just returned from West Bengal where he had heard allegations of vote-rigging and threats by party workers. One elderly woman, Rehki Ghosh, told him: 'My [grown up] children don't go out to vote because they will be beaten up.'

A man, Abdul Razzak, told him: 'They [party workers]

usually come at night a few days before voting and threaten us if we go out and vote.'

And another villager, Kiran Ghosh, said: 'For the last many years we have not gone out because when we go and put one foot inside the voting booth, the officials say your vote is cast, go away, so we come back home.'

It appeared that villagers were told to stay at home because their votes had been duplicated and already cast for the party. An opposition candidate claimed to have unearthed 8,000 duplicate votes with forty-seven pages of double entries.

No substantive research has been carried out on how wide-spread this is throughout India. In conversations, Elliott was told that West Bengal-style vote-rigging would only be possible for about 10 per cent of the electorate and that any winning party that tried it would need to have about 40 per cent support anyway.

'This isn't like Pakistan under Musharraf or Mugabe in Zimbabwe,' said Elliott. 'The elections are far from clean, but they still allow voters to throw politicians out of power.'

Election rigging would blot the legitimacy of governments in many countries. But India absorbs it as it does its poverty, its corruption, its rotting infrastructure, its film, music, food, culture and, more recently, its multinationals that are now beginning to punch their weight on the world stage.

In May 2009, India's Congress Party won a decisive election victory against a rival BJP-led coalition. Congress fought on a secular platform of continuing economic reform. The BJP was still seen by many as being rooted in communal Hindu nationalism.

In recent years, India has suffered a series of well-coordinated terror attacks traced back to insurgents in Pakistan. One, in 2001, on the parliament in Delhi killed six policemen and a civilian, together with five of the attackers. In late 2008, gunmen struck Mumbai, killing more than 170 people and taking over the luxury hotels. The impact was devastating for those involved and their families. It gripped both the Indian and world media. But the country absorbed it. Unlike even 9/11 in the United States, the Mumbai attack became part of the texture of India.

This is very different from its neighbours, countries that set out to build post-colonial democracies and instead became embroiled in ethnic, religious and territorial wars that seemed to stop their development dead in its tracks.

In January 1948 Burma gained independence from Britain. It became a military dictatorship in 1962 and the army has run the country ever since. It is hopelessly poor, corrupt and isolated while its democratic figurehead, Aung San Suu Kyi, has spent most of the last two decades under arrest.

August 1947 saw the India of the Raj split along religious lines into two nations, India and Pakistan – itself divided geographically between East and West Pakistan. In a little over a year a massive area where some 1.5 billion people now live was given its democratic freedom. More than a million died during the partition in communal riots as Hindus, Muslims and Sikhs fled from one country to another. India and Pakistan have since fought three major wars with frequent border skirmishes and low-level fighting. The conflicts include the 1971 war in which India gave its full support to the liberation movement in East Pakistan, leading to the creation of the new state of Bangladesh.

Six months after partition, in February 1948, Ceylon, renamed Sri Lanka, was also given independence. Often described as a teardrop hanging off the edge of India, Sri Lanka is a template of how things can go wrong if you don't get the original model right. It has been embroiled in both political and communal uprisings and fought a civil war from the early 1980s to 2009.

Sri Lanka's majority population, the Sinhalese, formed two dominant political parties along ideological lines – the right-leaning United National Party and the left-leaning Sri Lanka Freedom Party. While they regularly swapped power, there was a large Sri Lankan minority – the Tamils – which felt excluded from the political process. The Tamil sense of exclusion was worsened because they were generally favoured by the British as more efficient administrators than the Sinhalese. But after independence, even if a Tamil joined one of the dominant parties, ethnic differences would prevent him from rising far.

The Tamils are concentrated in the north and east of the country and comprise just under 20 per cent of Sri Lanka's population of just over 20 million. But more than 60 million Tamils lived just to the north in the Indian state of Tamil Nadu. Therefore the Sinhalese, while a majority in their own country, were instilled with a fear that they would be overrun by invading Tamil hordes from the north and eventually 'pushed into the sea'.

When one or other of the Sinhalese political parties were faltering, they could use a tougher anti-Tamil policy to win support. This prevailing atmosphere stumbled along for many years, with the Tamil card being played more and more harshly by Sinhalese politicians backed by conservative Buddhist clergy.

On the ground, it translated into sadly predictable scenarios. Buddhist Sinhalese troops went on brutal patrols in Hindu Tamil areas, just as Christian Serb police harassed Muslim Albanians in Kosovo and Buddhist Thai soldiers were sent down to quell Muslim insurgents in southern Thailand. Once things reach that far it's difficult to pull back.

Sri Lanka erupted in 1983 when Tamil insurgents ambushed a military convoy on the northern Jaffna peninsular. Thirteen soldiers were killed. Hundreds of Tamils died in subsequent riots in the capital Colombo and elsewhere. Three years later, the BBC posted me to Sri Lanka. It took another twenty-three years for the Tamil insurgents to be defeated, but the political problem remains unresolved.

At the start, there were half a dozen insurgent organizations forming a loose independence coalition demanding a separate homeland for Sri Lankan Tamils. One by one they were wiped out by the most ruthless group, the Liberation Tigers of Tamil Eelam. Because of atrocities carried out by Sinhalese troops, the Tamil cause commanded much sympathy among Western democracies. I regularly covered massacres in which the army murdered dozens of Tamils, including women and children, for no apparent reason at all.

The Tamil Tiger leader was Velupillai Prabhakaran, who staged the 1983 attack. Over the years he became a cult figure, with huge portraits of himself hanging in Tamil areas. He became obsessed not with any big nation-building vision but with the mechanisms of war.

Instead of drawing up a blueprint for development that would win the support of Western democracies, he concentrated on designing explosive suicide vests and vehicle bombs, brainwashing child soldiers, killing politicians and building makeshift aeroplanes to bomb Colombo. The areas his militia occupied were dreadful places. Despite the years that the Tigers ran whole swathes of the country, they did very little to improve basic standards of living. Instead, Prabhakaran kept his people suppressed with executions and beatings of anyone who stepped out of line. Denying children schooling, he sent them to war while deploying his militia into Sinhalese villagers to kill families who had no connection whatsoever with the military.

Throughout all this, Tamil communities in Britain, America, Australia and elsewhere sent back millions of dollars to finance him. They would hold legal fund-raising rallies in which Prabhakaran's portrait together with models of Kalashnikov rifles were put in display above fund-raising bowls. Living otherwise straightforward professional lives, when it came to the Tamil Tigers these expatriates created a moral blindspot for themselves.

I remember talking to one organizer in London who argued without a flicker of remorse that the massacre of Sinhalese civilians, including women and children, was a legitimate weapon of war.

It took years before the Tamil Tigers were internationally banned as a terrorist organization. But even then, as the Sri Lankan government was carrying out a final offensive against them in 2009, British politicians stood shoulder-to-shoulder with Tamil demonstrators in London calling for the military action to end, the Sri Lankan government to be investigated for war crimes and for a settlement to be negotiated.

On the surface, therefore, Sri Lanka's democracy works, in that elections are held and political parties regularly exchange power. But the country doesn't work because of the exclusion of the Tamils, and that in turn skews political debate away from issues of development to those of ethnicity.

At least, however, Sri Lanka's violence was confined, unlike that of India's other violent neighbour – Pakistan.

On a glorious spring afternoon in 1999, I was kneeling on a drawing-room floor in Islamabad with a former diplomat, as we pored over maps of Pakistan and India. My host, who shall remain nameless, was retired and we were brainstorming for a book I was writing about what might lead to a nuclear war in Asia.

At first, with a city map of Islamabad, we plotted a coup, deciding where to park the armoured vehicles, how to take the television and radio stations. Then we wrote the speech of the new military leader, one which would be accepted – at least in part – by Western democracies.

Then we moved on to the nuclear bomb. This was less than a year after India and Pakistan had carried out nuclear tests, which made future confrontation between them so lethal. 'You see what would happen in reality,' said my host, 'that although we say the use of the bomb would be our last resort, it would in fact be our first resort.'

'You mean you have plans . . .' I began to ask.

He interrupted. 'We would have no choice. India would completely overpower us in a conventional war. The only way to save our nation would be by going nuclear.'

Perhaps he had said more than he should, because suddenly there was a strange tension, as if we had never been talking about a fictional scenario and that we were both staring into the abyss of Pakistan's actual future.

I spent that evening with a former head of Pakistan's powerful security agency the Inter-Services Intelligence (ISI), who spoke enthusiastically about the Islamic 'greening' of Pakistan. To achieve that, he said, Pakistan needed to conduct military operations inside India that would begin very soon. This was all long before 9/11 and Osama bin Laden and the Taliban became household names.

Just a few weeks later, in May 1999, Pakistani troops invaded India in a remote mountainous area of Kashmir in what became known as the Kargil war. By October, it was over; Pakistan had lost and its democratically elected government was overthrown by a military coup, led by General Pervez Musharraf. The speech he gave on seizing power was generally accepted by Western democracies.

Musharraf installed himself as a military dictator and became one of America's most trusted allies. The contradiction that this was a man who was Chief of Army Staff when Pakistani troops invaded a flourishing Asian democracy and whose security apparatus had close links to the Taliban and Islamic extremism was a truth that few Western leaders had the courage to acknowledge or the wit to resolve. The consequence was that almost a decade later Islamic terror in Pakistan was reaching the levels of that in Iraq. Musharraf stepped aside, leaving a vacuum from which Western powers continued to insist that a healthy democracy could grow.

Throughout the Cold War and much of the War on Terror, the West chose to prop up Pakistan at the expense of India. The United States bankrolled Pakistan whether it was run by autocratic generals or corrupt politicians; even while it was creating a nuclear bomb and exporting the technology; even while it was organizing insurgencies in a neighbouring democratic nation; and even while it was encouraging a brutal Islamic regime in Afghanistan.

Yet during this time, the West failed to help build institutions of note that would guide Pakistan towards becoming a stable democracy. Education, in particular, was a scandal because many schools bereft of funds became reliant on Islamic religious charities that taught anti-Western hatred to a generation of young people.

So when Musharraf stepped down in 2008, there was a vacuum. Benazir Bhutto, one of the key political figures slated to move in, was assassinated and her place taken by her husband, Asif Ali Zardari. He was steeped not in experience of good governance, but in being jailed on corruption charges. Although never convicted, Zardari had spent eleven years in prison and when he got out he lived not in Pakistan, but Dubai. Pakistan's two dominant parties immediately began fighting between themselves, while the economy foundered and Islamic extremists took territory close to Islamabad itself. At that stage, after a quarter of a century of flawed foreign policy, the West conceded that Pakistan had become one of the most dangerous global threats.

After a long journey from Delhi, I stepped from a train in Amritsar near the Pakistan border into a swirl of cold, night-time mist that was blurred with yellows and oranges from different hues cast off by fires and lights around the station. Lying all along the platform, stretching far into the station concourse, I made out huddles of people, hundreds, possibly thousands. They were so tightly packed together that I had to pick my way through, trying hard not to step on a hand or a foot protruding from bundles of clothes.

I had made the same journey a quarter of a century earlier and I'm pretty sure it was as bad if not worse now. If this was what it took to become a nuclear power, why bother? Or if this is what democracy delivers, why boast about it? I had covered many authoritarian injustices, the arrest of an activist for example. Yet often, when travelling to do a story on repression of political freedom in, say, Singapore or Malaysia, I appreciated the well-paved roads and working telephones. Yet in the democracies of the developing world, I had often found myself treading through the poor and the homeless, just like that night in Amritsar. But then across the border in Pakistan it was no better – or worse – and that, too, had became a nuclear power and had tried both democracy and dictator-ship.

Pakistan is less than twenty miles from Amritsar. There is a station, Atari, right on the border, with customs and immigration booths. But when we got there cobwebs hung in broken windows. The telephones were unconnected, and bullock carts and motorcycles criss-crossed the railway line outside.

The road border near the town of Wagah was functioning, but in a crazy way. Workers lined up on either side carrying boxes of fruit on their heads. On the Pakistan side, they unloaded boxes from trucks parked some way away. They walked up to a thick white line painted on the road at the exact border point and handed over the boxes to Indian workers who turned around and carried them to a truck.

A full truck could have passed in minutes and been in Delhi six hours later. This archaic system took hours. The Wagah crossing could have been Berlin at the height of the Cold War. Two governments that should have been working together to try to end poverty had instead created a barrier of mutual fear. Not only did it impact on India and Pakistan, but it sliced the whole of Asia in half.

'We are unfortunately in a geopolitical situation which is compounded by inadequate leadership on our side,' said Pradip Shad, an Indian economic analyst and fund manager in Mumbai. 'We need to be a little more statesmanlike. We have come across as being obsessed with Pakistan. Pakistan is puny by Indian standards. We should let go of that obsession and concentrate on growing our own markets so that we can become relevant both as a market and a supplier to the Western world.'

In the past ten years or so, India has been steadily doing that. First Bollywood and then *Slumdog Millionaire* have become world famous. The Indian company Tata developed the world's cheapest car. Indian call-centre staff have become familiar voices in our everyday lives. Hi-tech Bangalore and

Hyderabad handle everything from instant medical scan analysis to feature-film computer graphics; and the Indian-born industrialist Lakshmi Mittal has frequently been cited as the world's richest man.

Back in Delhi, I went to see George Fernandes, then defence minister, and asked him why India couldn't shake itself free of the obsessions with Pakistan. 'Sure, we can,' he replied. 'Once Pakistan stops backing terrorism and once the borders become secure, the roads and railways can be fully open. That having happened you can go from Paris, from Rome or from Moscow and drive straight through to Bangkok. Why not?'

Tarun Das, who ran the Confederation of Indian Industry, unfolded a map of South Asia across the coffee table in his office, pointing out the key land and sea trade routes that could be opened up. 'If India and Pakistan could get over their relationship issues,' he said, 'we have a huge development potential for all the countries in the region. It's very exciting. It would be like a United States of South Asia, an economic zone and a common market and everybody would benefit.'

Had Das outlined his vision in Europe in 1945 he might well have been laughed out of the room. But half a century later, Europe had managed to achieve exactly what he was planning, and India was edging toward it.

But to what extent was democracy the main motivator and how much were other factors involved? India has its democracy, but there is little evidence that it has done much to alleviate poverty. In fact, it might have worsened it. For most of the time since independence, India has been governed as a socialist economy, protective of outside investment and influence. It made as much as it could itself, such as its own cars in the form of the sturdy, rotund and world-famous Ambassador. Economic reform only began in the 1990s. India embraced it, although its democratic checks and balances, coupled with manipulation from vested interests, often held back its growth. China, next door, was the long-distance runner who was pacing too far ahead for India to feel comfortable. China's success began to seep down into all areas of Indian society, and soon cities like Bangalore, Mumbai and Chennai were getting serious economic makeovers.

China had a particular resonance in the vast Indian state of West Bengal, whose 80 million people had been ruled by a coalition of left-wing parties for more than thirty years.

Statues of Lenin have been pulled from dozens of plinths around the world, but not in Kolkata. The leader of the global Marxist revolution stands on a high maroon platform centre stage in a city park, his head slightly turned, looking across toward a heaving intersection. He is wearing a three-piece suit and tie with his left hand gripping the lapel of his jacket.

Grubby red hammer and sickle flags flew from the railings around the park that were also draped with the bedding of the homeless who lived there. I visited in 2006 and the left-wing coalition led by the Communist Party was celebrating yet another election victory. Its policies were mapped out at the Communist Party headquarters in a poor Muslim neighbourhood nearby. The corridors were lined with portraits of party members who fought British colonialism and portraits of Lenin, Marx, Engels, Mao and Ho Chi Minh adorned the main meeting room.

'Do you still admire these men?' I said to Subodh Roy, an eighty-eight-year-old party worker whose job was to file press cuttings. A little over five feet tall, he stood up to greet me, holding down the edge of a newspaper to stop it being blown about by the ceiling fan.

'Yes. The name of our party is "Communist Party of India – Marxist",' he said.

'But I thought Marxism had failed?'

'No,' he said with a smile. 'That is your fault, not Marxism's fault.'

'My fault,' I said with an incredulous cadence, assuming he meant either the West or more specifically his former colonial masters.

'So Stalin?' I asked. 'Was he a good leader?'

'Yes. Yes. Stalin was strong,' he replied, his confidence unwavering and his eyes straight on me.

'And Mao Zedong of China?'

'Yes. Mao. He was good. He fought for communism, too, in the Chinese way.'

We were interrupted by the arrival of West Bengal's chief minister, Buddhadeb Bhattacharya, here for a series of post-election meetings. In his early sixties, he was a small teddy bear of a man who shuffled into the room wearing a simple white cotton top and trousers.

For many years the Communist Party had been popular in the rural areas, but had been losing out in the cities. Under Bhattacharya, it had spread its focus to urban voters, particularly the middle classes, by talking about the economy and foreign investment, a break from past policy. The West Bengal Communist Party had held off economic reform because of loyalty to communist ideals. But now even China had turned those on their head.

'The Chinese government has initiated new programmes,' he said, 'and we are learning from some of their policies. China has used its socialism to now include private ownership and foreign investment, and we have been observing very closely what is going on.'

'But China is far ahead of you,' I said. 'Wasn't it a mistake to wait so long?'

'Yes,' he acknowledged. 'We thought for too long that we should stick to our untrammelled path that only state ownership would work; that we must not allow private investment; and that we must disassociate ourselves from the world economy. That has now changed. The point, though, is that if we seek capital then we must ensure the benefits reach the poor, because that is what has gone wrong in the capitalist world. We must be careful not to make that mistake. So we must continue to apply Marxism, but in our own way.'

'What's the difference now between you and China?' I asked.

'The Chinese economy has an inner strength when it is negotiating with the West and with America,' he answered. He let out a small laugh and touched his chest to make his point. 'Our position is not like that. We are begging.'

Our interview finished, Bhattacharya's staff swarmed into the room to get him to another meeting. But he waved them away, sat silently for a moment, then looked up me. 'The problem with China is the absence of the right to dissent. That would not work here and that is our dilemma.'

Autocratic but successful, China focused Indian minds on the choice between freedom and economic development, and it percolated right through Indian society. Direct foreign investment into China then was over ten times that going into India – US$60 billion a year against the US$5 billion for India. For every cellphone in India, there were thirteen in China, and Bhattacharya was envious that the Chinese were getting richer faster than his voters in West Bengal.

At a maternity clinic in Kolkata, a doctor explained how they were having some success in persuading families to have just two children. In China, there was no persuasion. The limit was one child and it was enforced by law.

But then, outside the city, I asked a classroom of Indian children how many of them had more than one sibling, and every hand went up. Most had about five.

Across the road from the school, two slightly built women

were carrying a huge sack of rice. It was far too heavy for them. Their faces were drenched with sweat. Both were barefoot. One had a bleeding gash on her left ankle. Their saris, one pink and one dark green, were filthy and torn. They put down their sack and I asked if they would swap their right to vote for better working conditions.

'Yes,' said one. 'This is too much for us.'

'But if you could no longer vote?'

'No,' said the other, talking quickly to the other. 'No. We will do this work and take the vote.'

Other villagers, hearing the question, gathered around. 'We must vote,' said a bare-chested man, clenching his forefinger and thumb together. 'If we cannot vote, we have nothing.'

'Vote,' chipped in an elderly man leaning on a roughly hewn walking stick.

'Yes. Vote,' said a boy, leaning on his bicycle. More came up, nodding. 'Vote,' they all agreed.

'Really?' I challenged. 'But compared to China . . .'

'If we choose the right people, then our lives will improve,' said the older man.

'But then . . .' I began, but trailed off because on each of the faces I was seeing a sense of ambition more complex than just material wealth. Each of them had very specific individual ambitions. One wanted to own a sewing business. Another said he was a poet. One was saving to buy a motorcycle rickshaw and his friend asked if I could help him get a guitar from London. He wanted to be a rock star.

In a mall in a Kolkata suburb, we found the middle classes who were shopping amid posters for luxury apartment developments, designer labels and cellphones. They were more articulate – many fluent in English – but the sentiment was the same.

'The more we get to know about China and its policy,' said

a middle-aged woman in a light yellow sari, 'we realize that they do not practise human rights.'

'But isn't it a human right to have more money and a better place to live?' I asked, to which a young man in red and white sports shirt responded unequivocally: 'We are not willing to sacrifice human rights in order to get people out of poverty. No.'

After 9/11, India's loyalty to the democratic ideal finally percolated through to Washington. During the Cold War, India had been categorized as an enemy because of its friendly relationship with the Soviet Union. Pakistan was America's South Asian ally and complained vociferously whenever the relationship between Washington and Delhi showed signs of improving. But with America's proclamation to support democracies around the world, and Pakistan, a military dictatorship on the cusp of becoming a failed state, the American position became untenable. In a move compared to Nixon's 1972 policy change on China, America reached out to India and declared it a strategic ally.

'We think it is in America's interests for India to become a great global power,' America's ambassador to India, Robert Blackwill, told me in 2003. 'This is a great democracy. It has our values. Our long-term relationship with India is very stabilizing for Asia.'

As India's democracy, trade and new alliances gave it a global influence, Pakistan's unimaginative leaders – whether generals or politicians – were causing the country to collapse on itself. Yet neither country has managed to tackle the problem of poverty. What democracy has given India, though, is that safety valve of free expression and creativity that dictatorships repress. Cutting through the economic and political jargon, much of it was about that very natural emotion – hope.

'The people from the top to the bottom have not yet lost faith in the system,' said one close friend. 'It might not work for them now. But they believe the odds are stacked that it could in the future. In Pakistan, many have lost faith in the system and that is why they are moving to the Taliban.'

'In India, everyone is a minority,' said another friend. 'And minorities have to learn to get on with one another.'

'Every shade of opinion is accommodated and appeased, even if only symbolically,' said the author Namita Gokhale. 'The millions of Hindu gods give space to all kinds of psychological states, promoting and condoning all kinds of contradictory behaviour. There is no place for a single prescriptive morality.'

'Look at our poor,' said an Indian diplomat friend, living in the Middle East. 'There is something in our society that gives them hope. If you go to a slum, there is not hatred, but energy.'

What, then, was the tipping point of hope? I wondered. For, isn't it the loss of hope in an individual life that motivates a suicide bomber? In Delhi, I went to see a psychiatrist, Dr Ahchal Bhagat, who specialized in social development and was familiar with life in the slums. I told him the story of Sita, whom we had met at the quarry, and asked where he thought her breaking point would be on the issue of hope – or for that matter the breaking point of her parents.

'It is when they lose the interface between good and bad,' he said. 'Either they begin to see the world as completely good or completely bad. Or they look at themselves and they see themselves as completely good or completely bad.'

'But what happens to the children who grow up in that environment?' I asked.

'They develop a template that you must not trust anybody. If you trust someone you will be hurt. You create a scenario thinking "I'm not good. My world's no good. My future's no good", and that's a very depressing state to be in.'

I took Bhagat's analysis down to a Delhi slum to see how it played out there. When I had done similar tests in Iraq, Latin America or even the Balkans, individual human emotions such as love, hope and trust often get lost, because of violence, poverty, or a general sense of nihilism and victimhood – the interface that Bhagat referred to.

The slum carried a pervasive smell of mud, rubbish and urine. Children who should have been at school were everywhere. The shacks were made up of material looted from city garbage dumps, car doors, corrugated iron and wooden slats. Propane gas cylinders stood with rotting rubber tubes running off to cooking stoves. People shuffled down narrow paths.

I was lucky enough to be with two Indian colleagues, Smita Choudry, who was translating, and Ravi Leki, our Delhi cameraman. We stopped an elderly man who was walking past. With his shock of grey hair and beard, Smita was certain he was a community patriarch of sorts. As soon as we started talking others gathered around.

'How do you define fear and love?' I asked him with Smita translating.

'Fear means you have nothing,' he said straight away, not put off at all by the question. 'And love means taking everyone along with you, which is what we do in this community where we love each other.'

'I think fear means that a person who is poor has to be afraid,' said a younger man with dark, close-cropped hair. 'It means he is not educated and if anyone threatens him he becomes afraid.'

'What about hope?' I asked.

'Hope is about encouragement,' said the patriarch.

'People need to feel they can be uplifted,' said a middle-aged man in a loose grey shirt who joined us, pushing a small trolley. 'And love means embracing someone. A person feels happy when they are embraced.'

A young man, in his early twenties, set down an old television he was carrying. 'I think love is living together without fighting, which is what we all do here.'

'And hope?'

'Hope is that tomorrow may bring something good for me. Hope is that we may rise higher in life.'

A mother passing by holding the hand of a young boy over-heard and stopped. 'Hope is what poor people like us have,' she said. 'Because what else is there?'

Her name was Salma Bano and her son was Mohammed Nasim. He was ten. He wore a dark T-shirt and grey shorts and walked with a limp. A smudge of dirt ran down his cheek. His hands were covered in dust. He had tousled black hair. His face was expressionless. His eyes kept referring up to his mother. Salma explained that Mohammed was not at school because he was bullied there because of his leg. He would come home every day in tears. So she took him out.

'After he was born his leg became thinner and thinner until it was like it is now,' said Salma. She took us to her shack where carpets were laid out on the ground. Bed-rolls were piled onto a single iron bed. There was a small stove outside. Salma's sister squatted next to it, washing dishes in a bowl of water.

Salma and Mohammed had been out rag-picking, scavenging through rubbish tips. It was how she earned a living. 'She's saying that she teaches Mohammed to be polite and to eat well and use his mind for studying so that when he grows up he can work at his own business,' translated Smita.

Mohammed stayed quiet. When we asked him a question

he answered in a monosyllabic 'yes'.

Salma kept talking. 'She says she tells him to obey his mother and obey everyone,' translated Smita. 'That her life has been destroyed so he should take care of his life. She says she will educate him to trust everyone . . .' She broke off. The sister was interrupting from outside.

'But her sister says there's no one around to trust,' said Smita. 'So Mohammed should learn not to trust.'

'What do you teach Mohammed about fear?' I asked.

'No one has ever told me about this,' Salma answered. 'I don't know what it is.'

Smita asked her about hope.

'I told you about hope. It is all we have,' she said brusquely. 'Are you trying to take that from us now?'

'No, we're not,' assured Smita.

Smita said that nearby was a charity that had a lovely big hall where children could play. She asked if Mohammed would like to go there for the afternoon. He said he would.

We promised his mother to deliver him back safely. Mohammed rode in our minivan in silence. Smita tried to talk to him, but he stayed within his shell.

The centre was in a school-like building, two storeys high and set back within its own grounds. We slid open the van door. Mohammed slipped off his seat, and Smita helped him keep his balance with his bad leg. A charity worker called Pari, dressed in a bright-blue sari, came out to meet him. She hugged Mohammed, then helped him walk up the steps towards the entrance.

On the outside wall was a faded orange and blue mural. Mohammed stopped and looked at it. 'It's a picture of a bird in the sky,' explained Pari, opening the main door. 'Come on, Mohammed,' she said. 'Come and look at this.'

Inside was a fantastical scene. The entrance hall, the corridors beyond and another hall beyond that were filled with images of fish, dolphins, elephants, giraffes, seas, woods, rolling hills and deep-blue skies and suns. Mohammed stopped dead, then wriggled away from Pari and ran, just a few steps, before stopping and managing to balance himself.

'He's never seen colour like this before,' said Pari. 'The environment in the slums is very bad and the children grow up feeling that nothing good can ever happen to them. But if you bring them into an environment they can trust, they will know it immediately.'

Pari went over to Mohammed and put her hands on his shoulders. 'What do you like most?' she asked.

'I love it all,' he said excitedly. 'Perhaps the birds.' He let his eyes wander over the pictures. 'Or the man there flying the kite,' he pointed, turning round and looking her. 'Who made this? Did the children make it?'

'Yes,' said Pari. 'We helped them. But it's their work.'

The entrance hall itself was slightly raised and looked down on a large space where other children were playing. 'I like it here,' he said, breaking away from Pari again and limping enthusiastically to a safety rail. He gripped it while getting a better look. A teacher below gathered the children to stand in lines in front of her. They scampered into place.

'I like it here,' said Mohammed again. 'Are these children at school?'

'Yes,' said Pari, catching up with him, her hands back on his shoulders. 'They are about to go into class.'

'Can I go with them?' His tilted his head up toward Pari, his eyes alive with expectation. 'Is there a bicycle here? A small one will be fine. I can keep it here and cycle from home every day to study.'

Looking at Mohammed's tiny frame and the way he only just kept up on his bad leg, it was difficult to see how he could ride a bicycle. But he spoke about it as if it were an achievable dream.

'We'll see what we can do,' said Pari with a smile. 'But why don't you go and join the class?'

'Really?'

'Yes. Off you go.'

'You mean I don't have to go rag-picking?'

'Not today, you don't,' said Pari.

'What happens now?' I said to Smita.

'They'll take him back and ask the mother if he can come to school here,' she said. 'She'll complain about losing the money Mohammed makes from rag-picking. But it's only a few rupees. So they'll probably pay it and Mohammed will come to school here.'

We watched as Mohammed made his way down a set of steps and across the hall to join the other children. The teacher asked two children in a line to make way for him so he wasn't left at one end. Mohammed took his place, raised his head and put his hands down like a soldier standing to attention.

Above India's bustling city streets, billboards advertise cellphones, health spas and luxury-living apartment blocks, while down below the textured blend of chaotic humanity reigns untouched. It was as if the hoardings paid lip-service to China's dollar ideology. India absorbed it, took note, but just kept going. In China, the wealth-creation mission was all-encom passing, while for much of India it is a margin-note, merely part of a greater mix. India's benchmarks are more subtle and nuanced, touching far more on that Greek concept of *emos*, the human need to have, not a fast car and a computer, but an identifiable place in society.

One day we were returning to Kolkata from the countryside and bumped into a demonstration blocking off the intersection presided over by the statue of Lenin. We diverted down small roads, crammed with market stalls.

Walking through the crowd, head high, eyes curious, arms swinging confidently and oozing self-esteem, was a man without a stitch of clothing on. Those nearest to him – mothers, children, shoppers, traders – didn't flinch. In China – in fact, in most places in the world – he would have been arrested. But this was India, where freedom and human dignity were measured in a different way.

India's melting pot of chaotic coincidental revolutions is living proof that democracy can take root in a poor society.

But, given America's policy towards India during the Cold War, it could have been very different. During India's intervention in the creation of what is now Bangladesh in 1971, the United States sent a carrier group of warships into the Bay of Bengal to warn India off. India was strong enough to withstand the outside pressure.

In other parts of the world, however, America would have gone further. Indeed had India been in Latin America, might its democracy have survived?

LATIN AMERICA

ARGENTINA – Democracy's Debt

Marita Falabella banged a wooden spoon against the bottom of a saucepan with a fury. The free-market system that she had believed in for all these years had been a sham. Marita was angry and frightened. Her hair was tied up in a bun. Wearing jeans and a yellow top, she was sitting cross-legged in front of Argentina's pink colonial-style presidential palace where once walked a series of sash-uniformed dictators who had killed with abandon. Now, it had become an icon of Western free-market democratic values, which had led the country into one of the worst economic crises of modern times.

That day, in early 2002, thousands of others were with Marita in the Plaza de Mayo, the central square that runs down from the presidential palace through trees to a wide-curving city boulevard. Well dressed and non-violent, these middle-class protesters banged their saucepans or frying pans against each other or with spoons, making one hell of racket. Inside the palace, Argentina's government was hunkered down and foundering. It had had three presidents in two weeks and no one knew who was running the country.

Marita was thirty-six, married with two children, and six years earlier she had been diagnosed with diabetes. The disease is caused when the body fails to produce insulin, the hormone that controls blood-sugar levels. Insulin is a common drug, easily available all over the world, and without it a diabetic can fall into a coma and die. Marita was at the demonstration

187

because Argentina had run short of insulin. Most of the country's supplies were made by foreign companies and imports had stopped because the money had dried up.

Argentina had just defaulted on the biggest debt default in world history – a total of US$132 billion. It might not seem much to us now that we have been living with bail-outs of hundreds of billions.

Banks limited withdrawals. Those who thought their savings were in US dollars suddenly found them converted back to the shrunken Argentine currency. The peso, which had been artificially pegged one-to-one to the dollar, ended up a quarter of its value, meaning that millions lost 75 per cent of their savings. Argentine goods had become too expensive for foreign buyers and imports, such as insulin, had become unaffordable. Companies closed like dominoes. Millions were thrown out of work and, as money became worthless, the barter trade boomed.

The West took precious little notice. It carried on business as usual for another seven years until it, too, found out that its own financial system was as vulnerable as a house of cards. Then it reacted in the way the rich world does far too often. It tore up the rule-book so often used to lecture poor countries and bailed out its own people in order to cushion the fall and retain social stability.

After the protest, Marita took us back to her home in a reasonably wealthy suburb. Her house was set back from the road with a sloping garden and a small swimming pool. A black Labrador bounded out to greet us and a maid was making a snack for her son.

She opened the cupboard where she kept her insulin supplies. Only one small white box was there. The rest – and it was a large space – was empty.

'When my supplies ran out, I went to the chemist,' she said.

'But he told me he didn't have any insulin either. I managed to get one dose only off my doctor. It was a sample. He had run out, too. If I had had any idea at all that insulin would have been hard to come by, I would have stockpiled a year's supply.'

Marita shook her head, weeping. The boy ran over and gave her a hug. The maid touched her arm and gave her a tissue. Marita smiled, realized she had left the saucepan from her protest in the car. The boy ran off to get it.

'Our insulin is imported and the company that makes it is refusing to send it without payment. But I depend on insulin for my life. How can they leave people without it like this?' She dabbed her eye with the tissue. 'How can you simply not supply people with insulin?'

But they could because that was how the free-market worked. This was why Marc and Fabrice Kwame were child slaves in the Ivory Coast and why Marita feared for her life because of a lack of insulin. In 2002, before the flaws in the financial systems had percolated in the West, the market was thought to be always right. Money goes where it gets the best deal. I was standing in the house of the very middle class that the developing world needs to build a strong civil society that anchors an effective democracy in place. Yet, Marita, together with millions of others, felt betrayed.

Her son came back with the saucepan and spoon. Marita took it. Her fingers curled tightly round the handle. 'We have to know as a country that we can always get supplies,' she said sadly. 'Can't we make all our own insulin?'[1]

It was a good question. Firstly, why was Argentina with its

---

1 According to Argentina's National Institute of Census and Statistics (INDEC) the country imported 60 per cent of its insulin supply from 1999–2001 – about twice as much as in the decade before the crisis. For many years Argentina had made its own insulin, but not enough. Since the collapse, this situation has been reversed.

population of more than 35 million not making enough of
this very basic and life-saving drug? Second, why was its
foreign supplier not obliged by contractural safeguards to keep
supplying the drug regardless of the economic circumstances?

Over the previous years, the free market had ended up
flooding Argentina with dollar debt and investment and a
reliance on foreign goods. The centre of Buenos Aires was
filled with signs of the global economy. Foreign multinationals,
including banks such as HSBC and Citibank, were seen as
selling themselves to their Argentine customers on their global
values, the notion being that money was safer and the service
better in a global bank than in an Argentine bank.

Yet, as soon as things turned bad, the very banks that had
been advising on this economic formula stood accused by
their customers of abandoning them and leaving them broke
and swinging in the wind. Graffiti on their walls read: 'Banks
are thieves' and 'Banks = Shit'.

Back then, most of us trusted the banks to handle economic
complexities and make sure our money was safe. In Argentina,
they failed abysmally. There is no other way of describing the
devaluing of private savings accounts by 75 per cent, which
is more in tune with what happens in Zimbabwe and
Burma.

Many more of us are now more sceptical about the professionalism and morality of people working in the banking business. But it raises the question as to whether economists,
bankers or political leaders in Western democracies looked at
what was happening in Argentina and asked what our own
financial institutions were doing there?

After leaving Marita Falabella, I called the press office of
HSBC in London and asked if they could help me with a
question. 'If my money was not safe in the HSBC branch in

Buenos Aires,' I asked, 'could HSBC supply a list of those branches of the bank in which it would be safe?'

'What do you mean?' said the press officer.

'I mean, I would like to see a list of banks where my money would be safe,' I said. 'Or if it's easier, the list of those branches in which money would be at risk.'

'I don't understand,' he said.

'Like Hong Kong,' I countered. 'If the Hong Kong–US dollar peg suddenly goes, what will happen to my money?'

He laughed. 'Don't be ridiculous. That would never happen.'

'Well it happened in Argentina, didn't it?'

He said he would see what he could do, and I headed off to meet a free-market economist, from a think tank that had been advocating the policies that had left Marita without insulin.

Carlos Melconian's office was in a high-rise block with a view across the Buenos Aires skyline. It was a modern building that towered over the lower-rise, older structures designed during the turn-of-the-century industrial revolution boom. I told him about Marita Falabella and her problems in getting hold of imported insulin.

'Argentina used to be the star of the emerging market economies,' I said. 'Now it is in crisis. What happened?'

'It's not easy to say why,' he answered, 'Our convertibility law was good. It protected us against external shocks. When things are running well, nobody likes to change. You never know when is the best time to change. Maybe a year ago, we should have done something. But who knows?'

We talked some more, but it came out in complex economic jargon. While I was crystal clear about Marita's plight, I had a hard time making head or tail of what Melconian was telling me. 'Convertibility' ran into 'fiscal deficit' that ran into 'capital flows' that became 'setting price caps' and 'extensive margins' that ended up as 'macro-economic form models' and so on – until I was completely lost.

'So what, then,' I asked, 'is your message to those people who need medicine but can't buy it?'

'I don't know if this is a fiscal issue,' he answered, 'or a social issue or an economic one.'

'It could be a life or death issue,' I contributed.

'If the economy does not grow, nobody will receive medicine. For me the first issue is growth, then we resolve social problems, which would include the medical problems.'

I left unconvinced. Rationally, I am sure he was right. But as with the cocoa belt of West Africa or the unreconstructed streets of Iraq, the economic theory did not translate to the grit of the field – which was why we decided to head off to the small farming community of Casilda 230 miles north of Buenos Aires.

Shattered glass from the front window of the bank lay broken on the pavement. Its ATM machine was smashed and the metal door frame buckled. Rioters had been here a couple of days ago, but the debris had yet to be cleared up. The bank stayed closed. Argentina was still broke; the cause of the protest was unsolved. Those who ran Casilda – the police, the rubbish collectors, the bank tellers – were still not sure how things would turn out.

'Here,' said Victor Morena, one of the protesters, pointing at jagged glass jutting out from the frame. 'This is where I threw a brick at the window.'

Morena, thirty-five, was a bricklayer who couldn't find work because the money had dried up. 'People are tired,' he said. 'That's why we came out onto the streets. It's an expression of what we're feeling. We are tired of just sitting back and taking it peacefully.'

As he spoke, a lone glazier arrived with a ladder. Morena looked sharply across and reprimanded him. The glazier propped the ladder up against the front of the bank. He shrugged and unfolded an old wooden measure. 'I have to earn a living,' he said gruffly and started work.

'He shouldn't be here,' Morena muttered. 'We have to show solidarity. We should leave the bank as it is to show that we are fed up with being used.'

'But is smashing up banks the best way?' I asked.

'It's an expression. I don't know if it's the solution.'

We left the glazier measuring the broken window, and Morena took us to meet his fellow activists in a cafe down a side street.

Casilda is a lush town of about 30,000 people who live off producing wheat, soybean, corn, as well as honey and rearing cattle. It's 30 miles west of the provincial capital Rosario, birthplace of Che Guevara the revolutionary, synonymous with dangerous Latin American politics.

The cafe was a small room, half a dozen tables or so. On the wall was a huge faded Hollywood poster of Clark Gable and Vivien Leigh against the backdrop of burning Atlanta from the film *Gone with the Wind*. In the corner by the small counter was a hammer and sickle flag, its edges frayed but its bright-red dye fresh. Morena explained it had been furled up for years, but opened again since the riots began.

'Are you movie buffs or Marxists, then?' I asked lightly pointing at the poster and flag. Morena didn't answer, but deferred to two men sitting in the back corner. Both were in their late forties and said they were veterans of the 'dirty war' when left-wing activists were killed in their thousands, snatched from homes, thrown out of aircraft, buried in mass graves and became known as the 'disappeared'.

In the late 1970s, across Latin America, US-allied dictatorships formed an alliance against the Left called Operation Condor, which worked like Interpol. If activists fled, say, from Argentina to Paraguay, the details would be sent though and they would be picked up, jailed or killed. It was an entrapment net that nipped communism in the bud by giving its foot soldiers no place to hide. I had met those who survived in Paraguay and Brazil, and the two trade unionists in the cafe wore a similar look, the faces of men who had lived on their wits for years to escape capture. They wore drab T-shirts and jeans. Their eyes were unsettled. They're bodies were wiry and strong, but the recent more secure lifestyle, washed down with cold Argentine beer, had given them both slight pot bellies.

'Yes, we are Marxists,' said Daniel Scopetta, topping up his beer, and spreading his hands on the table. He said he was a steelworker, but now his aim was to steer Argentina towards becoming a socialist, if not a fully fledged communist state. His colleague Antonio Luraschi stood up and pulled out chairs so we could sit down.

'The protest was part of a long series of demonstrations,' said Scopetta. 'The problems started in 1990s when the economy was growing, but so was unemployment and social problems. And it's now come to this point.'

'Ultimately, what do you want to achieve?'

'People have had their bank accounts frozen. So if they want to buy food, clothes for their children, fix up their houses, they can't get the money to do it.'

'But, how would turning Argentina into a Marxist state fix those problems?'

Luraschi answered. 'The economic system we have now doesn't solve our problems,' he said. 'Vast sectors of society are excluded. The Marxist system would give all the population a chance.'

'Even though it failed dramatically before?'

'No, it didn't. You have to think of it in the context of many years of capitalism which has also failed. We've looked closely at what went wrong in the Soviet Union and are convinced we won't make the same mistakes again.'

'Will you have to fight again?'

'The situation is very different to the 1970s. A lot of the people in the armed forces now agree with us. This free-market system is too aggressive for our society and it has reached a point when it is exploding.'

The views of these two campaigners in a small Latin American farming town would soon be resounding through Washington and right to the Oval Office. They brought into question not only the checks and balances of the international banking system (that we now know were deeply flawed) but also the professionalism of that guardian economic institution for the developing world, the International Monetary Fund.

The IMF oversaw the economic policies of dozens of countries emerging from the Cold War. But very often, these governments were not able to keep up with repayments on money loaned for their modernization. The issue came to a head when debt repayments to foreign banks made deep cuts in funds the country needed to build basic infrastructure and services. This was worsened by a general assumption that much of the loaned money had simply lined the pockets of the elite. It wasn't unusual, as in Argentina's case, for a new government to find itself saddled with debt run up by its corrupt predecessors under the auspices of international banks and the IMF. Then, in negotiations to reschedule debt payments, the IMF would insist on rigorous spending cuts that impacted on the poor. If you ask on the streets of Britain what

IMF stands for, many people might be hard-pressed for an answer. If you mention it in Latin America, they would often bristle.

'What do you think of the IMF?' I asked Scopetta, who cupped his hand around his beer glass when he heard the question.

'An Argentine government official can't even take a piss without getting authorization from the IMF,' he sneered. 'They talk about globalization. Well, we used to call it imperialist oppression. We are an oppressed country, so the best thing the IMF can do is not help us any more.'

'Let's put it this way,' added Luraschi. 'The leadership in Argentina allowed the IMF to get involved and now our economy is devastated. Once you involve the IMF in anything they will look after their own interests, which are not our interests.'

Morena, who had stayed quiet, brought more beers from the refrigerator behind the counter. As we talked some more, I tried to put my finger on something about the three men that was different from many activists I'd met, people frustrated and on the cusp of turning violent. And it was this. They were convinced they had now been proved right.

'Never let in the IMF,' Luraschi repeated, summing up his thoughts as we finished up.

'You both look very relaxed, though,' I said.

'Because this time we will win,' he said.

Scopetta and Morena took us to a settlement called Villa Miseria, a generic name for a poor neighbourhood that translates literally as the 'misery village'. It was a shanty settlement on the edge of the town. They wanted us to see how the economic collapse had impacted on the very poor. As we were leaving the cafe, half a dozen men arrived. We stepped out. They filed in. A curtain was drawn across and the door was bolted from the inside.

The wreck of a saloon car turned on its side, its chassis scorched by fire, marked the border of the misery village. The scrubland behind it had been cleared around metal and wood huts. Electricity was pirated from nearby poles and the kitchen was a campfire fuelled by a propane gas cylinder.

Maria Isabel Llanos was a mother of seven children. From her drawn face and long grey-black hair, I judged her to be in her late forties, until she said she was only twenty-seven. One of the children, aged about four, trotted towards us from behind a hut. A dog that had been sleeping in the spare tyre of the wrecked car jumped up and ran toward the child. Maria intercepted it with a whack on the neck. The dog yelped and slunk back. The child clung to his mother's dress. Maria showed us cakes she had been making for a local food store.

It turned out that Scopetta wanted us with him because he was on a recruiting drive. He began his pitch, referring to the way Maria lived, asking where her husband was, pointing to the rusting corrugated iron that made up the roof of her hut.

'The state has the obligation to provide food to your family and all those without employment,' he said. 'But they're making repayment of the foreign debt a priority and they're leaving the Argentine people in the worst of all possible poverty. When we protest we are set upon by the police who are part of the establishment of the dominant classes. How can we make people understand that a country that is as rich as ours, that produces millions of tonnes of sorghums a year, that has 50 million head of cattle also has mothers living like this and their children going hungry? It is completely incomprehensible.'

Maria stared at him, half listening, half an eye on the child. She hooked her long hair behind her ears, pointed at Scopetta and turned to our interpreter. 'Is he a politician?' she said. 'They've been coming here all the time and they promise and they promise and then when they get elected you hear nothing else from them.'

Scopetta broke off from his argument. 'She's right,' he said. 'Politicians do break promises all the time. That's why we need the alternative system.'

Three more children appeared. They were wearing grubby handed-down clothes. Maria reprimanded them. Two melted away. A third joined her sibling and her mother.

'We need people to support us and be aware of our struggle,' attempted Morena.

'So we're asking you to join us,' added Scopetta. 'Baking cakes does not provide a good living.'

'I agree with that,' said Maria, but, like the African cocoa farmers and the housewives in the Morocco slum, she seemed far from convinced. Far away ideologues might be discussing Islamic caliphates, Marxist panaceas and democratic values, but all Maria was looking for was good governance.

Back in Buenos Aires, I got a call from the HSBC press officer. It was very late in London. He didn't have a written statement, but wanted to give me a verbal explanation that began on the premise that I had asked the wrong question.

'We have to work with the laws of the country in which we operate,' said the HSBC spokesman.

'But the deposits were in US dollars, not pesos,' I said.

'It was the Argentine government's decision.'

'And you just did it?'

'Our hands were tied.'

The argument reminded me of the chocolate companies in that both they and the banks put responsibility on governments whose institutions they must have known were weak and ineffective. With the Ivory Coast civil war, the cocoa industry headed off to South East Asia and Latin America to identify secure supplies. With the Argentine collapse, the banks turned their spotlights on the emerging economies of Eastern Europe and the booming phenomenon of China.

The Argentine crisis accompanied a predictable move throughout much of Latin America toward the Left. After a series of ineffective leaders, Argentina opted for Néstor Kirchner, a former socialist governor of the southern Santa Cruz province. Anticipating the economic crash, Kirchner had deposited his provincial government's surplus not in any bank in Argentina, be it international or foreign, but in Switzerland.

In 2002, Brazilians chose trade unionist Luiz Inácio Lula da Silva as their leader, and earlier in 1999 Hugo Chávez had become president of Venezuela. In 2004, Tabaré Vázquez took power in Uruguay. In 2005, Evo Morales was elected in Bolivia. In 2006, Daniel Ortega, who had been a key target in the US–Central American wars of the 1980s, won the presidential election in Nicaragua. Left-wing politicians became powerful opposition figures from Chile to Peru to Mexico.

The socialist swing offered up a problem to Washington, but, given the challenge at the time from Iraq and extreme Islam, it chose not to deal with it head on. Latin America is a vast area with almost 600 million people. Most countries won their independence in the early nineteenth century. But unlike in Africa, the Middle East and Asia, the new rulers were simply the European colonizers who had settled there and not the indigenous people.

The region is mainly European and Catholic in its thinking, but with a less-developed civil society. For much of the twentieth century, power remained with the land-owning classes, thus setting out the divisions between the Left and Right. The Right found a natural home in the United States and its multinationals came to Latin America for the cheaper work-force and raw materials. The Left looked to the huge numbers of the impoverished and, during the Cold War, towards inter-national trade union movements, Marxism and the Soviet Union. Its heroes were – and still are – Che Guevara and Fidel Castro.

America fought this trend with the Monroe Doctrine, a foreign policy dating back to 1823, long before Soviet com-munism or Islamic terror was seen as a global threat. President James Monroe introduced it to keep European colonizers in check, decreeing that no foreign power should have more influence in Latin America than the United States itself. In 1904, President Theodore Roosevelt added a 'corollary', saying that the United States would intervene militarily in Latin America when US interests were seen to be at risk.

Since the Monroe Doctrine's introduction in 1823, the United States is believed to have stepped in to overturn more than forty Latin American governments.[2] Cold War examples include coups in Paraguay and Guatemala in 1954, the 1961 abortive Bay of Pigs operation to try to overthrow Fidel Castro in Cuba; the 1973 coup in Chile that killed President Salvador Allende; the contra war against Nicaragua's Daniel Ortega in the 1980s; and the Grenada invasion in 1983.

A generation later, Latin Americans were voting in the same types of leaders that had prompted those interventions, indi-cating that the general sentiments of those societies were towards the Left, a quest for a social safety net, a fairer sharing of the economic pie, a political system similar to that already chosen by much of Europe.

Except this time round, there was no obvious foreign force onto which it could latch. The new rhetoric coming from

---

2 Gavin Esler, BBC, 3 April 2006, 'How the US Lost Latin America'.

Venezuela's Chávez and Bolivia's Morales blended with the old from Castro's Cuba. In 2008, both Venezuela and Bolivia expelled American ambassadors and, when relations between Moscow and Washington were at a low point that year, Venezuela and Cuba played host to Russian long-range ships and warplanes – conjuring up memories of the 1962 Cuban missile crisis.

In 2004, two years after the Argentine crash, when Iraq had been invaded, and President Bush was running for re-election, I headed back to Argentina. The peso had edged up to be worth three to the dollar and the new president, Néstor Kirchner, was just about keeping things together, although another fight with international bankers was looming.

We headed to an industrial area on the outskirts of Buenos Aires, where a shoe and clothing factory called Gatic had gone bankrupt, but the staff were trying to keep the business going. The building was cavernous with huge warehouse-sized spaces, pitch-black in places because of no lighting. Shelves were empty, with idle forklift trucks parked against them. The lift didn't work and we walked up several flights of stairs to the executive floor. At the end of a corridor flanked by empty glass-walled offices was the chairman's office marked by a platformed showcase of what the firm produced – sports shirts, shorts, stylish jeans, trainers, beach towels and all the paraphernalia of modern, sporty living, most bearing the logos of famous multinational brands.

Under the boom days of the high-spending President Carlos Menem, Gatic had been Argentina's leader in sportswear with seventeen factories created from free-flowing bank loans.

The plush conference room next door was thick with cigarette smoke. Around the table sat a dozen men in jeans and casual shirts with an array of sports shoes in front of them. The scene looked out of place for a boardroom, designed more for besuited Ivy League financiers whose pack-of-card concepts had bankrolled the company through its years of boom-and-sham.

These were factory staff, gritty men from the shop floor who were overseeing a rescue policy decreed by President Kirchner. Instead of the company being handed over for outside administration, the staff were allowed to see if they could get things up and running again themselves.

With them were a couple of representatives from a local trade union. If it worked, they sensed they could be rewriting a new economic formula for the country. The purpose of this meeting was to decide which of the shoes should become the new company's flagship brand, then try to get it sold through the biggest shoe seller in the country, a firm called Grimaldi. They had already designed a bright yellow sun as their logo, representing the Argentine flag. But they needed to raise funds to convince Grimaldi to take it.

But what was totally incredible was how little was involved – just 500 pesos, US$160, to get back into business again when the company collapsed with up to US$300 million in debt.

'If we can do it, we'll be planting seeds which we will harvest in the future,' Jorge Omar Torres, the cooperative president, was saying. 'This is our chance of creating a really great company.'

'I was talking to Grimaldi yesterday,' said Ernesto Paret, the trade unionist who had handled dozens of similar rescues. 'If you can move quickly, they'll close the deal for 500 pesos. But you still have to sort out the problem of cashing cheques.'

These were uncashed payments left over when the company went broke. Many banks were refusing to honour them.

'We've got the paperwork in place, together with tax

numbers and all that,' said Torres. 'It would be better to cash them in the banks, but if they refuse we can just take them to the money changers, except there we lose money.'

'That should work anyway,' said Paret, lighting a cigarette. 'At least you'll get the 500 pesos in time.'

'We need to aim to get the staff back onto salary again,' said one of the workers, Adrian Pascucello. 'No one can live on bartering for ever. It might be all right for day-to-day needs, but it's not a good way to live.'

'Everybody who deals with us says this is a great project,' reassured Torres. 'So I'm confident we can get people back on decent salaries just like it was in the old days.'

We went down to the shop floor with Adrian Pascucello, who was thirty-three and married with two children. His job was cutting the soles of the shoes and overseeing the machine that embroidered the new logo. Before the economic collapse the workers were paid 600 pesos a month, which was then US$600. After devaluation, that became about US$150. When the company went bust he got nothing, but he kept his job. Six hundred people worked at the factory before. Now only 150 were left, getting paid not in money, but in shoes.

Adrian took us back to his small terraced house where his wife, Marcela, was making out a shopping list. Stacked against the wall were dozens of pairs of shoeboxes. Marcela shook hands with us, then turned to Adrian. 'If you get two litres of milk, a dozen eggs, butter, three loaves of bread and a pie, how much will that be?'

'About half,' said Adrian. 'We have to give him a whole pair. One shoe is no good to him. So we could get some pies and I'll bring in some beer, too, and we can leave the rest on credit.'

Adrian picked a blue Adidas shoebox from the pile. Inside were a pair of Gold Star trainers with the now obsolete logo that his new company had abandoned. We walked down the street to a small grocery store, and Adrian handed the shopkeeper the list together with the Adidas box. Adrian had slightly underestimated and ended up carrying back an extra case of canned beans.

Barter was keeping Adrian and his family alive and millions of Argentines had come to rely on it as a system that worked – compared to the IMF-led one that hadn't.

But it wasn't until that evening when we went out with rubbish collectors that a fundamental, possibly simplistic, difference dawned on me between the struggle going on in Argentina and the one going on in Iraq and parts of the Islamic world. It was about human dignity.

Before the collapse, Meera Argan ran a team of factory cleaners. Now she was the head of a cooperative that rifled through rubbish at night and bartered it for food and clothes. On the rubbish heap in Morocco, the same thing was going on, but the people there were not part of any recognized organization. Meera, however, carried an ID card showing that she was a member of the 'Cartoneros' – known throughout the city as the cooperative of rubbish pickers. In the same way, Adrian was part of the Gatic cooperative and Victor Morena (whom I'd met two years earlier after he threw a brick at the Casilda bank) was a member of his local trade union and various other political parties.

Their livelihood might have been taken from them, but not their dignity. That was retained through membership of their left-wing organizations. Had little Souffian, the boy who slept in the tyre in Morocco, tried to pick rubbish with Meera Argan around, I have no doubt she would have taken him under her wing, given him a hot meal and found him a place to sleep.

Meera worked from rubbish sack to rubbish sack, using street lamps for light with the sleeves of her maroon top rolled up beyond the elbow and her hair pinned tightly back. When she found a frozen chicken, she held it up like a prize. 'You see,' she said, 'this is a good country. I tell you why it's good because the people who live here know that I'm not a beggar. They know I'm a Cartonero and they wait for us to arrive before putting out their rubbish because they know we can use it.'

Meera talked non-stop, bossing the other Cartoneros around, working, searching, tossing anything that was worth anything into the cart she pulled behind her. Her income was about US$1.30 a day, in line with almost half the Argentine population that lived on less that the official poverty rate of US$2 a day.

'I have a sixteen-year-old daughter and a nineteen-year-old son, so I need to work because they have to study. I run a train full of Cartoneros. We have our own train. The train people gave it to us because they know how necessary our job is. They issue us with a rail pass that costs between ten and eighteen pesos a month, depending where you travel from. But it should be free.'

She finished one line of rubbish bags out of which she had plucked several T-shirts, a pair of shoes, and several more frozen chickens which were deliberately left as gifts from local people.

'I would prefer to be doing this than worrying about how to feed the kids,' she said. 'I didn't have to leave my job. My salary was 450 pesos a month. But by becoming a Cartonero, it meant that the jobs of seven other people were saved. So it was a good thing to do.'

Meera moved along the road to another line of sacks, then grumbled about how they were arranged. She shouted a greeting across the road to the doorman of a small hotel who waved at her.

'What else am I going to do in this mess?' she continued. 'They tell me no one's got money any more. So am I going to become a crackpot and sit on the street and put a gun to my head and beg for someone to give me two pesos? That sounds really screwed up to me.'

'What do you think of President Kirchner,' we asked, interrupting her flow.

'I don't know the man. But if he's the new president and if you're meeting him, tell him the Cartoneros need to have free train passes.'

For weeks we had been trying to arrange an interview with President Kirchner and had got no reply at all from his office. So we decided to head off to his hometown and try to doorstep him there.

President Néstor Kirchner came from Río Gallegos, the capital of Santa Cruz province. It was a speck of a city on the wild southern landscape of Patagonia, just one aeroplane leg away from the far southern province of Tierra del Fuego and the Antarctic. Kirchner had been city mayor of Río Gallegos for four years and governor of the province of Santa Cruz for twelve, throughout which he showed little trust in the corrupt central government – hence his decision to bank Santa Cruz's budget money, not in Argentina but in Switzerland.

Río Gallegos has the air of a small, developed rural town with clean pavements, well-paved roads and old election posters of Kirchner himself, his sinewy, face staring down next to billboards for hotels and sightseeing spots.

Kirchner, fifty-four, was squaring up for another fight with private bankers and the International Monetary Fund. In September 2003, he had taken negotiations to the brink of another default and, surprisingly, the IMF had caved in. Now another deadline was looming and no one was sure how things would pan out.

Kirchner had been elected as a man of the people. His promotional material showed him being cheered by farmers, coalminers and factory workers. His manifesto was to allow Argentina to become a strong moral voice on how financial institutions should behave towards the poor and that was upsetting conventional economic thinking.

Just as Iraq had come to symbolize a cultural battle between Western and Islamic values, so Argentina had become an economic one between how wealth was shared, and by whose rules. To prevail in both societies, Western governments wanted to create their style of democratic government. But experience was showing that the people, particularly at the grass roots, had something very different in mind.

Argentina, of course, was a far easier task than Iraq, but it remained fraught with problems. Kirchner was befriending America's sworn enemies such as Hugo Chávez of Venezuela and Cuba's Fidel Castro, both of whom were given places of honour at his May 2003 inauguration. Months later, he stated bluntly that on the debt repayment issue, the priority would be given not to foreign bankers but to the livelihood of Argentines.

'No one should expect from us an automatic friendship,' he said. 'International organizations do not seem to understand that our economy needs to grow in order for us to pay our debt. If we compromised we would just create more poverty and if our economic problems worsen no one will benefit. That would kill our hopes and everyone knows a dead man earns no money.'

Or as Martín Redrado, Kirchner's trade secretary, put it to me less floridly: 'If we had abided by the recipes of the IMF we would have had less growth and more social disruption than we've had in the last twelve months,' he said. 'For sure the social situation would have deteriorated.'

For the world of international finance, this thinking was the equivalent of a declaration of war.

We flew to Río Gallegos on a Friday because I had heard that Kirchner might be there for the weekend, and waited on the pavement outside his modest house in a residential street not far from the small town centre. It was a modern single-storey corner building with a small, neatly mown lawn that had no fence and ran gently down to the street. Kirchner had flown from Buenos Aires, like us, in a commercial commuter plane, economy class only, and proved not to be a difficult man to bump into.

His SUV pulled up in the driveway. He got out and as soon as he saw us he came over. He was wearing a dark blazer with brass buttons and an open-necked light-blue shirt. His hair was salt-grey and swept back. He had no security with him whatsoever. He wore a huge smile, his right hand outstretched for me, his left touching the shoulder of my interpreter. He was about to say something when he recognized a family who lived nearby. He broke off to greet them, bending down to say hello to each of the two young children. The family didn't linger or fawn. There was no celebrity status. They headed off and Kirchner turned back to us.

'Are you going to reject the IMF formula?' I said.

He threw back his head and spread his arms, feigning despair. 'Come on,' he said. 'It's the weekend. We're all trying to relax.'

'Do you need to reject the proposals to help the country's poor?'

'Let's talk about this next week,' he answered, his hand on my elbow. 'When we're back in Buenos Aires.'

I threw in Meera Argan's question on the off chance of

starting a conversation. 'Any chance of free rail travel for the Cartoneros?'

He laughed and clasped my hand with both of his. 'It's better to talk without such a rush.'

'Could you say something now?' I asked.

'In Buenos Aires,' he said.

'Is that a promise?'

'It's a reality,' he said, raising his hands to his lips and blowing out a kiss of goodwill to my interpreter. As he walked away, he turned back to give a thumbs-up as if to under-line his promise. He went into his run-of-the-mill house through the garage and pulled down the roller door behind him.

It was irritating, but Kirchner was astute enough not to answer questions off the cuff to an international reporter, and he never kept his promise for the interview. I found out later that this was his style. He often kept ambassadors and heads of government waiting and had never even held a proper cabinet meeting.

Our driver had kept an eye on the family he had greeted. They lived just around the corner. We asked if we could speak to them because they clearly knew Kirchner and I wondered if, like him, they had known that Argentina's economy had been on the precipice of an unprecedented collapse.

Luis Avela and his wife, Gabriela, had been married for seven years. The two children Kirchner had greeted were Maria, four, and six-year-old Santiago. Luis worked for the local gas company. His main job was checking meters. They also knew our taxi driver, Guillermo, so we piled into their kitchen and sat around the huge white table while Gabriela brewed up a green tea known as mate yerba that was as thick as treacle. We made a bit of small talk about the Patagonian wind and considered why there were no trees on the pampas, but when I changed the topic to the IMF, everyone became animated.

'Of course we knew it was going to happen,' said Guillermo, the taxi driver. 'Kirchner made no secret that he was taking the Santa Cruz money out of the country. It's been proven that every time the IMF or any bank loaned Argentina money, we were not in a position to pay it back.'

'There has to be something of a deal,' said Gabriela, bringing a pot of tea over to the table. 'They have to realize that they are drowning us.'

Luis poured the tea into his own cup and passed it round to Guillermo. 'That's it,' he said. 'They have to stop pouring water on us. Kirchner isn't looking for a fight. He's saying we can pay this, but only so much now, so don't ask us for any more.'

'Yes,' said Gabriela, flaring up the gas ring again. 'But they don't understand basic things like that. They don't know about people being hungry and suffering.'

'What should happen to the IMF officials that supported the high lending?' I asked.

'They should be fired,' said Guillermo straight away.

'Are you talking about Anne Krueger?' asked Gabriela.

'She's the one who backed the investment projects for all those years,' said Guillermo.

'I don't know if it's just Krueger,' said Luis. 'Horst Koehler, too, is to blame.'

'What about the Argentine government?' I asked, impressed that they knew so much detail about the IMF. Krueger was the acting managing director of the IMF, often lampooned in the newspapers as if she were a colonial governor. Horst Koehler was its former head.

'If your friend was a gambler or thief, would you lend him money?' said Luis. 'They knew what type of government we had. They lost sight of what they were meant to do. The result is that those who had the least suffer the most.'

We drove south out of Río Gallegos onto the Patagonian grasslands which stretched unprotected and untamed for as far as the eye could see. A perfect horizon curved ahead under a big sky wisped with the faintest of white clouds. The wind was everywhere, buffeting gulls in the air, whipping up white water on the rivers, and when we got out of the car to see if I could spot the farm we were heading to, the wind slammed the door as soon as I let go.

In the distance, a hillside shimmered strangely, the green turning into dirty white then back again. We drove on and, as we got closer, I realized it was actually full of sheep being rounded up by farmhands on horseback with dogs.

Down the slope, by a fence, his thumb pushing tobacco into a pipe, was Paul Gallard, his leathery face etched and windburnt from years of working a farm on the steppe.

'So you made it?' he said, by way of greeting. I had expected Spanish-accented English at best. But Gallard was the son of English settlers who came to Argentina after the First World War. I zipped up my jacket against a fresh gust. Gallard wore a thick windproof coat, a tartan scarf, dark glasses and a cloth cap. Once his pipe was packed, he cupped his hand, struck a match and, amazingly, kept enough flame to light the tobacco.

We sat on the terrace of a wooden farm shack, made of light yellow clapboard and a maroon corrugated-iron roof. It was a resting place for farmhands with bunk beds and a small cooker. Behind us a windmill spun round to pump water. Inside was a shepherd from Chile, two cowboys from Peru and an Argentine foreman. Up on the hill three farmhands on horseback with dogs were driving the sheep down to a pen on flatter land near our shack.

In 2002, Gallard's farm was on the verge of bankruptcy. It produced beef, lamb, mutton and wool, the key commodities of Argentina's export industry, and I wanted to know if, like Kirchner, Gallard, too, saw the crisis coming.

'We knew,' he said. 'We all knew. We who lived and suffered it – yes – we knew. It's hard to believe they didn't know. It was cheaper to import than produce anything here and it meant we couldn't compete in the export markets. Eighty per cent of our wool, for example, is exported, but it became too expensive for our overseas markets. And we're not subsidized like European farmers, so our whole business was going down the drain fast.'

Gallard's blunt economic analysis was easy to understand. But just to make it crystal clear: while investors were hailing Argentina as a model for growth people knew it was a sham. The peso–dollar peg, four times higher than its market value, made Gallard's exports of meat and wool too expensive for his main markets in the Middle East, China, Russia and Europe.

'You couldn't have one peso to the dollar,' he said. 'I mean it was stupid.'

'When the collapse happened, what did you think?'

'Thank God. We had been hoping for it for a long time because we couldn't carry on like that. Everything was going bust.'

'But if you knew that, why didn't the bankers know it?'

He drew on his pipe and thought for a moment. 'Yes. They must have known very well what was happening. I'm just a common citizen and I knew that as time went on we had less and less means of paying them back.'

Something caught Gallard's eye and he slid off the verandah rail on which he was sitting. The sheep were almost inside the pen. A dog tore up the hill to coax down one left behind.

A farmhand leant down from his horse to open the gate. Gallard tapped the tobacco inside his pipe and lit it up again.

'What about President Kirchner, do you trust him?'

'I do. Yes. He comes from here, as you know. I think it's a damn good idea to stand up to the banks. I'm not completely against them. If you have debts you have to pay them, but you can't let people be run into the ground, not in a country where 50 per cent live in absolute poverty.'

'What credibility do the banks have now?' I asked.

'Not very much.'

'Would you trust them again?'

'No. I don't think they know what they're doing, not with these developing countries. This business of lending millions of dollars to somebody they knew was going downhill.' He paused, testing the tobacco in his pipe. 'But, then you would hope that bankers are intelligent people.'

'Then what should the IMF do?'

'I don't know. You'd better ask Anne Krueger that.'

Anne Krueger seemed to be the name on everybody's lips. It was time, I thought, to drop by the IMF in Washington and see her.

The IMF is a key part of what has become known as the global financial architecture or the system that overseas the international economy. It was conceived in 1944 at the end of the Second World War in Europe at the Bretton Woods conference in the United States. Its purpose was to address issues of reconstruction and see how to avoid another depression like the 1930s. At the same time, the World Bank was created and confusion had reigned about their respective roles. The World Bank is meant to concentrate on overall development, whereas the IMF deals more with the details of how the money works.

The crisis of 2008–9 prompted calls for both institutions to be overhauled. Much of the developing world regards them as having a top-down Western-centred view that didn't have a great track record. The head of the World Bank is tradition-ally American. The head of the IMF is usually European. But the 600 million people in Latin America, or the more than 3 billion in Asia, the Middle East and Africa have never had one of their own in the top job – even though much of the policy was directed towards them.

During the Cold War, the IMF happily dealt with Western-backed dictators. Afterwards they pushed through economic programmes linked to the free market. Even in times of crisis, this doctrine appeared to be completely inflexible. Malaysia, for example, ignored IMF recommendations during the Asian banking collapse in 1997 and pulled through, whereas neighbouring Thailand followed IMF advice and suffered badly.

After the Argentine crisis, the IMF carried out an internal review on how it could have handled things differently. It traced its involvement back to 1991, when the plan to fix the peso to the dollar was put in place through to 1998, at which time Argentina's growth began sliding into recession.

'Until shortly before the crisis, the country had been widely praised for its achievements in stabilization, economic growth and market-oriented reforms under IMF-supported pro-grammes,' it said in its official report. 'The eventual collapse of the convertibility regime and the associated adverse eco-nomic and social consequences for the country have, rightly or wrongly, had a reputational cost for the IMF.'

That is about the clearest IMF-written English I have found on the issue. The guidelines of what should be done were obviously written for bankers and not for people like Paul Gallard and his colleagues farming livestock or for Victor

Morena in Casilda, trying to work out whether he should throw more bricks through bank windows. In other words, there was no attempt to explain to a wider constituency outside the banking world.

Here's one example published under a section called 'Lessons': 'Decisions to support a given policy framework necessarily involve a probabilistic judgment, but it is important to make this judgment as rigorously as possible, and to have a fallback strategy in place from the outset in case some critical assumptions do not materialize.'

And here's another (please feel free to skip it) listed as a 'Recommendation': 'Medium-term exchange rate and debt sustainability should form the core focus of IMF surveillance. To fulfill these objectives (which are already current policy), the IMF needs to improve tools for assessing the equilibrium real exchange rate that are more forward-looking and rely on a variety of criteria, examine debt profiles from the perspective of "debt intolerance," and take a longer-term perspective on vulnerabilities that could surface over the medium term.'

I'm pretty sure that addresses Gallard's point about it being cheaper to import a steak than cut one off his stock because of the bogus exchange rate. But I would be hesitant to go in to bat on that against an IMF lawyer.

Anne Krueger was both fierce and matronly. In a strange way, she reminded me of Meera Argan, the Cartonero in Buenos Aires. Both were matriarchal figures with iron wills in charge of their empires. Krueger came into the IMF's massive conference room in Washington with an entourage of advisers whom she then dismissed, and they crept away out of sight into side rooms. Her hair was reddish-brown and short, and she wore rimless glasses and a beige suit. She had just turned seventy, at the evening of a career where she had been chief economist at the World Bank and a substantive figure in academia, most recently at the prestigious Stanford University in California. Now she was standing in as head of the IMF until a new managing director was found.

'Argentina,' I asked. 'What happened? Why didn't you know things were going wrong?'

'Well, I was at Stanford University at the time.'

'Sorry,' I stumbled. 'I didn't mean you personally, but the IMF.'

'I gather some staff did have major concerns,' she said, 'and I gather more than one staff member did privately communicate and there are copies of those letters looking specially at 1996 and 1997 when growth was very strong and asking if now was the time to make the fiscal correction. So it's not true there was none of that.'

'What happened, then?'

'Nothing.'

'Why?'

'I don't know.'

That threw me. I hadn't expected the acting head of the IMF to admit outright that she had no real idea about this important background to the biggest debt default in global history.

'Everything about Argentina is precedent setting,' she said. 'There is nothing routine about it. There has never been anything like this.'

I explained that I had just come from Buenos Aires and asked if she thought the IMF was now being too tough in what it was asking.

'I think not, of course,' she said.

'What's the risk of being too tough?'

'Let me turn it around. What's the risk of being too soft?' she answered. 'That's hard, too, because in the Argentine case that could be the formula for the next set of problems and there's a range in which it's a judgement call.'

We weren't really connecting. I wanted to hear something that would resonate with the many people in Argentina who thought the IMF was a bad thing, something to sell the institution to those who felt the impact of its policies. I tried again. 'But it's a fine balance, isn't it, when you have people taking to the streets because they've lost their jobs and livelihoods?'

'I'm not so sure. I think the reason those people are on the streets is because Argentina's fiscal policy was disastrously bad earlier. It is the crisis that put them on the streets, not the fund programme.'

I tried again: 'But when you're dealing with an emerging democracy, you know there's going to be corruption and other bad policies, you know it's not going to be like dealing with the developed world.'

'Then what you're saying is that the fund should stay out completely.'

No, I wasn't. What I wanted know was whether lessons had been learned and economists were looking for another way of doing things. I had hoped that Krueger, with her well-documented intellect, would throw around some thoughts. All I was looking for was a glimpse of a new idea that might have emerged from this unprecedented crisis. But she didn't want come out to play.

I wasn't the only one mystified. A few months earlier in September 2003 the Argentine economic crisis ended up on the White House agenda. While the IMF and international bankers were pressing Argentina to pay its debt and Kirchner was rolling up his sleeves for the mother of all fiscal fights, intervention had come fast and efficiently from none other than George W. Bush himself. Apparently, at a White House meeting of his closest advisers when minds were focused on

Iraq, Afghanistan and Homeland Security, Bush asked why he was being asked to spend time on a spat between Argentina and the IMF.

'The point of the view of the US government was that Kirchner needed time to establish his own credibility,' explained Richard McCormack, a former under secretary of state for economic affairs and close adviser to the administration. 'Kirchner needed time to get a clear understanding of the domestic economic situation in this country and what it was possible to accomplish politically. He also needed time to build his own political base from which he could then make decisions. There was a lot of objection from the IMF, but that is what we did.'

Just in case this was a line being spun from Washington, I checked the story with Martín Redrado, Kirchner's trade secretary whom I had interviewed in Buenos Aires. Did the White House support Kirchner over the IMF? I asked.

'Yes,' he said. 'That's what happened. I think they saw Argentina becoming isolated and if we went down the drain it wouldn't be good for anybody, not for Latin America, not for the region. Not for the world.'

Now that was language that I understood.

But something deeper was wrong. The West knew precisely the democratic decision of the Argentine voters who chose Kirchner because of his record of handling the economy while pulling people out of poverty. The West knew that if Kirchner was to honour his manifesto he would have to renegotiate Argentina's debt obligations. To give it a civilian analogy, to keep his promise to his electorate, Kirchner needed to hand over less than the minimum monthly amount due on its credit-card repayments.

Despite repeated warnings, the West ignored the voters' decision. Rather than working with Argentina's democratic choice, it tried to reverse it without examining the consequences. On a far less violent level, this was the economic comparison of the refusal to recognize Hamas's democratic legitimacy in the Palestinian territories.

Despite the checks and balances put in place by American and European democratic institutions, the Argentine debt problem was not addressed until the US president got involved personally. Even then, George W. Bush viewed it not through a lens of democratic values but through one of strategic importance. He already had his hands full with extreme Islam that threatened to set alight the Middle East. He could ill afford to open a second front against extreme socialism in Latin America.

Memories of America's Cold War involvement in Latin America were still fresh. Some of the architects, such as former Secretary of State Henry Kissinger, and Oliver North of the Iran-Contra arms scandal, remained players in the US political scene. This was not some fantastical disaster scenario, it was a region that forty years earlier, with the Cuban missile crisis, had brought the world to the brink of nuclear war.

Waves crashed against the sea wall of Havana's corniche, unexpectedly drenching a couple walking along the pavement. They jumped back, laughing, kissed and the girl brushed water off her boyfriend's face. Then she slipped her arm around his waist as they walked on chatting. It was 2002, and we drove past in a purring, large 1960s Cadillac, painted a deep-sea blue with a white streak, with the gear lever next to the steering wheel and a smell of faded, but lovingly polished, leather from the seats. We were on our way to meet the president of Cuba's National Assembly, a philosopher and diplomat called Ricardo Alarcón who was also a close friend of Fidel Castro's.

To our right was the restless sea, and to our left the waterfront skyline from another age. The wooden shutters of colonial-style buildings dating back to the sixteenth century were flung open in the morning sun. Sea salt in the air had washed out the paintwork long ago. With our Cadillac windows down, we heard Latin music, perhaps from a street behind, guitars and a female singer that became louder then faded away as we passed. Soon we were driving around a square with a massive poster of Fidel Castro, instantly recognizable with his military fatigues and grey hair and beard. He was making a speech, jabbing his finger down towards a microphone with the Cuban flag flying behind him.

We got stuck for a few minutes in a traffic jam, a time-warped image, where every vehicle was a huge American car from the 1950s or 1960s when sanctions were first imposed on Cuba. None has been imported since. We edged out, headed down a hill and then drew up at government offices and were shown into a large meeting room for the interview.

Die-hard, defiant Cuba, lying just ninety miles off the Florida shoreline, stood as a stark reminder of America's failure to keep its enemies at arm's length. It was still governed by the twentieth-century visions of Mao and Marx. In 1962, the Soviet Union tried to install nuclear missiles here. President Kennedy threatened war and President Khrushchev backed down. Only in 2009 did President Obama, with his personal knowledge of how the developing world and its alliances are less than black and white, begin to unwind fifty years of hostility, sanctions and enmity. Havana might have posed an ideological challenge. But it was not a direct military threat.

Cuba is a Marxist enigma. It did not self-destruct like the Soviet Union. It did not cause mass starvation like Mao's China. There were no outbreaks of disease and war, as in Africa. Routine communal killings, as in India, were almost unheard of and unlike the Islamic movements of the Middle East and South Asia, it did not send bombers and saboteurs across to America to blow things up and kill people. And Cuba had no problems with the IMF and Western bankers because it was barred from using them.

Yet, when I went there in mid-2002, the United States government had just expanded its list of the world's most dangerous countries to include Cuba, which, with Iran, Iraq, North Korea, Syria and Libya, comprised the Axis of Evil.

Ricardo Alarcón was sixty-five, had a doctorate in philosophy from Havana University and had lived for more than ten years in New York as Cuba's permanent representative to the United Nations. He walked into the room wearing a loose-fitting white shirt holding a huge unlit Cuban cigar. It was just past eleven in the morning.

'Is your government evil?' I asked.

'No,' he said, breaking out into a long, throaty laugh. 'But then I would say that, wouldn't I?' He fired up a lighter, lit the cigar, checked the draw then let it hang in his fingers over the arm of the chair.

'We are not evil, but neither are we God's chosen government. This good and evil concept might be the way a child looks at the world, but it's better to have a more mature approach, particularly when those making the accusations happen to be so powerful and have so many resources that affect your life and my life.'

'Are you saying America is being childish?'

'To be generous to them – yes.'

He talked about a recent international development report that praised three lingering communist regimes in Cuba, China and Vietnam for doing more than other countries in pulling people out of poverty. He spoke proudly about how Cuba had resisted American attempts to interfere for more than forty years because, he said, the Cuban revolution had the support of the people.

'Tell me,' I interrupted, 'is it possible to get that sort of result in ending poverty if you have a free-market democracy?'

'So far I don't think God has created such a country,' he answered. 'Do you know of any case where it's happened? Where is a country in Latin America that has succeeded in resolving the real problems of the people and at the same time developed what you refer to as this Western kind of democracy?'

'But if you released all your political prisoners tomorrow what would happen?'

'Nothing, but the next day there would be others. We are not talking about big figures. Those critics of Cuba may have more political prisoners at this very moment than those in Cuban jails. At this very moment to be Muslim, to have dark skin, to be a foreigner appears to be sufficient cause for being arrested in several Western democracies and those people are not identified or charged.'

We spent some time working out the numbers. Cuba was then accused of holding about 400 political prisoners, which Alarcón didn't deny, and America admitted to having more than 750 terror suspects in Guantánamo Bay.[3]

'We are dealing with crazy things here, Humphrey,' he said. 'This Guantánamo Bay which has been an American base since 1903 – it is in Cuba, yet we are meant to be an evil country making weapons of mass-destruction. Our army has a hilltop position that looks down on the base. We could shoot at them any time. But we don't. Cuban and American soldiers speak every day and America says this is the most secure place to keep these prisoners. Does any of that make sense to you?'

---

3 The United States took control of Guantánamo Bay under a 1903 Cuban–American treaty, which gave America a perpetual lease on the area. Cuba says it has never agreed to the arrangement because the treaty was signed under force. But it has generally cooperated with the American presence there.

He drew on his cigar, but put his hand up to make sure I didn't interrupt. This was Ricardo Alarcón, academic and senior Cuban politician, insisting that his point be heard.

'And does what happened in Argentina make any sense?' he said, thick smoke clouding around his face. 'Is that democracy when you can make the whole economy of a country disappear without consulting the people; when you eliminate entire branches of the nation's economy without consulting the workers? Is that democratic freedom? Of course not. Here, in Cuba, our economy is our own and will remain so. It will never belong to the multinational corporations or the International Monetary Fund, and in Latin America people know that. Cuba is here to stay. We're not moving to another planet. There is more thinking now that the world will have to change in the direction of trying to find alternative models to the present prevailing one.'

'What is that?' I ventured. 'Russia? China?'

He let out his throaty laugh again. 'You want a crystal ball, and I don't have one,' he said. 'The Russians before had our kind of socialist approach. But they abandoned that. The Chinese have their own kind of socialism and we have our own. Right now, obviously, we are closer to the Chinese kind than to the Russian.'

Cuba is at the heart of the debate that I have heard throughout the developing world. If you live under an authoritarian system and you speak out against it, you will be punished. But your children will be educated. They will receive basic health care and live relatively secure lives. Everybody would like there to be a better balance, but the awkward choice is there, plain for all to see. This system was being ridiculed everywhere not so long ago, but perhaps now we're not so sure.

As Alarcón pointed out, in recent years the United Nations,

the World Bank and other institutions have conceded that Cuba, Vietnam and China have done more to end poverty than most other developing countries. These governments, steeped in old-style Marxism, are tackling, better than any other, the type of hopelessness blamed for fuelling terror, disease and a raft of African wars. They are also addressing head-on the point raised by Usama Rehda the wedding photographer I met later on in Iraq. He would happily forfeit his right to vote, if other basic rights could be guaranteed.

After meeting Alarcón, we headed out to a farming cooperative where students were doing an obligatory one day a week of manual labour in the fields. They tended cabbages, radishes and peppers that were being sold at roadside stalls. They were bright and chatty and when asked about health care they reeled off the more than a dozen vaccinations they had all had, such as for hepatitis, meningitis and dengue fever. The drugs were made in Cuba, immediately addressing the crisis that Marita Falabella, the Argentine diabetic patient, had faced over securing supplies of insulin from a foreign company.

They didn't cringe when I asked if they want to head off to live with fellow Cubans in Miami. 'I'd like to visit,' said one, who was aiming to be a microbiologist. 'But not stay there. I hear it's very busy and crowded in Miami.'

'Havana, Miami,' joked another with plans to be a lawyer. 'I could take both. I'll jet-set between the two.'

Their boss was a veteran of Cuba's Cold War attempt to export its revolution around the world. Juan Miguel Garcia was forty-two, and in the late 1970s had fought with Marxist government troops in Angola. He looked as if he knew a bit about global poverty.

'This system is the best for us. Yes, there's the free education and health care, and my son, he's a farmer like me, but he's studying to become a doctor and my nephew will become an agronomist. So both of them will end up with better jobs than me. That can't be bad.'

Less than a hundred miles separate Cuba's 11 million people from another Caribbean island with a different modern history. While Cuba has remained rigidly authoritarian and protective, Haiti's 9 million people have had everything free-market democracy has to offer – including, in 1994, a negoti-ated American military intervention called Operation Uphold Democracy. Haiti has continued to be riven by factionalism, corruption, attempted coups and since 2004, 9,000 United Nations police and troops have been deployed there.

Haitians have an average lifespan of fifty-seven years, whereas Cubans live twenty years longer until they're seventy seven. Despite its Marxist doctrine, Cuba's per capita income is about US$4,500 a year against Haiti's US$1,300. Haiti is the poorest country in the region, with 80 per cent of the popu-lation living under the poverty line and more than 50 per cent in abject poverty.

One of the most fundamental benchmarks of any society is infant mortality rates. In Cuba 5.82 out of every 1,000 babies die before they reach a year old. In Haiti the figure is almost 70 – more than ten times worse. To put that in context, the United States is slightly higher than Cuba at 6.26.

Different systems deliver different benefits, giving rise to a basic question: What is most important for you?

Before Fidel Castro came to power, Cuba was ruled by the dictator Fulgencio Batista. He was the last of a series of dicta-tors who had made Havana a playground for the rich, whose speculative, dirty money flowed into the country to build nightclubs and casinos and prop up self-centred politicians and sycophants that kept the elite in power. Frank Sinatra and

Al Capone partied there. Ernest Hemingway lived there and Graham Greene wrote part of *Our Man in Havana* there. But ultimately the dictatorship couldn't hold because little or nothing was reaching the poor. In 1959, Fidel Castro, his brother Raúl, the charismatic and brutal Che Guevara and their guerrilla forces swept into Havana and set up the system of government that has endured until today.

At about the same time Haiti, too, was being ruled by a series of dictators. The most notorious was François (Papa Doc) Duvalier, who governed from 1957 to 1971 and held power through his private militia known as the Tonton Macoutes. Some 30,000 people are believed to have been killed and many more fled to America. Other presidents followed, some legitimized by elections, but none was able to break the mould of violence, corruption and poverty.

Recently, at a seminar of British Foreign Office economists I asked them to imagine that the Apocalypse was nigh; that the only surviving area was the Caribbean and there were only two countries where they could go to build a new life for themselves and their loved ones. One was Cuba, the other Haiti.

'Who would choose Haiti?' I asked. No hands went up.

'And Cuba?' About half the people in the room raised their hands, then many swiftly brought them down again because their bosses were watching. Choosing a dictatorship over a democracy might not look good on the CV. But, in a comfortable meeting room in Whitehall, they didn't actually have to make the decision, nor even think about it very hard. In Iraq, in Casilda, others like the wedding photographer Usama Rehda and the bricklayer Victor Morena were thinking about it all the time.

The thought also weighed heavily on the mind of Gisela Delgado, who ran a private illegal library in a small apartment in Havana. People visited to borrow banned books on philosophy, religion and politics, by authors such as Thomas Mann, Ernest Hemingway, and George Orwell, whose *1984* was her most borrowed book. Gisela, in early middle age, elegantly dressed as part of Cuba's educated middle class, was openly breaking the law. The government decreed what books should and should not be read and it classified most of those in Gisela's library as counter-revolutionary.

'Why are we only given these bad choices?' she said. 'Why are we asked to choose always between the United States system of government and the Cuban one? Look at us, we had Batista who was tyrant and now we have Castro who is a dictator. If you're giving us a choice, give us something that works.'

'Do you see yourself as a dissident, then?'

'Yes, I am,' she said defiantly. And so was her husband, Hector Palacios, who was in the kitchen cutting up vegetables for dinner while we were talking to his wife. Hector was a large, towering, irritated man, who was in constant confrontation with Castro's regime. He had already been jailed twice and later he was jailed again for more than three years.[4]

'Are you a danger to Cuba?' I asked, half thinking he might treat the question lightly as Ricardo Alarcón had done. But his face tightened and his eyes narrowed and bore into me. 'I am just a simple Cuban who wants to change Cuba,' he said.

'What is most important to you – free medicine or free speech?'

'I don't want health without freedom. That is the main thing for a human being and for mankind.'

---

4 In March 2003, Hector Palacios and more than seventy other human rights advocates were arrested, tried, and sentenced to up to twenty-eight years in prison in the most severe crackdown the island had seen in recent history – according to Human Rights First. Palacios was released in December 2006.

'But to get the health care and education, do sacrifices have to be made about other rights?'

'No, you're wrong,' chipped in Gisela. 'All rights are important. Look at the conditions in our schools where children are forced to follow a particular kind of ideology.'

'Exactly,' said Hector. 'Supposing I want my child to go to a religious school or another type of school; that's illegal here.'

'OK, then,' I asked them both, 'give me an idea of the type of government you want in Cuba?'

'We don't want what they've got in the US,' said Gisela. 'We want more a European model. We want the government to free things up so people can own their own land and run their own business and we want respect for human rights, freedom to think how we want and say what we want.'

'But you have the freedom to speak to me now?'

'After you've gone, I can be arrested and put in jail,' said Hector sharply. 'What freedoms do I have?'

'You seem to be an angry person.'

'Yes, because I've been imprisoned twice because of the way I think. I haven't committed any crime. Wouldn't you be angry?'

It would be impossible and presumptuous to put ourselves in the shoes of Hector Palacios or, for that matter, in the shoes of the many individuals in this book who have lived on the raw end of this issue. Yet, spending time in Hector and Gisela's Havana apartment, with Gisela's book-lined study, a kitchen filled with food, taps through which water ran and electric lights that turned on with the flick of a switch, it was clear that the democratic debate varied depending on the level your society has reached.

In the Ivory Coast, Sangone Lamine's aspiration was to be

paid a fair price for his crop. His basic needs were a road, electricity, water and schooling. In Iraq, Usama Rehda wanted water, electricity and security, all of which the government was failing to provide. Neither Usama Rehda nor Sangone Lamine believed that voting in new politicians would actually solve their problems. In Cuba, Hector and Gisela had those basics, and wanted to take things to another level. They were putting their lives in jeopardy because the government wasn't yet ready to travel that path with them. Yet without the bravery of people like Hector Palacios and Gisela Delgado, many governments would never be pushed into reform.

In Paraguay, in the same region and with a similar culture, I met a young mother in a dreadful hospital who would have given everything to get the sort of health care available in Cuba. Her name was Carmen Martinez. She was an indigenous Indian and her two-year-old daughter, Maria, was suffering from hydrocephalus. Her skull had ballooned out to at least twice, maybe three times, its normal size, because cranial fluid was not properly draining away through the body.

Even now, I don't have to look at a photograph of Maria to remember vividly the pain drawn across her vulnerable little face, stretched out of all proportion by the hydrocephalus, making her head so huge that her neck and tiny body couldn't support it.

In developed Western democracies a small, routine operation would have cured Maria. In Paraguay, Carmen Martinez had twice brought her daughter on a gruelling journey from her village 150 miles away to this hospital in the capital Ascunción, pleading for medical help. No one had answered her call.

In the hospital, beds were empty and mattresses were rolled up and damp from the rain and humidity. No doctor was there. There was just one Paraguayan nurse, disgusted with her own government for failing to supply medicine – even bed sheets.

'I've been asking for help ever since she was born,' said Martinez. 'All I know is that Maria needs an operation and then she'll be better. Her head is so heavy that she has never been able to sit or crawl like a normal child.'

Paraguay had followed the pattern of many Latin American countries. Its military dictator, Alfredo Stroessner, ruled for thirty-five years until 1989, with the familiar result of some development, high corruption and widespread human rights abuses. Stroessner was ousted in a coup by another general, Andrés Rodríguez, who in 1993 handed over to a civilian president, Juan Carlos Wasmosy. Wasmosy ended up being convicted of corruption and jailed. As the World Fact Book, compiled by the CIA, puts it, without a hint of irony: 'Despite a marked increase in political infighting in recent years, Paraguay has held relatively free and regular presidential elections.'

This was the world into which little Maria was born. Her hospital had been built mostly with Western aid money in order to satisfy demands that Paraguay did more to help its indigenous Indian people – who made up about 5 per cent of the population. The minister in charge of the Indian portfolio was a ferocious blonde Paraguayan, Olga Rojas de Baez.

After meeting Maria we went to de Baez's office in Ascunción. Outside the office groups of Indians were waiting to see her. Many had travelled for days from their faraway villages. De Baez was late for our meeting, and when her car pulled up she walked straight past the Indians into the building, saying nothing and avoiding their gaze.

Her air-conditioned office was decorated with sketches of Indians, the women bare-breasted and the men in headdresses with spears. She gave us a colourful woven bag and insisted we visit an Indian handicraft centre. I cut the small talk short because I was still stunned at the way she had treated her constituents outside.

'Why, with the Indian community being so small, aren't they properly integrated into society?'

'It's up to them to take the first step,' she said. 'They won't do that because they don't like to get close to Paraguayan culture.'

'But what I don't understand,' I went on, 'is why you head this department and not an indigenous Indian?'

'Oh, an Indian couldn't do that,' she said. 'The Indians don't have the university education. I don't know any accountants or economists among them.' Even de Baez thought she might have overstepped the line and added, 'It's not that Indians don't have access to education, it's that they don't use it.'

I then raised the case of Maria, and without drawing breath de Baez took a pen from her desk and wrote down an address and handed it to me. 'We will send her here,' she said. 'It's our new hospital for the Indian people. It is only three years old. We built it completely for the Indians. The doctors are wonderful. It's a fantastic success.'

We left her with Maria's name and outside my interpreter studied the note. 'It's the same place,' he said. 'I'm sure of it.'

'All right,' I said. 'But let's just do what she says and go to this address.'

It was indeed the same hospital. Maria was already there, and two days after first meeting her, no doctor had seen her because none had been there. Nor, said the staff, had Olga Rojas de Baez. They hadn't seen her since the hospital opened. Over the next few days, we tried to get a private doctor to go to the hospital to, at least, examine Maria. But none would.

Back in London, I asked a doctor to look at our pictures

of her. He said that eighteen months earlier, when Maria was six months old, she could probably have been cured. But now – by the way her eyes moved back and forth – she was almost certainly brain-damaged and living in terrible pain. In another six months, without help, Maria would most likely be dead.

Over the next few weeks, my producer in Paraguay, Andrea Maicham, kept banging the phones to find a doctor who would help. She eventually tracked down a neurologist who was willing to carry out an operation. At the same time, my report on Maria on the BBC's *From Our Own Correspondent* programme was heard by Dr Stephanie Taylor, a senior clinical lecturer at St Bartholomew's Hospital in London. She raised the money for Maria to have the operation and medical care afterwards.

A surgeon drained the cranial fluid, and Andrea told me Maria had become chatty and was recognizing the names of the people around her. But six months later she was dead. Doctors believed the immediate cause was a urinary tract infection caused by reusing dirty nappies, and that Maria's hydrocephalus might initially have been caused by poor nutrition for the mother during her pregnancy.

Little Maria Martinez was not a child caught up in war or famine. She was a victim of something far more basic – bad governance.

This horrible story speaks of everything a government should be doing for its citizens, but doesn't. Carmen Martinez was uneducated and had not been taught even the basics about child care. The state had no mechanism for making sure Maria received treatment for her condition. The politician in charge had no respect for her constituents. And the medical profession was such a weak institution that there was no safety net for children like Maria.

As I said, it is impossible to put ourselves in the individual shoes of Hector Palacios and Carmen Martinez, but the issue at stake here is what comes first – saving a child's life or holding elections, because as I was beginning to learn, in some societies, you can't do both.

In the Cold War, Latin America was a proxy battleground between the Soviet Union and the United States. Now, the combination of poor societies and left-wing movements is seen by many in Washington as a cloud to be watched – particularly as communist China is making inroads there with both political and economic influence. Some American politicians view this as a strategic threat looming in their backyard.

Unlike the Soviet Union, post-Maoist China has never publicly stated any ideological goal beyond its borders. But its need for raw materials and energy has sent it out to Africa and Latin America and where big sums of money go, alliances and friendships tend to follow. China's slogan for its expansion is 'peaceful rising', and the China factor was finding an audience among governments that have watched its growth leap and their own stagnate. Some of China's poor of twenty years ago were now taking out mortgages on first homes while their own were still scrabbling around for a pair of shoes. China's wallet has become a real presence in the developing world, often moving into slots left empty by the Soviet Union.

For many years after the Cuban missile crisis, the Soviet Union ran an electronic listening or spying station near Havana at a complex called Lourdes. It gave Moscow an ability to eavesdrop on much of the United States and across the Atlantic Ocean to Europe. Lourdes was the biggest Soviet signals intelligence (SIGINT) facility outside of the country, covering almost thirty square miles and employing up to 1,500 Russian technicians and military personnel.[5] They intercepted telephone calls, faxes, emails and other computer communications. They also had equipment that could target specific telephones and computers and they listened particularly to American naval and aircraft activities.

The details of what happened are classified but in 2001 Russia announced it was pulling out of Lourdes. At about the same time, possibly earlier, China began building its own spy base nearby. By then the Lourdes equipment was outdated and China came in with the latest state-of-the-art technology.

It was not clear exactly how intrusive and strategically damaging this was to the United States, but when I interviewed him, Ricardo Alarcón, the National Assembly president, mentioned that Cuba felt close to what he called the Chinese style of socialism.

Then, in 2009, as the global economy shook down into recession, an alliance between two big beasts on opposite sides of the democracy argument was needed to pull things back from the brink. China and America were thrown together knowing that each had the power to either wreck or rebuild. In international conference jargon they became known as the G2 – the world's two most prevailing economies.

The recession proved to be a yardstick of the post-Cold War era. Other powers had been given a chance to create what jargon called a multi-polar platform, meaning a counterweight to America's supremacy. But none had. The other beasts of balance could have been Russia or India. But they were still fumbling and not ready. It could have been the

5 www.globalsecurity.org

European Union, but the member states rarely agreed among themselves on the big issues.

The financial crisis also skewed traditional strategic thinking, mainly that the chequebook and treasury bond had replaced the missile silo and nuclear weapon as the base of raw power. The concept of Mutually Assured Destruction had become economic instead of military.

This meant two things. First, the West eased up the pressure on China over human rights and democracy. It had already been happening for some time as cash-rich Chinese corporations bailed out failing Western ones, and Chinese-made goods stocked the shelves of our supermarkets. Second, questions were asked as to how it had come to this. A nation that killed hundreds of its own citizens in the glare of television lights around Tiananmen Square just twenty years earlier was now calling the shots at the top table.

China has played a very different game from Russia or India. It took a single-minded longer view of what it wanted to achieve, based almost entirely on economic growth. Its political reforms have been next to non-existent, although a wealthier middle class and technology such as the Internet have opened up channels of new expression.

When asked weighty, direct questions about democracy, the Chinese leadership often replies with opaque answers. But in Beijing one evening some years ago I found myself sitting next to the son of a powerful minister. He had just come back from the United States and was telling upbeat stories about its openness and freedom. So I asked him outright: why was China refusing to give its people the same and let them vote for a government of their choice?

'We don't like your democracy,' he said, 'because in open confrontational debate one side ends up humiliated and proven wrong. It is against our culture to lose face. So we are finding another way to govern and we want you to work with us through our successes and our tears and when we have found this way it will be a truly wonderful system under which to live.'

'So where will it end up?' I countered. 'Are you saying that eventually you will create a society run by an authoritarian regime that is not repressive, where dissidents are not jailed and executed, where free speech and science can flourish unchecked, and students can protest in city squares without fear of arrest and jeopardizing their future?'

He barely blinked at my long, slightly frustrated question. He folded his napkin neatly, put it on his side plate, took a sip of water and eyeballed me in a very American way. 'Yes, Mr Hawksley. That is exactly what I am saying.'

But the United States viewed China's influence in Latin America with a very different strategic eye than it did in Asia or Africa. Even now, US interests in Latin America remain protected by the Monroe Doctrine, which ensures that America remains the sole foreign power of influence in the region. So with Cuba defiant, Argentina bruised, socialist leaders on the rise and the dust again being brushed off the Monroe Doctrine, in 2006 I headed to that big-hitter Brazil to try to see how things might play out if China raised its profile in Latin America above the parapet.

Charles Tang, chairman of the Brazil–China Chamber of Commerce, cut an arresting figure, negotiating the uneven pavements of São Paulo. He wore a well-cut pinstriped suit, a tall man, in late middle age with a head of stylishly cut black hair. As he crossed the road to his office, Tang's gait seemed to sway and keep time with street music coming from a building nearby. He was a Chinese man who walked like a Latin.

Tang came from a powerful Chinese family that had played both sides of Mao Zedong's communist revolution and was now reaping the benefits. Tang himself left China as a child, went to Hong Kong, then to the United States, where he became a banker. Thirty years earlier he had fallen in love with Brazil.

He was now playing both sides by arranging deals in what was becoming known as the Second World.[6] A rising global influence, it incorporated countries like Brazil, Turkey, China, India, South Africa and Russia, all of which were trading, negotiating, exchanging ideas outside the traditional Western paradigm. While the West was talking about creating a global alliance in a league of democracies,[7] the Second World was thrashing out ideas of how to move forward, regardless of whether they were democracies or autocracies.

Charles Tang had been brokering deals which had technicians for Brazil's Embraer aircraft company setting up a factory in China and Brazilian farmers selling the Chinese huge quantities of sugar cane ethanol as well as a myriad of other arrangements – from hi-tech to raw materials. In recent years, China had become Brazil's third biggest trading partner after Argentina and the United States.

After an exchange of visits between President Luiz Inácio Lula da Silva and China's Hu Jintao in 2004, a Sino-Brazilian strategic partnership was announced that Tang described as a natural alliance, mainly because of the lead China could show in poverty alleviation.

'The Chinese government has removed 400 million people

---

6 Parag Khanna, *The Second World: Empires and Influence in the New Global Order* (Allen Lane, 2008).
7 Suggested by Senator John McCain in his 2008 presidential campaign.

from poverty,'[8] he said expansively. 'These people now participate in economic growth and they live with dignity.'

'Are you saying that this is what Brazil should do?' I asked.

'Absolutely,' he replied, 'because that is the true victory for human rights. That's what human rights are all about.'

'So do Brazil and China form a natural strategic partnership?'

'The strategic and commercial alliance between the giant of Asia and the giant of South America is crucial.'

'But will that cause problems in Washington, with China being a communist country and everything?'

'We all know China is not really communist, and we have to remember that the United States is China's number one trading partner and probably the number one financier of the US government. I don't see any animosity there. China simply wants to become a wealthy nation and so far the Chinese government, with its success in dealing with poverty, has achieved the greatest conquest in the history of human rights.'

I put the same questions to the Brazilian trade minister, Luiz Fernando Furlan, who was more measured because he understood the issues swirling around the US Congress – the ones that I, too, would soon see for myself.

'Maybe they're jealous up there,' he said, referring to America. 'Maybe China is more aggressive in Latin America because it's expanding its economy faster. We deal with them on a business basis and if we have opportunities for their

---

8 A 2007 World Bank report described China's progress in reducing poverty as 'enviable'. Between 1981 and 2004, the fraction of the population consuming less than a dollar a day fell from 65 per cent to 10 per cent, it said, and more than 500 million people were lifted out of poverty.

investment in our railroads, ports, general infrastructure and pipelines, then we will take them. It's just business after all.'

Many of the deals were slow to work out or were hampered by bureaucracy on both sides. But China's trade with Latin America grew at about 30 per cent a year and the region became the destination of about half of all China's foreign investment. This kept up throughout the financial crisis, with recent examples being US$12 billion for Venezuela, US$1 billion for Ecuador, US$10 billion for Brazil's national oil company and a US$10 billion reserve for Argentina from which to buy imports from China, that may otherwise have come from the United States.

Down in São Paulo's Chinatown, Francisco Marten, a slight, shy man, was stacking herbs and rice on shelves in a small supermarket. Marten started work in Chinatown because of an affinity he felt for Mao Zedong and communist ideology. But that was some time ago and it was now just a job that he was happy with. He was deeply involved in local Brazilian politics and took us back to the potholed streets of his poor neighbourhood. He had voted for the winning Lula da Silva in the presidential elections, but now felt betrayed by him and had joined an even more left-wing movement – the Socialist Urban Workers Party.

While we talked, children played barefoot in the road; men drank at a makeshift bar; cheers from a soccer game came over the rooftops.

'Look around us,' he said. 'Nothing has changed. This is the same street that I have always known. And the people do not change because the government does not give them education and without education they cannot know about their rights.'

'So what will happen in the next election?' I asked.

'We will go more to the left. This is the mood of Latin America. More of it will happen, believe me.'

*

James Schlesinger, former director of the CIA and Defense Secretary, knew a great deal about how America dealt with perceived threats and about Latin America and the Monroe Doctrine. He had been in office during Operation Condor and worked against other backdrops such as Vietnam, the Israeli–Arab Yom Kippur War, Saddam Hussein's rise in Iraq, the continuing hostilities against Cuba and the conglomeration of Cold War threats that made up US foreign policy.

I went to see him about a story I was planning about the military dictator of Panama, Manuel Noriega, who came to power in 1983 as a buffer against the spread of Cuban communism. This was the time that Cuba was sending doctors, nurses and troops around the world as part of its attempt to spread communism. Noriega was fervently anti-communist and served America well. But as the Cold War faded, Noriega became a narcotics trafficker and the War on Drugs began to take precedent over the War against Communism. In 1989, US troops invaded Panama and installed a civilian president. An interesting side note to this Latin American military operation is that in the vacuum left by Noriega's removal, Panama suffered widespread looting similar to that in Iraq fourteen years later. Yet in both cases US military planners said they had not anticipated it.

While talking with Schlesinger, we got onto the topic of what the CIA calls 'blowback'. This is when a policy, put in place at a particular time, comes back to haunt you. One example of this was Saddam Hussein, whom the US supported as a buffer against Iran. But Saddam then invaded Kuwait and became a global threat. There was also Osama bin Laden, an anti-Soviet Mujahideen warrior in Afghanistan during the 1980s who went on to engineer the 9/11 strike in 2001 that launched the War on Terror.

Blowback and interventions have gone on regardless of who

is in the White House. James Schlesinger had seen the era of Kennedy's Camelot send troops to Vietnam and the dark days of Richard Nixon pull them out. George W. Bush went into Iraq and Barack Obama is stepping up the heat in Afghanistan. No one yet knows what the blowback will be from that.

'I don't think we ever thought of Noriega or Saddam as altar boys,' said Schlesinger. 'In Saddam's case he ended up doing what all our Middle East allies said he would do and invaded a fellow Arab country and at that point we turned against him.

'In Noriega's case we were prepared to use him against Castro, but he ended up misbehaving against us and gradually his arrogance grew to the point that we turned against him, too.'

'But is that any way to run a foreign policy?' I said.

'That is indeed the basis of foreign policy in all countries,' said Schlesinger. He was in his early seventies and there was a twinkle in his eye as he spoke – the look of a veteran who had seen it all, knew things went wrong, and accepted that that was the way it was. 'There are temporary alliances. There are alliances that reflect opportunism and there are more deep-seated alliances. The first two types are indeed a cause for concern. We supported the Afghan Mujahideen fighters until such time as the Soviet Union departed from Afghanistan and suddenly we lost all interest in Afghanistan and that was a mistake. In Noriega's case, suddenly we decided that the practices that he may have been long inclined to follow should be brought to an end. He didn't change. But we changed.'

'And this has always happened?'

'To the best of my knowledge,' he answered. 'Let's go back to the 1930s when a substantial part of British and American society thought that helping Adolf Hitler rise to power in Germany would keep communism under control in Russia.

Now, if you want to talk about blowback, that's blowback for you.'

I sat in on a congressional hearing about China and came away feeling somewhat uneasy about America's future relationship with the Chinese. Both countries may have made huge efforts in finding common ground, but they still fundamentally disagree about how societies should be governed. In the hearing room, while looking into China's influence in Brazil, I heard senior elected politicians whip up scenarios of a hostile China that was an enemy of the United States. Whether credible or not, these men had an authority to sway American opinion and drive through policy, just as they had on the Iraq invasion and their predecessors before that on Vietnam, Chile and other world-shaking US initiatives.

The purpose of the hearing, as laid out by the chairman, Larry M. Wortzel, was to assess 'China's acquisition of military hardware and technologies and consider the implications of these actions for the United States and its allies.'

It unleashed a stream of accusations about the high level of Chinese threat and how America should deal with it.

'The basic fundamental disconnect between us and China is that we have a conscience and they don't,' said Republican Senator Lindsey Graham. 'As a nation we need to understand that this communist dictatorship is a government without a conscience. If Ronald Reagan had taken the position with the Soviet Union that we are taking with China, the Soviet Union would never have collapsed.

'We need to decide early on how to deal with China. The status quo cannot be accepted and tolerated by this country any more than the Soviet Union's practices were tolerated by Ronald Reagan.'

His fellow Republican, Congressman Thaddeus McCotter, agreed. 'I still believe that communism is an inherently evil system. I still believe it is against Western democratic capitalism. My view is quite simply to equate the Chinese communism to the rise of the Soviet Union in the 1950s. The question then was whether the Soviet model would prevail. Now history is repeating itself with the Chinese communist super-state, rising militarism and a rising economy that is fuelling antagonism. The only difference is how our government is dealing with this.

'Under the pretext of being a different type of communist government they are doing everything they can to manipulate, to get the resources and to steal technologies. They are competing for energy resources around the world that have huge strategic value, and much of the hard currency China receives goes into its militarization. We are engaged in that struggle and must use whatever means we can to rectify the situation.'

They came and went, but there was not one voice that disagreed with the fundamental premise laid down by the two Republican politicians.

I went from there to meet Dan Burton, chair of the US congressional committee that handled what the United States calls the Western Hemisphere. He worked in Rayburn House where congressional members' offices run off wide corridors and are decorated with the American flag and emblems representing their campaigns and constituents.

'It's extremely important that we don't let a potential enemy of the United States become a dominant force in this part of the world,' said Burton. 'You can rest assured the US is going to do everything it can to make sure this hemisphere is safe.'

'What exactly is your concern?' I asked.

'We continue to have concerns about Chávez, Castro,

Ortega, Morales in Bolivia, and there are concerns too, now, with their connections with communist China and I think we need pay particular attention to that.'

'Is there a line that you would not let China cross in its involvement in Latin America?' I asked.

'From a security standpoint we should always look at Latin America in relation to the Monroe Doctrine.'

'Could you be more specific?'

'The specifics are not something to discuss in a media forum,' he said. 'But there are already military exchanges and hardware being sold or given to Latin American countries by China and we're watching that very closely as far as what we would do if and when, if certain things should happen.'

'Isn't this view a bit backward looking? Hasn't the world moved on from this sort of thinking?'

'Not at all. The number one responsibility of the president and Congress is to protect the people of our country, to make sure that peace reigns and survives. So, no, I don't think it is backward looking to examine every aspect of this issue.'

In Latin America in the early twenty-first century, democracy has led to socialism in many countries. In the Middle East Islamic parties were doing well. Yet both are seen as potentially hostile to American values and interests.

The problem is not new: Eisenhower predicted a massive communist victory for Ho Chi Minh if Vietnam held nationwide elections in 1956 – as laid down in an international agreement two years earlier. Encouraged by the United States, South Vietnam cancelled the elections, prompting an insurgency by the north that turned South East Asia into a battleground and ended up later with America's defeat in the Vietnam War.

The issue of elections producing unfavourable governments, therefore, has to be addressed if democracy is to flourish. But the growing global influences of Islam and socialism might not make that easy – particularly as there are few benchmarks to define when these ideologies, although popular with voters, actually cross the line to be perceived as being hostile to the West.

In 1997, I read a piece by the young academic and journalist Fareed Zakaria that talked about the phenomenon of 'illiberal democracy'.[9] Zakaria was responding partly to a dilemma posed by the US diplomat Richard Holbrooke when trying to end the 1990s civil war in Bosnia. Suppose the election was free and fair, Holbrooke had asked, but those elected were 'racists, fascists, separatists' who were publicly opposed to peace and reintegration. Holbrooke was talking about ultra nationalism, whereas a few years later elections in Iraq produced hard-line religious blocs, and Latin America, in the eyes of many in Washington, was producing unacceptable levels of socialism.

Zakaria explained that it was difficult for the West to recognize the concept of 'illiberal democracy' because for almost a century our definition of democracy has meant 'liberal democracy – a political system marked not only by free and fair elections, but also by the rule of law, a separation of powers and the protection of basic liberties of speech, assembly, religion and property'.

In an illiberal democracy, therefore, the government was legitimately elected but ignored the spirit of democracy and often its constitutional limits of power, thus depriving citizens of rights and freedoms. Robert Mugabe's Zimbabwe is an obvious example of this.

In his essay, Zakaria warned that 'democracy without

---

9 Fareed Zakaria, 'The Rise of Illiberal Democracy', *Foreign Affairs*, Nov./Dec. 1997.

constitutional liberalism is not simply inadequate, but dangerous, bringing with it the erosion of liberty, abuse of power, ethnic divisions, and even war'. He set America the task of making democracy safe for the world, suggesting that instead of 'searching for new lands to democratize and new places to hold elections, to consolidate democracy where it has taken root and to encourage the gradual development of constitutional liberalism across the globe'.

One region in which this appeared to be happening was South East Asia where, following the Vietnam War, a spectrum of authoritarian and democratizing nations with Muslims, Christians, socialism and capitalism all living and working side by side began to blossom.

But how were they managing it and would it last?

SOUTH EAST ASIA

INDONESIA – Democracy's Lure

Just before midnight on 28 August 1987, I got a call that the Philippine military was about to try to overthrow the newly democratized government. From a restaurant in Remedios Circle, just back from the panoramic waterfront of Manila Bay, I took a taxi with Gwen Robinson of the *Australian* newspaper towards Malacañang Presidential Palace, the seat of power and the obvious target of any military rebellion. As we were about to cross a bridge on the palace's outer perimeter, there was a flash followed by a sharp crack. The taxi driver hit the brakes. Two truckloads of troops sped past and vanished into the smoke caused by the explosion. As it cleared, the lights of our taxi illuminated three men on the ground. Two looked dead. One was just alive, his intestines spilling out. They were civilians. One was a cigarette seller. His tray of cigarettes had spilt onto the road. All three wore sandals and faded T-shirts – the clothes of the poor.

The troops who killed them were working under the command of Colonel (Gringo) Gregorio Honasan, a charismatic young colonel who had earned a reputation for daredevilry by parachuting out of an aeroplane with a python wrapped around him. A year earlier he had been a key figure in overthrowing Ferdinand Marcos, who had been the Philippines' dictatorial president for more than twenty years. Marcos was a pro-West Cold War warrior. He ran the sprawling archipelago as a series of enfranchised territories. He rigged elections, imposed martial law and lined his pockets, while his wife, Imelda, partied with film stars, built resorts and collected shoes.

The Philippines was the first country in the recent cycle of modern history to carry out a 'people power' revolution to rid itself of a dictator. In February 1986, after Marcos declared victory in yet another rigged election, the streets of Manila filled with protesting students, businessmen, nuns and priests. Soldiers were sent out to stop them. But, under the orders of officers like Honasan, they changed sides, stuck flowers in their gun barrels and joined the protests. Helicopters flown by rebel pilots buzzed the Presidential Palace, and Ferdinand and Imelda Marcos fled to Hawaii.

It took only a few months for Honasan to turn from being a 'people power' hero to a military rebel. The night of his coup, we visited a commandeered television station, spoke to hesitant soldiers at army camps whose loyalty was unknown and watched a nationwide address by a group of unnamed soldiers claiming they were fighting for the future of their country. John Mills, from the Australian Broadcasting Corporation, with whom I was sharing an office, managed to speak to Honasan himself, and asked why he was trying to oust a democratically elected government.

'For our children and our children's children,' said Honasan.

'To achieve what?' said Mills.

'Wait and see,' said Honasan.

By the end of the next day, Honasan was in hiding and the coup attempt had ended. But the Philippines' democracy was far from secure. Over the next eighteen months, I covered four more coup attempts, numerous political assassinations and demonstrations, civil wars on two fronts and interviewed player after player who believed that democracy gave them the right to do whatever they wanted regardless of the cost to others.

A few days after the August coup, we tracked down one of Honasan's fellow rebels, a helicopter pilot. I won't name him. He supported Honasan but claimed he wasn't involved in the military action. He had led the helicopter squadron that had buzzed the Presidential Palace, prompting Marcos to leave. To get to him, we were sent on a runaround of changing cars, shifting rendezvous and being separated, only to end up in a housing estate of military homes on the outskirts of Manila. A batman served lunch and he talked confidently about the appalling impact the new president, Corazon Aquino, was having on the country. He boasted how he and his men had the power to control the skies over the Philippines. He had a pot belly and a frog-like face with dancing little eyes that never settled anywhere. He answered each question by pompously reciting economy or land-reform slogans. He often lost his thread.

'All right,' I asked. 'Once you take control of the government, then what?'

He blinked and looked at me, his brow furrowed. 'We will have freedom,' he said.

'Yes, but do you have your own economists, educationalists, agronomists, city planners lined up to govern better than President Aquino is now?'

There was silence. A Filipina journalist with us translated to be absolutely sure he understood, and a conversation started up between them. It became heated, with the journalist banging her hand on the table and the helicopter pilot shaking his head and retreating to a freshly lit cigarette.

'No,' said the journalist eventually. 'They haven't even thought about it.' Her face looked drained. She had been raised and schooled during the Marcos years and lived through the exhilaration of his overthrow. She had experienced the confusion and disappointments of the new democracy and she had held a candle of sorts for the glamour and easy visions of the military rebels.

This was two years before the momentous events of 1989 – the crushed attempts at democratization in China's Tiananmen Square and the successful ones in Europe with the pulling down of the Berlin Wall and the domino collapse of European dictatorships. At the time of our scrappy little coup attempt in Manila, few in the West had first-hand experience of how societies reacted to sudden post-dictatorial freedoms and what human dreams and fears kicked in that lead to street celebrations during the day and killings and kidnappings at night.

Marcos's downfall began in 1983, when either he or one of his henchmen ordered the assassination of a charismatic young opposition leader, Ninoy Aquino – shooting him on the steps of the aircraft that had just flown him back from exile. Ninoy Aquino's housewife widow, Corazon, stood against Marcos in elections that he had rigged. When Marcos fled, she became president, announcing a new constitution and offering land reform for the poor. The once repressed communities went on the rampage. The communist New People's Army killed businessmen. Right-wing oligarchs struck back with their own private death squads. The military, confused as to their mission, kept trying to overthrow the government.

Some weeks after the Honasan coup, I tracked down a lieutenant who had appeared in the nationwide address we'd watched on television. He was in his early twenties, very bright, and planned to spend a year at the US War College near Washington – that is if he got a pardon. I asked him why he did it. 'None of us understood the meaning of democratic space,' he said. 'So we thought we needed to stop it.'

'Why?' I asked.

'We were frightened,' he answered. 'We were afraid that we would lose everything we had.'

Writing this now more than twenty years later, I've since interviewed many special interest groups all over the world who lash out because they are afraid of losing the status quo. After the insurgency broke out in Iraq, the post-Marcos Philippines came more to mind than the scenes of jubilation, on a par with the liberation of Paris in 1945, envisaged by the Bush administration.

There is a difference between ridding your country of an occupying power, as in the Second World War, and ousting a clever, home-grown dictator, as in the cases of Saddam Hussein and Ferdinand Marcos. If Filipino troops, who still had their pensions and most of their power, kept rebelling again and again, what was likely to happen to the much more bloodied men of the Iraqi military when they were sacked, losing their jobs, pay and status?

With the departure of Marcos, President Corazon Aquino faced three distinctive violent threats. One was from the military. One was from the revival of centuries-old rebellions in the Islamic south. And one was from the Soviet-inspired New People's Army (NPA). Suddenly, each had been given the space to test the limits of new freedoms.

The NPA was one of the dopiest insurgencies I had ever encountered. Its spokesman would drop round to our office in the Manila Hotel offering a facility to an NPA military camp that never materialized. He was a dull-faced, monosyllabic character who took for granted our alliance to his cause. We would give him a meal and let him sleep on the sofa. Then he would vanish, leaving a phone number that was never answered only to reappear a few weeks later with the same promise of access. It turned out he was having problems with his wife, who kept throwing him out of the house. When she did, he would bed down at various foreign news bureaux around Manila.

The insurgency was Latin American in style with the guerrillas representing the poor and many having links to left-wing NGOs and the Catholic Church. As Cold War politics subsided, so did the NPA. But Islamic unrest in the southern Philippines rumbled on, ever vigilant, watching to see whether democracy administered from Christian Manila would do the business in the faraway south.

Muslim settlements in the country pre-dated Spanish colonizers by several centuries during which a well-administered sultanate stretched across an area that later became the southern Philippines, Indonesia and Malaysia.

Many Islamic leaders had refused to recognize the Philippine government, whether run by the Spanish, Americans or the predominantly Christian post-independence politicians. Their long-established militia, known as Moros, regularly took on government forces.

Ferdinand Marcos waged a brutal but inconclusive war against them in the early 1970s, after which there was an uneasy peace. Now President Corazon Aquino, with the heady confluences of her new democracy, again wanted to try to bring the Muslim community into the mainstream. A fragile ceasefire had been declared and I headed off to see them with my colleague John Mills. Our destination was the remote island of Jolo on the Sulu Archipelago that stretched between the Philippines and Malaysia.

A Jesuit priest met us off the plane and took us through a military checkpoint. Four of our Moro hosts were bantering on the other side with Filipino soldiers who let us through with barely a look. We got into the back of the Moro pick-up truck and headed off. The camp was halfway up a mountain, a cluster of wooden huts, with a fleet of Toyota trucks parked in a clearing. The fighters wore brand-new camouflage uniforms, bought in Belgium, apparently. Their leader spoke fluent English and told us they would fight until they were granted an independent Moro homeland.

On the way back, bumping along in the back of the pick-up, we joked with the two Moro fighters escorting us. We sat amid a stack of boxes, some of which stank to high heaven. We drove down out of the wooded area and saw that at the bottom of the hill the Filipino military checkpoint has been moved forward a couple of hundred yards and the mood was very different. As we pulled up, there was a sharp exchange between a soldier and the driver. The faces of the two men with us tightened. One slipped his hand into his tunic and curled his fingers around a pistol butt. A Filipino officer stepped out from the checkpoint and pointed toward us: 'You two, out,' he said in English. As we jumped down from the back, the officer said, 'Over there. Run.'

Troops poured out from the checkpoint. 'Get down!' John shouted, his hand on my back pushing me to the ground. The wheels of the pick-up skidded. It reversed hitting one of the soldiers. There was a shot, followed by a burst of gunfire. A Moro in the back returned fire. The other was flopped over the boxes. The driver crunched the gears and carried out a sweeping forward turn, weaving the vehicle to avoid the fire coming from the soldiers. Soon they were out of range and, I was pretty sure, carrying a dead or badly wounded Moro guerrilla fighter.

The Jesuit priest, whom we had met earlier, arrived in his jeep and took us to the airport. He didn't speak to the soldiers. His Catholic credentials let him pass unhindered. When we were well away he said, 'Young men with guns. What should we expect?'

Our flight, an old prop-driven short-haul plane, had already landed, bringing back families from the Haj in Saudi Arabia. The tiny airstrip, encased in the jungle hills, was a mass of white-clad people embracing each other and exchanging gifts. The pilot, in a smartly pressed airline uniform, walked over and talked to the priest in Tagalog. 'He's asking if you have a durian with you,' he said.

'What's that,' I said.

'You wouldn't miss it,' said the pilot, breaking into perfect English with an American accent. 'It's a fruit, and it has a bad smell.'

Oh my God, I thought. That's what we were carrying in the Toyota pick-up. The priest and the pilot spoke some more. The pilot's face dropped as he heard the story. He peeled off some notes and pressed them into the priest's hands.

We learned that gunfight had been triggered because of an argument over the durian that was to have been taken on our plane. There was no higher political cause than that. It was apparently illegal to carry durian on the aircraft, but the pilot was doing it anyway and somewhere along this fractious line someone had not been paid.

Years later, I would be back in South East Asia, when the Moros were seen as a global Islamic threat and the island of Jolo was a surveillance target for the War on Terror.

South East Asia is a sprawling area with India and Bangladesh to the west, the Pacific to the east, China to the north and Australia to the south. Burma or Myanmar is a military dictatorship. Vietnam and Laos remain communist. Impoverished Cambodia is an experiment in United Nations-nurtured democracy, but has ended up with Han Sen the same strongman in power for thirty years. Singapore and Malaysia are authoritarian democracies. Thailand veers between corrupt democracy and military technocracy, and the Philippines and Indonesia are struggling new democracies, both having varying degrees of success.

The area has become a choice for the many multinationals setting up factories in the global supply chain while millions of tourists holiday there every year. For them its democracy is irrelevant. What matters is security and stability. Although vastly different in religion, culture and systems of administration, the governments of South East Asia no longer fight each other.

If South East Asian wars and hunger have vanished from our television screens, might it not be possible that at some stage those from Africa and the Middle East would no longer be there, too? Was there something to learn from South East Asia, particularly Indonesia, the biggest Muslim country in the world?

Indonesia's dictatorship ended in 1998. Violence broke out in East Timor, which in 1999 won independence under the efficient and fairly bloodless watch of the Australian military. Christians and Muslims were also fighting in Sulawesi, Ambon and elsewhere. Islamic terror had encroached with the 2002 bombing on the tourist island of Bali that killed more than 200 people, many of them Australian tourists.

The question then being asked was whether the violence was going to be as enduring and contagious as it seemed to be in the Middle East. One of the overarching issues in the debate over the West and Islam is how and why Islamic cultures have fallen behind in science and technology. In that respect Islamic South East Asia was some way ahead of the Middle East, and we headed off to meet a man in charge of Indonesia's plan to design and build a state-of-the-art commuter aircraft – the first ever to be made by a Muslim nation.

Indonesian Aerospace's factory was in the hill city of Bandung, a mix between old Javanese mysteries, tropical exoticism and the din of traffic and construction.

The gates of the plant were chained with rusty padlocks and outside were factory workers protesting about being laid off without pay. Inside, I walked across the vast, empty tarmac with the company's president, Edward Soedarno.

'I will show you that a Muslim country can develop high technology of its own,' he said. Yet the whole place was eerily empty – huge dirty-white hangars, tarmac-stained and pock-marked, sprouting weeds and no one else around. Sixteen thousand people had worked here. But almost all of them had been laid off with an economic downturn and Indonesia's own uncertain political future.

Even so, Soedarno was touchingly upbeat. Because of the heat I was wearing just an open-neck shirt and khaki trousers. He was in a dark double-breasted suit, with a light cotton shirt, silk tie and cufflinks. His company might be collapsing around him, but his enthusiasm for what he wanted to achieve was undiminished. We stepped into the hangar and in front of us was the N 250 prototype, a commercial turboprop aircraft that he hoped one day would fill a niche in the small-plane commuter market. Much of its technology had been designed and made by Indonesians. The project began as long ago as 1976, but the N 250 had flown only once, for less than an hour, eight years earlier in 1995.

As we climbed into the fuselage, empty apart from wires hanging down and loose pieces of paper on the floor, I couldn't help disagreeing with many of the comments I had heard from colleagues and others about this project and Indonesia as a whole. Some had looked at me aghast and asked why. It was failure. It would never get off the ground. It was symptomatic of the malaise that enveloped Indonesia, of the corruption and the dictatorship.

But, having spent many of the preceding months in the Middle East, I might have been eyeing things differently. There, Hamas and Hezbollah were digging tunnels and shipping in rockets with which to attack Israel. Iraqis were killing American and British soldiers, blowing up mosques and murdering each other. Yet, Indonesia was trying to build an aeroplane to ferry businessmen around Asia.

In the Middle East, I so often heard that things could not be done because of some problem that spiralled down to explain paralysis and hopelessness. Often it was because of Israel or America. Yet, here in this run-down hangar, not once did Soedarno blame any outside forces for the stalling of his aeroplane project. He could so easily have reflected the stench of failure all around us, but he didn't.

It was not part of Soedarno's thinking. He knew what he wanted to do. He knew there were obstacles. He planned to overcome them. He came over as a man who felt that as long as he was still in the game, he was winning. It has become increasingly fashionable to suggest that Muslim societies have failed to match the West with technology, but Indonesia had started doing something about it long before 9/11 broadened the debate.

'I am so proud,' said Soedarno, brushing his hand around the controls in the cockpit. 'I am so glad we have been able to design this.'

'What does it actually mean to you?' I asked.

'It is rare to see a Muslim country developing high technology,' he said. 'It means that we, from an Asian Muslim country, can sit at the same table and talk in the same language. We can talk about high technology. We can talk about aircraft. We can talk about outer space without feeling bad because we can now follow what the rich countries are discussing.'

For a moment, he seemed lost in his own thoughts. He spotted a stain on the windscreen, took out his handkerchief, moistened it with his saliva and rubbed the dirt off. Then he picked up his argument. 'You ask me what it means. I am an engineer, so for me this is a step for us to say to the world: "Yes, we can, because we are the same human beings as you."'

I liked Soedarno, but outside the padlocked gates, where his laid-off workforce was gathered, he was despised. Sitting on the back of a red pick-up truck was a papier-mâché effigy of him, shaped like a rat with floppy ears, whiskers and his pockets filled with money. The president of Indonesian Aerospace was portrayed as a stereotypical businessman, corrupt and uncaring about his staff.

The protesters were crushed up against the fence with police on the other side to stop them breaking through. They chanted slogans, raising their fists in the air, demanding retribution from a world of privilege, broken promises and bad leadership. There were at least 3,000, probably more, a sea of disappointment, anger and slogans. What they wanted was clear – their jobs back. Whoever could deliver that, would win their loyalty.

We noticed a lanky, sullen young man, in a sleeveless khaki jacket, pulling leaflets out his many pockets and working the crowd. His name was Rusdianto.[1] He had been sent to Bandung by his head office in Jakarta to recruit for the Islamic Justice Party, then the fastest-growing political movement in Indonesia. Rusdianto was neither charismatic nor a firebrand.

---

1 Many Indonesians, such as the late President Suharto, only use one name.

In fact it turned out he wasn't particularly liked by the aircraft workers. But in the past couple of days he said he had signed up 2,000 new members.

'Everywhere the Justice Party finds oppression we will help,' he said. 'Like today we are helping the families that once relied on the aircraft company. All around Indonesia we will help the underprivileged and the poor.'

Thirty years ago, he might have been inspired by socialism. Now Islam was his motivation. Washington sees both as dangerous. But Indonesia had been at this crossroads before and understood the repercussions should the country veer in the wrong direction.

Indonesia had been tenuously colonized by the Dutch, who lost it after the Second World War when Sukarno, the country's flamboyant leader, declared independence. He immediately created the institutions of a secular state under a unifying philosophy called 'Pancasila' designed to balance the aspirations of the military, the communists, the Muslims, the Christians and restless communities on faraway islands. Its tenets were national unity and social justice for everyone.

But Sukarno was also determined to give poorer nations a voice to balance American and Soviet power – and that led to his downfall. In 1955, he hosted an international conference in Bandung that created an organization called the Non-Aligned Movement. The term the Third World was partly hatched there, meaning a middle way of governance away from the competing capitalist and communist ideologies of Washington and Moscow. In the mind of Sukarno and the many leaders who went to Bandung, the Third World would be a force of balance emanating from Asia, Africa and Latin America. Interestingly, the key powers in those regions are now being referred to as the Second World.

Sukarno's dream created enemies in the West who

believed he was making South East Asia vulnerable to communism, particularly from China.

'If the British and the Americans remove everything from this area,' explained Lord Head, the then British High Commissioner to Malaysia, 'I think people would feel that the only power in the area would be communist China. There would be no balance and people would say we are bound to be dominated by communist China. What we're really doing in South East Asia is to ensure a balance in which the countries of South East Asia feel they can grow up and govern themselves the way they want to.'

Patronizing, perhaps, but reflective of a brutal Cold War policy that was to follow. Sukarno's idealistic middle way meant accommodating left-leaning, grass-roots organizations that risked empathy with Moscow or Beijing. The West was determined to stop it. First there were right-wing demonstrations against Sukarno, then, in 1965, backed by the United States, the army overthrew him. The coup was led by the little-known General Suharto. Indonesia became a staunch American ally. Washington stayed silent as hundreds of thousands of suspected communist sympathizers were massacred.[2] Free speech was shut down. The tentacles of the security forces touched all parts of society. The American policy that turned Indonesia into a pro-Western dictatorship was to be replicated throughout much of Africa, Asia and Latin America as lines were drawn in jungles, deserts and mountains against the encroachment of communism.

When Richard Nixon visited Indonesia in 1969, he proclaimed President Suharto a champion of freedom. He failed to mention the mass graves filled with the corpses of those who might have been looking to Moscow for an alternative.

---

2 National Security Archive www.nsarchive.org

Suharto ruled for thirty-one years but, like Marcos in the Philippines, as the Cold War wound down, his dictatorship ran out of steam. When he stepped down in 1998, Indonesia's competing forces flooded into the vacuum – although this time the front-runner was not communism but Islam.

While we were in Bandung with Indonesian Aerospace, President Bush was in the country mustering support for America's latest global cause. His reception was very mixed, because he immediately revived memories of Indonesia's Cold War American experience.

Bush stepped into a highly complex world. Indonesia's president, Megawati Sukarnoputri, was in office because she was the daughter of the idealistic leader whom America helped overthrow. She was acutely aware of what damage America could do to change the course her country wished to take.

Bush needed the world's biggest Muslim nation to be an unflinching ally. But this time America could not sponsor a coup and install a friendly dictator if things looked like getting out of hand. The very forces that Bush saw as being the enemy were powerful within Indonesia's political process. One example of this was the refusal of the Indonesian government to ban Jemaah Islamiyah, the Islamic organization held responsible for the Bali bombing.

Bush and Megawati made Bali the focus of the visit. Flanked by palm trees swaying in a tropical breeze, Bush sought to calm fears on his intentions. 'We know that Islam is fully compatible with tolerance, liberty and progress because we see the proof in your country and in our own,' he said. 'Terrorists who claim Islam as their inspiration defile one of the world's great faiths.'

In talks afterwards with Muslim clerics and academics, he was met with a wall of scepticism, which I was told later was one of the biggest wake-up calls of his presidency. They gave

Bush a lecture not only about Israel and Iraq, but also about the overthrow of Sukarno and the mass killings that followed. If America tried to do the same over Islam, Bush was warned, millions in South East Asia would turn against him and put at risk America's role in the whole of the Asia–Pacific region.

A few days later, I spoke to one of the academics at the meeting. Dr Azyumardi Azra was president of the State Islamic University, and I was partly expecting him to be wearing a full-length beard and white robe and cap. But instead, he wore a colourful batik shirt and was clean-shaven with close-cropped grey hair. He was quite happy to meet in the bar of Jakarta's Mandarin Hotel where, as we talked, a young bartender flamboyantly mixed exotic cocktails.

'These Americans keep saying that Islam is compatible with democracy,' he said, his voice hesitant with doubt. 'And that's what Bush told us.'

'Do you believe him?'

'Let's wait and see. I don't know if they're capable of making a clear distinction between radical terrorists and Islam. I don't know if they think like that. They think only in black and white – with us or against us – and Islam does not speak or think like that.'

The confluence of Indonesia's new democracy and expanding Islam produced strange bedfellows. Back in Jakarta we filmed in a suburban mosque where the former head of national intelligence had become an Islamic preacher. In his old job as an American ally, General Zahaumudin Maulani would have rigidly kept a lid on political freedom. Now with a white robe, beads and black fez cap, he stood on a mosque podium, his back ramrod straight, talking about the recreation of an Islamic Caliphate in South East Asia.

'Americans are unjustly accusing Muslims,' he said. 'Muslims must stand up to the superpower. It is their duty.'

Afterwards, when I talked to Maulani, he was full of praise for al-Qaeda, and angry at the United States.

'Al-Qaeda is the only organization in the Islamic world that has the courage and the guts to stand up and criticize and oppose American injustices in the Muslim world,' he said.

Soon we were carrying the camera gear through the lobby of a large cheap hotel to find out what President Megawati was promising voters and what she actually stood for. In the corner of a low-ceilinged conference room was a choir of girls, with bright red sports tops and white skirts. They were singing a political song about Indonesian nationalism, giving a lead to the rest of the room. Everyone was standing, all dressed in the same colours, with red blazers and name badges stuck onto the lapels. Gazing down on them was a huge portrait of a smiling and bespectacled President Megawati, who was drawing on her father's national unity doctrine of Pancasila as the means to stave off extreme Islam.

Her party's general secretary was the only person in the room not wearing a uniform. Pramano Anung was very much in the mould of Soedarno in Bandung. He was impeccably dressed in a tailored suit with a white shirt and red patterned tie. 'If you want to profile a modern Muslim,' he said, 'you've got one right in front of you. A typical liberal Muslim like me has been to university, maybe studied abroad. We get on with people. We're not suspicious of different cultures and ways of life. I drink. I collect wine. I have more than 250 different brands in my wine cellar. I love cigars, but . . .' and he held up his hand for a dramatic pause, '. . . I also go to the Haj.'

'Does that mean you're a good or a bad Muslim, then?' I asked.

'Neither good nor bad. It is a different interpretation.'

I told him what General Maulani had said in the mosque and asked why the government didn't stop him advocating al-Qaeda-style violence.

'It's difficult,' he said. 'We are a nationalist party, but we need the support of the Muslim parties to govern.'

'And if you didn't have their support, what would happen?'

'There would be protests and this would be a big problem.'

As in many cities throughout the world, the American embassy was cordoned off with bombproof concrete blocks and razor wire. Security involved body searches and scans that made us late for our meeting with Ralph Boyce, the US Ambassador to Indonesia. Unlike many ambassadors who were Republican Party political appointees, Boyce was a career State Department diplomat, with a high forehead and a bushy grey beard. His message carried nuances that set it apart from rhetoric then coming from the White House. I told him we'd just been interviewing a former intelligence chief who supported al-Qaeda, and asked him where Indonesia fitted into America's 'with us or against us' doctrine.

'Yeah, well,' said Boyce dismissively. 'That's a phrase where, in a place like Indonesia, there's a lot of grey in between the black and white.'

'Can America accept the grey?'

'There's a great deal of resonance – including with President Bush – that what is going on in Indonesia does require some understanding.'

'But he doesn't accept the grey in Iran and Syria.'

'That's because there's a sense that what's happening here is truly historic, that there are going to be bumps along the way and that we have to keep our eye on the big picture and that Indonesia has to succeed in this.'

'Would you then accept an Islamic party in power?'

'I think that's so hypothetical that we needn't deal with it now.'

But, with an election only a year away, it wasn't. Our final stop for the day was a strange anti-American rally held by President Megawati's sister, Rachmawati Sukarnoputri. Unlike Megawati, she had never forgiven the Americans for what they did to her father and wasn't afraid to show it.

'Bush is a symbol of neo-colonialism,' Rachmawati shouted through a microphone at a park in central Jakarta. She paused to allow the crowd to cry 'Allahu Akbar' (God is Great), and punch their fists in the air. 'This is the symbol which our founding father Sukarno put as the enemy of the Indonesian nation. If you people still believe in what Sukarno was saying, we have to say that America is an enemy.'

As Rachmawati finished she returned to the VIP area to join none other than the leader of the Justice Party, that fast-growing Islamic movement for which the humourless Rusdianto in Bandung had been signing up the Indonesian Aerospace workers.

Dr H. M. Hidayat Nur Wahid stood up, shook Rachmawati's hand, bowed and arranged a plastic chair for her. They sat side by side, under a cityscape of shopping malls and modern buildings, an odd couple, a cobbled-together alliance between the daughter of man who had vowed to keep Indonesia secular and a Muslim intellectual who wanted to turn it Islamic.

At first glance, Wahid carried no signs of extreme Islam about him. He had a small goatee beard. He wore nothing on his head. His brown batik shirt was like millions of others around the region. But his CV read like something from a CIA Islamic identity manual. He had studied Islam in Saudi Arabia, home of the extreme Wahhabi doctrine exported by al-Qaeda. He left with a PhD in Islamic philosophy. He had taught at a madrasa here in Indonesia and now planned to run for president on an anti-American ticket.

We met later in his tiny office, which bore the hallmarks of a new organization – the smell of new electronic equipment, desks without telephones, boxes half-emptied – and not much money in evidence.

'Before you start,' he said. 'We are not al-Qaeda and we are not a member of al-Qaeda.'

'How would you describe your relationship with America, then?' I asked.

'They are not our enemy, but they might make themselves our enemy. It is not that they don't understand us. It's that maybe they don't want to understand us. They talk about democracy, but they don't know what it means. They think it's something agreed by them, that it can only be practised the American way.'

A year later Islamic extremism had erupted into an insurgency in South East Asia. Rebellion in the name of Islam was tearing apart southern Thailand, an area which had a Muslim majority. A mosque on the east coast had been the site of a pitched battle between the Thai army and Islamic insurgents and low-level fighting was going on all the time. Close by was Malaysia's east coast, deeply conservative and the homeland of the Pan-Malaysian Islamic Party (PAS) that had become the country's official opposition.

There was a common thread, too – the creation of a South East Asian Caliphate which the former intelligence chief Maulani spoke of in the Jakarta mosque. The Caliphate would govern the region from southern Thailand to Papua New Guinea as a pan-Islamic state unfettered by colonization, Christian intrusion and the outside world.

I planned several stops this time. The remote island of

Pulau Sebatik had been branded by Western intelligence agencies as a terrorist haven. I would talk to The Justice Party that had failed to win the Indonesian election, but secured itself as a major political player. I put out feelers to meet the young men who were planning bombing attacks or sympathized with those who had carried out the Bali bombing. I would go to the mosque destroyed in Thailand's new civil war and talk to the head of PAS in Malaysia's Islamic east coast heartlands.

The aim was to see if, perhaps, there was something to the Western idea of a domino theory? Was America right to draw geographical lines against the encroachment of Islamic extremism as it had done in Iraq and Afghanistan?

Before leaving London, I interviewed the then Malaysian prime minister, Abdullah Ahmad Badawi, who had taken over from the far more legendary, forthright and eloquent Dr Mahathir bin Mohamad, seen as the founding father of modern Malaysia. It was on Mahathir's watch that Malaysia had become regarded not so much as a Muslim nation but as an Asian economic Tiger.

Malaysia began its existence under the shadow of a communist insurgency that lingered throughout the Cold War. In the 1960s it was wracked by race riots between the Chinese, who controlled much of the economy and made up a quarter of the population, and the Malays, who made up about half of it. Convinced that the violence would worsen, the Malaysian government passed laws positively discriminating in favour of the Malays, who were guaranteed jobs, education and economic rewards. Known as the New Economic Policy, it was criticized by Chinese, Indians and other minorities for making them second-class citizens. Both bin Mohamad and Badawi rigorously stuck to the policy. Malaysia avoided racial violence. Its economy regularly grew by 8 per cent year on year, enabling it to create cities with skyscrapers, motorways and airports, together with a health and education system that would be envied in many developing countries. Malaysia set a pace that has rarely been given the credit in the West that it deserves.

Badawi, a far softer character than bin Mohamad, was now testing how much he could loosen things up without Malaysia losing its economic punch or racial tension raising its head again. But in the middle of all this came the challenge from extreme Islam, pitting two faces of Malaysia against each other – the wealthy tiger economy against the conservative Islamic Caliphate.

'Are you an Islamist?' I asked Badawi in his suite at London's Dorchester Hotel.

'I don't like this word,' he said. 'Let's say I am a devout Muslim.'

He was a tall man with a gentle voice who had studied Islam at university. 'We have taken a stand on the subject of Islam, to offer Islam and to practise Islam based on moderation and respect for people from other religions, a willingness to coop-erate and share powers and an Islam that is progressive and that can show the way forward. We call it Islam Hadhari or hard-driving Islam.'

Some translated that as 'civilizational Islam' and it differed starkly from what I had heard so many times in the Middle East. It was based on what people wanted to achieve as opposed to what they wanted to avenge. It seemed to be nothing less than a psychological revolution in thinking, embracing reform, democracy, education, science, business and the economy. You could see it in the spring in the rush-hour step in Kuala Lumpur, the traffic jams, the designer shops, the sun glinting off the massive Petronas Towers, the call to prayer from the minarets, the eagerness to do business and get on with life.

'So will Islam Hardari help you win the War on Terror?' I asked.

'Yes,' said Badawi. 'I think we are winning this war. Not completely, yet, but we are watching very carefully and soon we believe we will see no threat.'

'What then is the difference between your type of Islam and that violent side we are seeing in the Middle East?'

'Our thinking is different,' he said. 'I don't want to say they are backward. They have been practising Islam for a long time. But you just have to see where they are now, what is the position of their countries. Then see what we are doing in Malaysia.'

The east coast city of Terengganu is territory of the Pan Malaysian Islamic Party (PAS). Together with the neighbouring state of Kelantan, PAS, rooted in religious and not secular ideology, had built up a power-base that won it state level elections and enough seats in the federal parliament to challenge Malaysia's ruling United Malays National Organisation (UMNO) head on. From being a small grass-roots party, PAS had become a major force in Malaysian politics. In PAS-controlled areas the clichéd texture of Islamic rule had appeared. There were bans on alcohol and women were mostly covered. The party also wanted to introduce laws that would include stoning, whipping and amputation, but the UMNO-run federal government would not allow it.

Terengganu is also a fishing town, so we took a small boat from its colourful port out to sea. I wanted to ask fishermen what they thought about an Islamic government and the popularly touted aspiration of creating a pan-Islamic Caliphate in South East Asia.

Halfway out, sudden thick cloud pressed down, darkening everything around. Lightning streaked in the distance and ripples drifted across the surface of the water. The air that had been hot and heavy still gusted, creating tiny white waves that tossed our small boat from side to side.

Our helmsman tightened plastic sheeting over our heads, closed a hatch in his tiny wheelhouse and glanced back towards the shore, now lost in a blur of rain. He turned the boat into the wind, cut the engine to a hum and lit a cigarette. Its herbal smell mixed with the tang of cold rain. Water splashed over the wooden deck. As the rain fell harder, the huge colourful fishing boats we had been heading to became invisible. We were soaked, our hair matted. We could see nothing around us. The noise of the rain blended with strains of Malay music coming from the boatman's CD player.

Our small boat was well maintained and the owner had a radio, CD player and a cellphone and other paraphernalia that showed he was part of the worldwide consumer society. Whose side would he and the other fishermen be on? What made them drop their nets into the sea in the morning? Did they have a tipping point? What made a person decide? Did they see themselves as part of that crucible where Islam, democracy and wealth-creation could dovetail into a success story?

The storm ended as suddenly as it had begun. The sun broke through and a jagged sky appeared, part brilliant blue and part dark clouds moving like spaceships. The boatman increased the throttle. A wave slapped against the hull, spilling water onto the deck. The sun's heat hit my face and we continued our journey out to sea.

The fishing boat we were making for wasn't shy in its colours. It had a yellow, red and white hull, a green wheelhouse and bright sun awnings stretching over the upper and main decks. Fishing nets were stored in bundles on both sides. Crew members perched on them like cushions, sewing up tears with huge needles. We bumped alongside and shouted up that we wanted to come on board. A fisherman hooked us in, steadying our smaller boat, as another held out a hand to help us over. We were an odd mix. My producer was Mages Swari, a Malaysian Indian who had a deep suspicion of her own government, and my cameraman was Jone Chang, a quietly spoken Singaporean. While I would fly back to London at the end of this trip, both Jone and Mages had a personal stake in the world that we were investigating.

The boat was spotless, its deck scrubbed; patches glistened where water had gathered from the storm. Coloured flags, each with its own meaning, fluttered down the stays. Mages began finding out where the fishermen came from, then tested the sensitive area of Islam.

We were in Malaysian waters, but the crew was from all over – Indonesia, Thailand, the Philippines. They went back and forth across borders, rivers and seas to wherever they could get work. Two were cooking up an evening meal. One fixed a metal plate across the deck at the front. The rest sat, bare-chested, in the middle of the boat mending a fishing net spread out between them.

We began cautiously, asking if they supported PAS and it's Islamic values.

At first, the fishermen were reluctant to talk. Political issues might be heart-felt, but they were not natural ground for conversation with strangers. Then one of the younger ones bit through a line of twine, spat out the threads, finished a knot at the end of his net and muttered something to Mages.

'He says that under PAS they didn't have any development,' she translated.

An older man, measuring thread through his hands, joined in. 'He agrees,' continued Mages. 'PAS didn't fulfil any of the promises they made in the last election.'

I asked Mages if we could ratchet up the questions. 'Sure,' she said breezily. 'But you know these guys are saying they support UNMO because they think we're from the government. I think it's because some might not have work permits.'

'OK, then. Can you check with this guy here . . .' I said, tilting my head toward the young fisherman who had first answered, '. . . if he supports the Muslims in southern Thailand.'

When Mages asked the question, everyone stopped working. The two crewmen who were cooking moved round to the front of the wheelhouse to get closer. A fisherman from the bow walked toward us and leant against the rail. Mages engaged in a long conversation with them all. Each wanted his say. They became animated, the discussion heated.

'They're not saying,' said Mages, breaking into English. 'They only say they don't support killing innocent people.'

'Which people?' I pressed because civilians were being killed on both sides, although far more Muslims were dying than Thai Buddhists.

'They're not saying,' said Mages.

'Then why are they suddenly so interested?'

'That's the point. Of course they support it, but they're not going to say it.'

'All right,' I said. 'Do they support the creation of an Islamic Caliphate in South East Asia?'

The level of discussion calmed. 'Yeah,' said Mages, 'they want to see the Caliphate.'

'Malaysia or the whole of South East Asia?' I asked, meeting the gaze of two Mages had identified as coming from Indonesia.

'They want the whole region,' said Mages. She asked for details, then said, 'Yeah. They want wherever the Muslims ruled before Westerners came, so that's Malaysia, Indonesia, southern Thailand, Brunei.' She spread her arms in the air. 'You know. Everywhere.'

'Do they all agree?'

Mages asked, and all of them enthusiastically nodded their heads. 'Yeah, that's what they're saying, they want to see an Islamic state in the region.' She turned her head towards a cry coming from our boatman, who was pointing at the sky and gesticulating.

'Come,' said Mages. 'He said we must go. The weather might change again.'

I shook hands with each of the fishermen, strong, confident grips. Jone climbed down onto our smaller boat, steadied himself in the swell, then I handed him the camera and climbed down myself. Mages was still with the crew, busily writing. The boatman started up the engine. I held us against the hull with a boathook, while Mages finished. Rain clouds were out to sea, but the view ahead of us was clear, and we could see the small skyline of Terengganu.

The fishing boat was one of many hunkering down for another bout of evening weather. The men were in work and skilled at their jobs. Compared with others in the developing world, they were doing well. The 9/11 attacks had blown images of an alternative world towards them. Yet they must have known something about the Taliban-run Afghanistan, that laboratory of an Islamic Caliphate that oppressed millions. It wasn't as if the Caliphate they spoke about would have delivered better fishing nets and mobile phones.

The fishermen were not starving. They were literate. They earned a living. They were not insurgents and probably had no plan to be. But something in human nature meant that the possibility was closing in.

As dusk fell with the call to prayer, our boatman manoeu-vred us into the small harbour. We ate on the Terengganu waterfront, alive with chatter and activity, with its crush of colourful fishing boats in the early tropical evening. Gas flames flared at roadside stalls. Motorcycles weaved back and forth. Families wandered with a freedom impossible to imagine in Iraq.

Why swap all this for car bombs and suicide attacks? Yet, all over the world, regardless of culture, race or religion, that is what some people say they want. The nugget of discontent I had heard on the fishing boat was universal. Sometimes it faded and people moved on. Sometimes it produced a Mao, a Castro or a Lenin. Sometimes it seeped down far enough to activate a very few, such as America's Timothy McVeigh who killed 168 people in the 1995 Oklahoma City bombing; or thirty-year-old Mohammad Sadique Khan who ten years later carried out London's 7/7 bombings as a protest against Britain's 'atrocities' against Muslims all over the world. Sometimes, as with Timothy McVeigh, there was no momentum. Sometimes, as with Khan, he was inspired by Osama bin Laden and his violence became part of a political cycle that others took up.

But into which category did the fishermen's discontent fall and how would it work through? What they did and how they felt could reflect the direction in which Malaysia and South East Asia might go. Did those men believe they were on the fringes of a long revolution which, as with Mao and Lenin, appeared to have a clear vision of how to create a better world; or had the fishermen responded as they had because they had been offered a rare occasion to complain?

Mages was talking loudly into her phone next to me. Suddenly and conspiratorially she dropped her voice, finished up and snapped shut the phone. 'Change of plan,' she said excitedly, slapping my palm in a high-five. She clenched her fingers round her phone and leant forward. 'Listen carefully,' she said. 'Tomorrow, we go to the madrasa that was used to store weapons to smuggle into Thailand. It was the imam there who wrote the instruction manual for starting the jihad in southern Thailand. He is the inspiration for the Caliphate.'

The next morning, above a deep-flowing river we walked precariously along a single trunk of a palm tree lain across as a bridge. Ahead was a desert-scape of sun-white arid scrubland. The sky was deep blue and wisped with white clouds and we were all drenched from the humidity. The village where we'd left the car was now a mile or two away. Ahead of us, across the bridge was the madrasa or religious school that had been the target of the anti-terror police for spawning Islamic violence.

Baharuddin bin Jalleh, a local fisherman, led us across. We had found him at the village, a tall man, in his early fifties, with grey close-cropped hair and clear brown eyes, unafraid of direct contact. He had worshipped at the madrasa mosque there and knew the imam. But he hadn't been there since a police raid some months back and was curious to see what we would find.

We stopped at the edge of the grounds that were marked by a broken-down fence, much of it collapsed, its wires tangled up in the dry dirt. Mages pulled her scarf over her head. As we walked on, palm tree shadows created sharp contrasts between sun and shade, and dotted round on a slope towards the mosque were small, slatted wooden huts that looked like large kennels. Inside one were torn pieces of paper and an oil lamp. Quotations from the Koran were painted on the sides. There was just enough room inside for one person to sit.

Mages turned to me from talking to Jalleh. 'He says the pupils sat for hours in these huts studying the Koran.' She swished a fly away from her face. 'My God, it must have been baking.'

I stooped and reached inside for a torn sheet of paper. It was written in Malay. Mages and I looked at it together. She translated: '"Warriors should stand up and unite to capture our beloved Pattani back."'

This was a reference to the town in southern Thailand where a mosque had been destroyed in a gun battle between Islamic insurgents and the Thai security forces.

Jalleh led us down to a slope between more of these huts to the mosque itself. The whole empty place carried an oppressive air, a world apart from the lamp-lit Terengganu waterfront and the shopping malls of Kuala Lumpur. It was a jungle version of bin Laden's Afghan caves.

Two women in green sarongs from a nearby palm oil plantation washed clothes on the mosque's concrete verandah. It was a small place of worship, windowless apart from the door and some slatted windows above. Dead palm leaves littered the concrete floor inside. Flies buzzed around the faeces of stray dogs. I asked if the women knew anything about the police raid.

'Nothing,' said Mages after talking to them. 'They heard that the police came but that they found nothing. Then one day they came to wash clothes and everyone was gone.'

'What was it like when people were here?' I asked.

'The people were nice. But they just came to wash clothes because of the well.'

'Do they know if the police found any weapons here?'

'No. They didn't hear that they found weapons.'

'Do they support the Caliphate?'

Mages asked them, but the women kept their eyes on the

clothes in their buckets, kneading them and staying quiet.

'What about Jalleh?' I asked, turning my attention to our guide. 'Does he support the Caliphate?'

Jalleh was looking at a notice framed on the wall outside the mosque and when Mages asked, he pointed to it as if that was his answer. 'It says "Don't waste your time on anything else"; translated Mages. '"Just concentrate on getting close to Allah."'

'I'll ask him again,' she said. They fell into deep conversation, with Mages creasing her brow, pushing him for clarification, then breaking out into laughter.

'You'll never be able to explain this to your viewers,' she said. 'OK. He's been an UNMO supporter all his life. That's the government's party. He thinks that PAS are useless and self-centred. But get this, he wants the Islamic Caliphate, yet he doesn't support violence.'

'He worshipped here,' I said. 'So he knew what all this was about.'

'Exactly.'

'And has he heard of Islam Hardari?' I asked. 'Hard driving or modern Islam.'

'He's heard of it,' said Mages, wiping sweat off her forehead with a scarf. 'But he doesn't know what it is.'

It seemed that Jalleh had already decided between UNMO and PAS, concluding that the Islamic-based party had failed him. Yet, like just about everyone I was talking to, he claimed to want Malaysian politics to go further towards an Islamic-based society than even PAS was suggesting. The Caliphate aspiration, though, was in such a different category that it was less part of routine political debate and more a dream-like longing to think about whenever life became too difficult.

'When are we seeing PAS?' I asked Mages as we began walking back.

'Tomorrow, after Friday prayers,' she said. 'Is that OK? After we get back from Pattani?'

'Fine,' I answered thoughtfully. Mages touched my arm to make us drop back out of earshot. 'Listen, from PAS you'll just get the party line, and we'll never get to this imam now. He's vanished. But I'm pretty sure I can get someone from KMM to talk to you.'

I looked at her sharply. Along with Jemaah Islamiyah, KMM, or Kumpulan Mujahidin Malaysia, was one of the key militant organizations threatening to bring more violence to South East Asia.

By midday, we were on our way north to Thailand. The roads were well maintained and marked with clear white lines and signs. People waited in bus stops built with shelters to protect them from the sun or a tropical downpour. We passed schools, clinics and police stations – a palpable seeping down of wealth, which in many other developing countries was siphoned off by corrupt officials. That might still be happening here, but the basics were being built.

Given that Malaysia was meant to be a sanctuary for the Muslim Thai insurgents and just north of the border lay the violence-wracked city of Pattani, everything at the border looked too relaxed.

On each side of the road were drab, modern immigration and customs buildings, but most of the traffic was ignoring them. Motorcyclists and truck drivers weaved past a battered border sign sponsored by Coca-Cola. No one seemed to be stopping.

We did because of our camera equipment. But there were no queues, and the immigration officials barely gave us a glance. Was it pure luck that Jemaah Islamiyah or KMM had not had more successes; or were the Thai and Malaysian intelligence so smart that they knew who was dangerous and tracked them before they even got here?

Once in Thailand, the atmosphere changed, as if a whole community had suddenly lost its spark. It was grubbier. There was more litter. Children, not at school, played barefooted in filthy rainwater. People walked with heads lowered. A woman, draped in black, was hunched over a tin washing bowl. A man carrying a ladder briefly met my eyes and immediately glanced away. We asked the driver to pull up at a fishing village and then walked down a filthy dank path to the riverside. Shanties of bamboo straw and metal clung to both banks.

This river community carried within it the drabness of oppression, a sense that however hard you try you cannot break through because people from another tribe, race or religion will stop you. Your success depends not on merit, but on birth. I had seen it among Catholics in Northern Ireland, Tamils in Sri Lanka, the Shia in Iraq, Albanians in Serb-ruled Kosovo. It pervades Britain's class system. It is entrenched in America's black and Hispanic ghettoes. It is all over caste-ridden India. It is intrinsic to human nature, although often the atmosphere of subjugation is as much perceived as real, so that even when resolved for the better, resentment, hunger for revenge and violence continue.

For some months, while travelling around the Islamic world, I had carried with me a stark number. The average annual income in Western democratic societies was US$30,000 a year. In Muslim ones, it was less than US$4,000 – barely more than a tenth. Was it because of Western oppression? Or was it because – as a grand ayatollah in Lebanon once conceded to me with a glint in his rheumy eyes – something within Islamic society had held its people back?

We tried, as we had on the fishing boat, to ask about the

Caliphate, but the villagers didn't want to speak. They answered us with silence.

A few miles beyond the fishing village, we tried to turn off the road, but ran straight into a Thai military checkpoint. The soldiers saw Jone's camera, turfed us out of the van, searched it, then let us go. Further up, set back from the road among tropical greenery, we spotted a Buddhist monastery and headed down its long driveway. But instead of being greeted by saffron-clad monks we drove into a Thai army camp set up in the grounds. Rows of trucks and armoured vehicles stood alongside military green tents with the white monastery and its ornately carved orange roof behind. A monk arranged joss sticks in an earthen pot that he was decorating with red petals. Nearby, three soldiers sat on white plastic garden furniture, smoking, and putting bullets into the magazines of their machine guns.

A soldier asked what we wanted. We told them we were making a tourist film on Thailand and wanted to film the monastery. A senior monk appeared and said we could film only the building. Jone shifted the camera to and fro between the temple and the army, while the monk explained the presence of the troops by saying that other temples had been attacked by insurgents. 'The army is here to protect us,' he said.

A few years earlier in Europe, while driving up a hillside in the Serbian province of Kosovo, we stumbled upon an artillery position of the Yugoslav army. Kosovo's 2 million population was predominantly Albanian Muslims. But, like in Pattani, they were ruled by an elite from a faraway capital and from a different religion – in this case the Christian Serbs from Belgrade. Down below from the Yugoslav guns was an Orthodox monastery where Serb villagers were taking refuge after being driven out of their homes by Albanian activists.

Many of the activists had come to Kosovo from abroad with a vision to start a war that would create a Greater Albania, just as some insurgents in South East Asia had come from Algeria, Afghanistan, Pakistan and elsewhere to create a global pan-Islamic Caliphate.

'The Albanians attack Serbian homes, so the army arrives to protect us,' a Serbian Orthodox priest told me then. 'Now their guns are here. Who knows what will happen?'

On the other side of the world in Pattani, Thai troops and Buddhist monks were living cheek-by-jowl against a restless Muslim population, inspired by war from outside its borders.

Killings were routine. Muslim insurgents attacked police and army checkpoints and patrols. In one, they blew up an armoured car, mowed down soldiers trying to escape, then began beheading the corpses, before reinforcements saw them off. We left the monastery and headed for our final destination, the Krue Se Mosque – or what was left of it – just outside of Pattani. It was a small building, 400 years old, set awkwardly on Highway 42, an arterial road in a residential suburb of the town. The mosque had never been more than a simple place of worship, but it had now become a symbol for South East Asia's Islamic struggle.

The gunfight at the mosque in April 2004 lasted nine hours. The mosque was now a roofless shell and a place of Muslim pilgrimage. More than thirty Muslim activists died in the shoot-out and about a hundred more died in at least ten other gun battles with the Thai security forces that day. It was the moment that a simmering insurgency turned into an all-out local civil war with the population taking sides according to religion and birth.

Muslims from everywhere were coming to the mosque, treading over rubble, inspecting bloodstains on pockmarked walls, staring skywards up through where the roof used to be and sitting quietly in the open in prayer.

'They should talk to the people first,' said a young Islamic scholar called Sharif. Dressed in a simple white ankle-length robe, he had travelled from the Thai island of Phuket. He clasped his hands as he spoke and shook his head from side to side in disbelief at what he was seeing. 'You can talk for one day, two days, five days. Why bomb?' he asked in broken English. 'What is the good in that when Muslim people die and Buddhist people die?'

'There was no jihad before,' said a friend with him. 'But now the government has a problem.'

We crossed through the traffic to a roadside cafe. A group of men sat around a table draped with a blue and white plastic cloth, smoking, their eyes shifting from our camera equipment to the damaged mosque and back again. Two motorcycles were propped up on the pavement outside. A woman in a pink top and black headscarf pulled soft drinks out of a freezer decorated with a Pepsi sticker. She was the teenage daughter of the owner, Abdul Rahman, an ebullient rotund man, who was holding court at the head of the table. His cheeks hollowed as he drew on his cigarette and raised his hand to wave us in. The cafe was half on the pavement and half inside Rahman's house. Curtains were drawn across a back room with the sounds of children and a reprimanding mother coming from inside.

'What happened over there?' I said, pointing toward the mosque.

'The activists had been hiding out there for two days,' he replied, pulling out a chair and insisting we sit down. 'Then, at five in the morning, they went out and started shooting at the police. The police returned fire. After that, the army came and serious fighting began.'

Rahman made a living by running a cafe and found a war landing on his doorstep. 'I felt sad,' he went on. 'They were all Thais. They weren't outsiders. The police could have talked to them. I watched it. They weren't even given a chance to surrender.'

'Is it going to get worse?'

Rahman dropped his cigarette to the concrete floor and put his heel on the butt. 'I have to look out for myself,' he said, his eyes shifting across to his daughter who was stacking the freezer. 'If I tell you everything I feel I will get into trouble, too.'

'They [the Muslim fighters] were wrong to use violence,' said a younger man sitting next to me who said his name was Mohammed. 'But they're not wrong in what they want. Pattani was once a Muslim state and now they want that back again. That is why they fight.'

'There's fighting every day,' said Rahman. 'One or two people are killed every day.'

'Is it war?'

'For the people who are out there fighting, definitely it's a war for them,' said Mohammed.

'Do you agree with them? Do you guys want an Islamic Caliphate?'

'Of course,' said Rahman. 'We are Muslims. We want an Islamic state, but we are powerless to do anything against the government.'

Half an hour later, we checked in to a local hotel and were back in Buddhist, or perhaps more accurately, exotic, sensual and hedonistic Thailand. A delegation was visiting from Bangkok. The garish foyer was filled with clusters of military officers and politicians, a brace of monks, and a swathe of beautiful women who sashayed around with drinks and food. Music wafted in from a bar and a singer pounded out the

Whitney Houston chorus 'I Will Always Love You'. We weaved our way to the lift through an atmosphere of back-slapping and laughter. War had brought them together and this was the winning side – at least for tonight.

The long day, though, was not yet over. It had started at the deserted madrasa in Malaysia and was about to return there. The hotel phone rang while I was in the shower. Dripping wet, and wrapped in just a towel, I answered it. 'Where are you,' Mages said excitedly. 'I've been banging on the door.'

'In the shower,' I replied, my tone tinged with apology.

'Then get dressed, because we're coming to your room.'

She arrived with Jone who had his camera. 'OK, I talked to Din,' she said, sitting on the end of the bed, spotting the confusion on my face. 'The guy from the militant group KMM. OK? He said to meet him at this ridiculously hard to get to place in three months' time. He wanted money. He was saying this and that. And I told him to grow up. This was the BBC. He had his chance to get his message across and he should stop messing around and just talk to you.'

She unfurled her fingers from her cellphone. 'So he's waiting for my call,' she announced triumphantly. 'We can put him on the speaker and Jone can film it.'

'And you know he's for real?' I asked cautiously.

Mages laughed. 'Sure he is. But I'll tell you the whole story afterwards.'

Din didn't quite not mess us around. He would only read from a statement and didn't want us to use his voice, even if we electronically disguised it. He didn't want Jone to film it. I agreed. There was no point doing otherwise. He spoke in slow, heavily accented English. He stumbled and asked if he could start again. He sounded frightened.

'I know this interview is for the BBC,' he said, 'and that people all over the world watch BBC. I want them all to know that the respective governments might have cracked down on us but that does not mean we are scared. We don't care about dying. Our aim is more important. We want to kill the enemies of Islam. We will continue fighting.'

He stopped abruptly and Mages spoke to him in Malay. 'It's all he's prepared,' she said. 'But I'm asking him something else.'

Din's voice was raised and Mages pushed him. The name of the Islamic party PAS was knocked back and forth between the two of them. Then the call suddenly ended. 'He didn't want to give them time to trace it,' she said, closing her phone. 'But I was asking him about PAS. You see Din was trained in a jihad camp in southern Thailand alongside PAS members. But PAS says they are not involved in the violence at all. So that's the question to ask them tomorrow, isn't it?'

'But they'll deny it, surely?'

Mages face broke into a smile. 'Yeah, but watch their damn faces.'

At dawn, we returned to Malaysia. By the time we arrived in Terengganu, the road outside the city mosque was jammed with rows of parked motorcycles. Minibuses pulled up to disgorge families heading for midday prayers. Women with their heads covered in white and light-blue scarves walked in single file between the vehicles. Men squatted against the wall of the mosque. One smoked, staring into a puddle. Another flipped through the pages of a local newspaper. Everyone was waiting for the cleric Dato Seri Haji Abdul Hadi bin Awang.

Not long ago Awang had been the chief minister of Terengganu, in charge of budgets, roads, schools and hospitals for the million people who lived here. But a few months earlier, in the first election since 9/11, PAS had lost control of Terengganu. In fact it didn't just lose, UNMO kicked it out in a landslide. He lost the state election and had returned to his day job of being a preacher.

Awang arrived not in a limousine, but by stepping out from a side building that we later discovered was his office. A queue of men curled around the mosque to greet him. He wore a cream robe, a white cap and huge spectacles. He walked slowly toward the mosque, carrying Islamic books under his left arm and leaving his right hand free. He paused for a moment at each man who bowed slightly, took his hand and brought it to his lips. Then he moved on.

He might have been too much of a revered figure to have ever been an effective politician. There was no way anyone in the crowd would question what he said, let alone throw a rotten egg or shout an insult that challenged him to doubt his own thinking. But then, was there any modern country where a religious leader held the skills to govern well, which was a different thing from simply holding power.

Mages wasn't allowed into the packed mosque. I stood at the back with an air-traffic controller, Zainal Yusuf, whom I'd met on the road outside and who had kindly offered to translate. Even though Yusuf's English was perfect, I found it hard to follow Awang's arguments. Little wonder: The focus of the address was on the Koranic rules of fasting.

Outside, I asked Yusuf if he believed the allegation, made by the insurgent Din, that PAS members had undergone military training as Islamic terrorists. The question both surprised and angered him.

'It's not true,' he said cutting his hands through the air in frustration at the question, his voice pitching higher with each sentence. 'We do not agree with the violence. Islam is a peaceful religion. Even if we lost elections we don't care. We don't burn down the town. We are not extremists. We are not violent people. We are not terrorists.'

Awang's small office was up some outside steps and decorated in green and orange pastel with simple rattan furniture. Malay fruits were laid out on a coffee table for us. I began by asking about the recent election in which PAS representation in the federal parliament fell from 20 to just 6 seats, and he lost the chief minister's job in Terengganu. He accused the government of controlling the media, buying votes and stealing oil revenues. But even against all that, he claimed, PAS had made huge strides in tackling poverty – although the Terengganu fishermen didn't think so.

Given that the government had interfered so much, I asked, did he then believe in the course of violence that some Islamic activists were advocating?

'We follow the teachings of the Koran,' he answered, 'which means we use only peaceful means. We do not accept violence to gain our objective. Anyone who advocates this will be expelled from our party.'

'So you support the causes but you don't agree with their use of violence?'

'The end doesn't justify the means. It's got to be true and done through proper channels.'

'If a member of Jemaah Islamiyah or the Kumpulan Mujahidin Malaysia walked in here today, would you hand them over to the police?'

'Yes. If it's proven that they are creating violence, of course we will tell the police.'

With each question, his eyes became more alive, switching from those of cleric to a politician's on the stump. And I believed him. When I'd asked similar questions of the generals of the Khmer Rouge they wore the dead-eyed expressions of men with too much blood in their memories to care. Awang was like a spirited uncle yearning for a last run around the track.

'What will happen, then, in South East Asia?'

'If democracy is given a real chance, and Islamic groups are given a chance to state their case, then I believe that peace will prevail. But if these governments want to stand and hold fast to their power, then it's going to be a difficult time.'

He stood up and saw us to the door, shaking our hands Western-style. A few steps out, I turned and looked back and saw him through the window adjusting his hat in a huddle with his advisers. He glanced up, met my eyes, waved and smiled.

Mages, Jone and I gathered on the road. It was baking hot. Motorcycles and vans pulled out of their parking spots spewing up dust. Mages wiped her face with her scarf. We were separating here. Jone and I were heading for the Sabah city of Tawau in Borneo. Our final destination was actually the island of Pulau Sebatik which was cut in half by the Malaysia–Indonesian border. Western intelligence agencies had flagged it up as one of the most dangerous places for terror activity in the region, a key trans-shipment point for weapons and people. Before I arrived in Malaysia, Mages had gone to recce it for us and returned saying she hadn't got to the island itself. It was too risky. Nor could she go back to that area at all.

'Is it safe for us to go?' I had asked.

'The guys I spoke to said you shouldn't go,' she had said. 'But, you know, I think you'll be all right.'

As we were heading for Terengganu's small airport, I asked her again. 'Are you sure you're not coming?'

'No way,' she answered. 'Listen, it might not be dangerous for you guys. I don't know. But for me as a Malaysian citizen, they can make my life hell. You just don't know what this government is capable of doing.'

*

Over the past year, I had discussed Pulau Sebatik many times with intelligence experts and the island was on all their radars. I received the most comprehensive briefing from a contact at the Rand Corporation that has close links to the intelligence world. Indeed, when you sign in to visit you have to specify whether the purpose is classified or non-classified. I can't name my contact, but I asked if there was a place that America regarded as being crucial in Indonesia or South East Asia. From a military perspective, he said, it was Pulau Sebatik. He laid out a map on his desk and pointed to a tooth-shaped island jutting out from a jaw in the Borneo coastline. 'Right here is a free operating zone for Islamic terror,' he said. 'They have thousands of weapons hidden. They can move freely. They use established smuggling routes to export terror.'

'Who are they?' I asked.

'Jemaah Islamiyah. They carried out the Bali bombing. They feed from the Muslim groups in the Philippines, particularly Abu Sayef. They have a branch in Malaysia. They are allied to al-Qaeda and are importing weapons and fighters into southern Thailand.'

I laid my hand over the island. 'And this place is the key?'

'If we got back control of this, their job would be a lot harder.'

The day after leaving Terengganu, I was in a speedboat with Jone zipping across the water towards Pulau Sebatik and, already, I was sensing that things weren't quite as they seemed from Washington.

For a start, we hired the speedboat with a young English-speaking tourist guide. When we said we wanted to go to Pulau Sebatik, they didn't bat an eyelid. On the way out our guide, the enthusiastic Abbas bin Lahiyah, referred to the smuggling routes and terror threats rather like a raconteur tells you about Jack the Ripper on a walk through London's East End. The excitement was good for business. We sped past dozens of fishing boats and small craft flying flags from Malaysia, Indonesia, Thailand and the Philippines, all of whom Abbas said would criss-cross the borders without checks. This was the route used by the Moro smugglers whom I had met all those years earlier taking their contraband between Malaysia and the Philippines.

It was early morning and the sun had yet to burn off the haze. Once clear of the cluster of boats, the helmsman opened the throttle even more, splashing us with cold salt spray.

'He wants to get there before the ferry,' said Abbas, pointing to the boat ahead of us. 'Or we may not be able to dock.'

We roared past the ferry from where the handful of passengers waved at us. The coastline appeared in a blur and within minutes we were hugging thick green mangrove swamps that led into rainforest covering most of the island. Abbas said if we wanted to stay longer we could camp out and see the gibbons. 'They like seafood,' he laughed. 'If you're lucky you'll see them come down to eat the crabs.'

I hadn't known exactly what to expect on the island. I wouldn't have been surprised to find a sandbagged gun emplacement, a police station or even a village deserted out of fear of terror raids. Instead, our boat pulled up at a neat little jetty where we jumped out, unloaded the gear and let the boatman push clear to make way for the ferry.

Ahead was a decked wooden walkway, flanked by single-storeyed clapboard homes built on stilts sunk into the seabed. Flower baskets decorated verandahs. The walkway gave way to a dirt road that rose up a slope. On the right were a clinic and a school with a soccer pitch outside. On the left, were more houses, their gardens alive with tropical flowers. Two children sped past us on mountain bikes. A mother carrying a child walked down to the ferry. We stopped by an elderly woman in a bright yellow dress busy watering her garden and asked if she knew where the village headman lived. She pointed to the house two doors up.

'You can't miss it,' she said, with Abbas translating, and she was right. Pinned up on the wall next to the front door was a poster of the Malaysian prime minister, Abdullah Badawi. The Malaysian flag, albeit tattered and sun-faded, hung limply from a pole on the roof. The headman's name was K. K. Abdullah, an UMNO Party loyalist who turned out to be a living example of how a mix of Badawi's hard-driving Islam and good intelligence operated on far-flung frontiers. We hadn't told anyone we were coming, but K. K. Abdullah was expecting us, with fruit, biscuits and tea waiting on a coffee table in his living room.

He was courteous, but perplexed as to why we were interested in his village. With the first few questions, we got into a bit of tangle until it emerged that the English fluency of our guide, Abbas, was confined to exotic stories about the island-hopping smuggling routes. Abdullah's brow furrowed. His message was serious. He needed to get it right. He suggested we ask the village schoolteacher to come and translate. In any case, he would prefer it if we interviewed him, not in his house, but outside against the backdrop of his village. Outside, we made broken-English and Malay small talk about the flower gardens, rain-forest and crab-eating gibbons while waiting for the teacher.

Sunaiman Marlan appeared walking across the soccer pitch, a small, thoughtful figure, in a black fez cap and a light brown shirt, ink on his fingers and his top pocket lined with cheap ballpoint pens. In the distance, his pupils, in white and dark uniforms, peered out from behind the school fence.

'What is it you would like to discuss?' Marlan asked.

'I'd like to know if you have a problem with terrorists,' I said. While Marlan spoke, Abdullah began shaking his head.

'No problem at all,' translated Marlan, 'because we have complete cooperation with Indonesia. We all work together. If there was a hint of anything happening, both our countries would fight these people from Jemaah Islamiyah. So we feel very secure.'

'Do you think anybody in your village supports Jemaah Islamiyah, or the idea of an Islamic Caliphate?'

They both shook their heads. 'I don't think so,' said Marlan. Abdullah put his hand on Marlan's elbow and explained more. 'Yes. That's right,' said Marlan. 'He talks to people here all the time. To the young and to their parents to make sure they have everything they want. We are very happy in our island village. We feel very safe here.'

Abdullah explained that the border itself was about fifteen miles away, deep in the jungle. It was unmarked and there was nothing there except rainforest. We didn't go there. If the finest electronic and human intelligence techniques couldn't crack the threat on Pulau Sebatik, then I doubted that Jone, Abbas, Marlan, Abdullah and I would make headway either.

The terror threat on Pulau Sebatik was not much different from anywhere else in the world – a largely uninhabited area where it was easy to hide things. But if the villagers were vulnerable to the al-Qaeda cause, or subjected to a repressive dictatorship, there would have been a very different atmosphere. There might be no regular ferry. The electricity would probably be intermittent. The road would be washed out with potholes. The clinic would not have medicines. There may be no school or certainly not one with a teacher as assiduous as Marlan. The police or the army would also have been there in some form. The flower baskets and gardens of individual homes, I suspect, would not have been so carefully tended, and Jemaah Islamiyah with their cries of the

Caliphate might have found an ear among the small population here.

The long-established US think tank Freedom House, set up in the 1950s, defines freedom as the opportunity to act spontaneously in a variety of fields outside the control of the government and other centres of potential domination. It also specifies two categories of rights. Political rights involve participation in the electoral process, including voting, competing for office, joining political parties and so on. Civil rights concentrate on the freedoms of expression and belief, associational and organizational rights, rule of law, and personal autonomy without interference from the state.

In the four countries I was visiting on this South East Asian journey, Indonesia and the Philippines ranked highest for political rights, but also posed the biggest threat in the War on Terror. Both were being exploited by democratic openness. Malaysia and Singapore on the other hand, had internal security laws on their statute books written by British colonizers, which meant that suspects could be locked up indefinitely without charges – Guantánamo Bay-style.

In many conversations in the developing world, it is the civil liberties that people found sacrosanct – a passport, a bank account, a school, a house. Political rights were often in a faraway second place.

Pulau Sebatik was a remote microcosm of this thinking. Its future lay with Malaysia's ruling UMNO party. You wouldn't want to cross it, but then it delivered basic freedoms, such as the ferry service, and it kept you safe.

The next morning we flew to Jone's home, Singapore, and possibly the most precise example anywhere of successful constitutional liberalism – or, if you took another view, oppressive authoritarianism. The citizens had little or no political freedom, but their opportunities to become rich, educated and well travelled were enormous.

I had two appointments there. One was with the US Ambassador Frank Lavin, a political appointee and a close friend of George W. Bush and his political adviser Karl Rove. The other was with the Singaporean National Security minister, Dr Tony Tan, whose job was to detect and stop any terror attack on Singapore.

Lavin was bristling. He was in his late forties, confident, plain-spoken, but surprisingly defensive as we talked in the US embassy conference room with a draped American flag as his backdrop. We found ourselves debating America's democratic paradox. Singapore was as fine an ally as the United States could want, whether it was battling terror, communism or drugs. Yet its success was as far removed as you could get from the democratic model America was trying to install around the world.

Created by the British colonizer Sir Stamford Raffles in the early nineteenth century, Singapore is an island city-state on the southern tip of the Malay peninsula. It won its independence from Britain as part of Malaysia, but the tension between the Malay and Chinese populations was so great that Singapore broke away in 1965 and became an independent nation. Its population is less than 5 million in an area of just 273 square miles.

Britain bequeathed it a system of parliamentary democracy, and, to keep dissent at bay, a skilfully written internal security legislation. The result was a political culture with parliament, courts, newspapers and elections, but all of it controlled by the government under the umbrella of the People's Action Party (PAP) that had never been voted out of office.

Singapore's pro-Western stability suited America well. The island sat on the Malacca Straits, the narrow stretch of water that runs between Indonesia and Malaysia, through which up to 80 per cent of Japan's oil is transported. During the Cold War, it was described as a choke-point. War-planners imagined scenarios in which just three or four Soviet submarines deployed around the Malacca Straits could paralyse world trade. Now, they were devising war games in which Malaysia and Indonesia fell to extreme Islam, Singapore was taken over and the choke-points were blocked.

Its critics describe Singapore as a one-party state but it is constantly rated as one of the world's ten least corrupt countries. When, in 1975 as a teenage backpacker, I crossed from Malaysia to Singapore, I was hauled in at the border to have my hair cut because it touched the top of my ears and the edge of my collar. Such rigid discipline, like the ban on chewing gum, walking naked in your own home, masturbation and others, became legendary.

But the thinking was far more sophisticated. Singapore had set out to show that repression of individual freedom created wider benefits for the community as a whole, emphasizing a political system and way of life that long before 9/11 began to challenge the Western view of human rights and individual liberty. The mantle of this argument has now been taken over by China.

Lavin had recently challenged the Singaporean government to ease political restrictions, warning that Singapore would 'pay an increasing price for not allowing full participation of its citizens'. At the same time, though, he was praising the island-state for being as good as it gets when keeping people safe from terror attacks.

'Why when you have a proven model of authoritarianism that works in Singapore and Malaysia,' I asked, 'do you think Western-style democracy will create stability in the Middle East and the developing world?'

'It might be troubling for the BBC,' he said, crossing his legs and holding my gaze, 'but the current administration has said that the problem in the Middle East is a lack of democracy – that is open media, people allowed to express themselves, open role for women, universities which allow people to discuss ideas. When none of that exists and everything's bolted down, people are pushed towards radicalism. They know that their system doesn't work. It is dysfunctional and they're prone towards one of these violent organizations.'

'But this sudden idea of democracy,' I queried. 'Will it work?'

He shifted in his seat. 'The approach to terrorism has to be multi-faceted,' he argued. 'You're not going to simply win it on the police and military side of things. Elections don't necessarily solve your problems, but they give you a process to solve your problems.'

'Have we learned anything from South East Asia?' I asked.

'Yes, we're winning,' said Lavin. 'The terrorists are much worse off in South East Asia now than they were three years ago. Radical Islam has been rejected. It seems that most people have the same concerns as people in the West. They want a growing economy, education for their kids and they did not tilt toward the radical Islamic parties.'

'What about this aspiration for a Caliphate?' I asked.

'It's not a realistic aim. It's endemic in an extremist group to have extraordinarily ambitious goals – whether you are a communist, a Nazi or an Islamic terrorist you are going to state some incredible goal that is going to transform mankind. It's a rallying cry and the adherents tend to be reasonably uneducated teenage males. So the point is, you are not going to seduce that group of people into violence by promising a better health care system.'

The foyer of Singapore's Ministry of National Security and Defence was decorated with posters of helicopter raids and special forces' gunfights that on closer inspection made me do a double-take. The images came across as being far more threatening than, say, similar military murals from Iraq, Vietnam or even Europe in the Second World War. Set against Singapore's aura of wealth was an HSBC logo on a skyscraper, spelling out exactly what was at stake and what, indeed, Singapore was protecting. There was nothing opaque about it at all. HSBC must be able to set up shop and feel safe. From all that, trade, wealth and freedom will flow.

The minister, Dr Tony Tan, his grey hair swept back and wearing large, thick, brown spectacles, had lived through much of Singapore's modern history. He had played a major part in its transformation from an impoverished Asian fishing town to an international trading centre. I wanted to know what impact he thought Islamic extremism was having on Singapore. Fifteen per cent of the population was Muslim, and seemingly integrated into Singapore's moneymaking, forward-looking society. Dr Tan, however, was worried.

'It's no good denying that there's been an impact,' he said. 'More Muslims are now adopting a strict form of dress for women. Parents are insisting that their daughters wear the headscarf and some are pulling their daughters out of school because they're not allowed to wear it. Dietary habits are changing, too. In the past, Muslims had a relaxed attitude and would sit and share a meal. Now, some are becoming very strict and they will not sit down at a table where liquor is served.'

'And that's something you can't control?' I asked. 'Like chewing gum?'

He laughed and shook his head. 'No. We keep an eye it. But we cannot speak for Islam. It is up to the moderate Muslims to argue that their interpretation is the correct one. This is why Malaysia and Indonesia are so important to us. Muslims have to show that Islam is not a barrier to progress, that you can be Islamic; you can make progress; you can be a modern country; you can uplift the standard of living of your people; you can increase trade; you can interact with other countries; you can still be a good Muslim; and that you must not give up hope.

'The final battle must be between these two groups to see who succeeds in meeting the soul of the Muslim population. In Singapore, we are 75 per cent Chinese, but we are surrounded by Muslim nations and 15 per cent of our own population is Muslim. It is very important that we make each group feel they are part of Singaporean society and that they have equal opportunities as everyone else.'

'But is your system of government designed to achieve that? You wouldn't describe it as a freewheeling democracy, would you?'

'We are a democracy, but we are not as loud a democracy as the United States or Britain.'

'You mean, you tend to nip things in the bud?'

'We have rules. There are regulations. We have to maintain this multi-racial harmony. We are a delicate, fragile society. We have seen how emotions can be inflamed. You can't have everyone shouting and creating chaos. Everybody has to have limits.'

I had heard the argument about moderate and extreme Islam many times, and about the limitations of full democracy. But somehow, here in Singapore, coming from a Chinese politician whose city-state was surrounded by Muslim countries, it was more salient. An Islamic insurgency was raging in Thailand. Militants were grouping in Malaysia, and just a few miles away Indonesia, the world's biggest Muslim country, was smarting from numerous bomb attacks. Singapore's population was less than 5 million. Malaysia had 25 million. Indonesia was vast – 240 million people sprawled over thousands of islands.

After seeing Tan, we headed to Indonesia for a meeting with none other than the Justice Party that was still calling for Islam to be central to Indonesia's public life and rule-of-law. We didn't fly to Jakarta, but took a ferry across a narrow stretch of water from Singapore to the rather bizarre Indonesian island of Batam.

Standing on a windswept deck, crossing the frenzied commercial waterway between Singapore and Indonesia, the contradictions, warnings and dreams gathered during that visit a year earlier seemed far longer ago.

Indonesians had elected as their president a military general, Susilo Bambang Yudhoyono, who had reinforced his reputation in his handling of the Bali bombings. The matronly Megawati had been thrown out and she conceded grudgingly, but without violence. Indonesians must have wanted to move on. They didn't want a leader symbolizing a bygone age, but a man who had muscle enough to guide them forward.

The US ambassador Ralph Boyce's caution over a hypothetical Islamic landslide had proved right. The Justice Party leader, Wahid, had never stood for the presidency. His fledgling movement, though, had done well in the parliamentary elections and won more than 7 per cent of the popular vote. Wahid's reward was to become the equivalent of parliamentary speaker, meaning that he had to step down as party leader. Power was balanced between Yudhoyono and Megawati's parties with other smaller parties, many with Islamic elements, holding substantial influence.

Batam was only an hour away from Singapore and couldn't have been more different. It was a whacky carnival of cranes and construction sites, of tourist buses driving along dirt roads to just-finished golf clubs and spas. It reeked of new money, flutters of investment from the Asian boom. It was an architect's paradise of weird, experimental buildings put up without haggling over planning permission. If there was a message of Indonesian identification in them it certainly wasn't anything close to a medieval caliphate. Even the mosque was unique. Shaped with layered terraces, set back in gardens with fountains and lush lawns, it looked like a cross between a pyramid and a pink birthday cake.

Our meeting was with H. Haris Hardy Halim, a member of parliament for Batam's branch of the Justice Party. We found him at the local legislature, itself a brand-new building. He was even more secular in looks than his party leader. He had short-cropped hair, no beard at all and wore an open-necked blue shirt and a dark suit. He reminded me of a more mature and weathered version of Rusdiantó from Bandung – dull, but loyal. We sat on the steps in the sun, and Halim told how the Justice Party had come second in regional voting.

'So who did you support for the presidency?' I asked.

'The election was about people's needs,' he said. 'So we put aside our personal interests and told our supporters to vote for a leader who would fulfil those needs.'

'And who was that?'

'Yudhoyono – the man who became president.'

Indonesia's was one of three key elections held in South East Asia in 2004, and each delivered similar results. In March of that year Abdullah Badawi won in Malaysia. In May, voters in the Philippines chose Gloria Macapagal-Arroyo, an economist. And in September, Indonesia opted for a military general with Yudhoyono.

The journey around Thailand, Malaysia, Singapore and

Indonesia reinforced my view that these countries had already shown paths ahead for the developing world, and were now doing the same in the crisis over Islam. The region was also a place that tipped slightly in favour of holding elections than not. Unlike in Latin America and the Middle East, elections in South East Asia were not delivering governments that posed a threat to the West. Far from it, they were giving a democratic voice to Islamic parties, thus preventing terror. The voters did not want that Islamic voice to prevail over the ones that were giving them an increasingly higher standard of living.

But stopping rebellion was not the same as turning a developing society into a wealthy one. Singapore had succeeded, so had Malaysia to a certain extent. But these were essentially authoritarian states. Poverty in the Philippines and Indonesia, identified as the two most democratic societies, remained a key challenge.

Yet somehow between them these South East Asian nations could lead to an axis where three opposing problems might actually be resolved: the creation of full democratic freedoms, the alleviation of poverty and the realization of Islamic aspirations – all achieved without violence.

Indonesia was the prize. If it could meet those three challenges, then there was no excuse for any other nation, Islamic or not, to fail. But it seemed to me that Malaysia, though smaller, might hold crucial answers and I went there to talk to two key players in the democratic debate. One was tipped to be a future prime minister and one was seen as the founding father of the modern nation.

Oxford-educated Khairy Jamaluddin had just turned thirty and was son-in-law to the then prime minister, Badawi. He was a member of parliament and a key figure in the ruling party's youth wing. Over the next generation, he would be close to power in Malaysia and probably become a leading voice in the developing world. We met just outside Kuala Lumpur in Malaysia's opulent and futuristic administrative capital city of Putrajaya.

'Could you imagine a time,' I began, 'when Malaysia would have two roughly equal political parties competing in a knife-edge election. In other words, would it be dangerous to move from a one-party to a two-party state?'

'It depends on the terms of the debate,' he answered. 'If the debate was based on ethnicity or religion then it could be dangerous. But if it were based on issues like corruption, development, poverty, it could happen. Unfortunately, if you look at the opposition party (PAS), they've defined the terms of the debate on radical religious terms that could be dangerous.'

'So you're arguing that you have to keep the lid on things in order to keep the peace?'

'I think in ethnically diverse and very complex societies with historical baggage and enmity there is a need for the government to legislate laws which actually keep the peace.'

'Do elections then help or hinder development?'

'It's a question of sequencing,' he said. 'Elections are the fundamental basis for democracy. But if the population has not been adequately educated and if strong institutions have not been put in place, the elections can throw up unexpected results that do not help development. What is truly needed in these countries, these failed states, where you're trying to re-create a credible administration, is good governance. Good governance overall is the panacea to the problems in these countries, and good governance is not just about elections. It's about a sound education system. It's about institutions of governance that are far above elections themselves. It's about poverty eradication, education, infrastructure and uprooting extremism.'

We were sitting in the morning sun on a hotel cafe terrace looking down on deep green jungle mixed with the modern architecture of Putrajaya. As we finished, Jamaluddin said, 'So you're off to see the big man now, are you?' He was talking about the former prime minister, Mahathir bin Mohamad. 'What are you going to ask him?'

'Your interview was about the future,' I said. 'I'm going to ask him what should have been done at the beginning.'

Mahatir, now in his eighties and recovering from a second heart-bypass operation, was a divisive figure. He locked up political opponents. His key rival, Anwar Ibrahim, was beaten in jail on trumped-up charges of homosexuality, which was still illegal in Malaysia. He muzzled the press, bullied judges, and was filled with venom for Western human rights activists. In the 1990s, when accused of taking a £50,000 bribe from a British construction company, he asked whether people thought he would be so cheap. When questioned about the intention of PAS to bring sharia law into Malaysia's eastern states, he said he wouldn't allow it for economic reasons. If you cut off people's hands they couldn't work and their health care costs would be too expensive. When challenged by a British human rights campaigner that Malaysian development was ruining the way of life of remote tribes in Borneo, Mahatir said he presumed then that the campaigner would like to be living in a cave. The campaigner was momentarily flummoxed, until Mahatir challenged him about the English way of life before the Roman invasion.

Mahatir was much frailer than when I had last seen him some ten years earlier. We met in his think tank, the equivalent of a US presidential library, and he was helped to his chair by an assistant.

'What would have happened,' I asked him, 'if Malaysia had

practised Western-style democracy straight after independence?'

'We would have seen racial fights all the time and destabilization. The whole country would not have been able to grow and people would have felt unsafe. Stability is the most important thing because without it you cannot develop a country.'

'But you were criticized by Western democracies for being too oppressive?'

'Well, what we did was nothing compared to what is being done in other countries today. By and large people accepted it because time and time again they voted us in knowing full well that we exercised this authority.'

'If you were looking at your general way of governing, you have America on one hand and China on the other. Where would you be on that spectrum?'

'Maybe in the middle between the two extremes,' he answered. 'It's always better to be moderate.'

'But what does the Chinese style of government have in common with your style?'

'One has to remember that China is a big country, 1.3 billion people, speaking very different languages. To govern such a country is not easy. You would think that the majority would know what is best for them but the majority is often influenced by ethnicity and ideologies and all that, so they are dealing with a very special situation and this idea that democracy will solve all problems is a lot of nonsense.'

'When you were prime minister, in repressing rights, did you go too far?'

He smiled and didn't answer exactly. 'You have to take heed. You have to be fair. You have to explain that it is necessary. But it must really be a necessity. Sometimes of course you are very suppressive of any opposition.'

'And the politicians in London or Washington – do they

have any idea of how to work in the developing world?'

'None at all,' he said with his anger visibly rising. 'They have achieved nothing. They have worsened the situation. More people who would have been alive today are dead now because of their very shallow understanding of the situation. They don't understand anything. Democracy is good, but in order to achieve it you shouldn't go around killing people. This is what is happening today. You are forced to accept one system – democracy – and if you don't accept it you say I'll bomb your country and kill your people.'

'Are they learning?'

'They must be very dense if they don't learn that.'

Far away in a small European country still recovering from war, they were learning pretty much what Mahathir was preaching about – how to curb the risk of racial violence and bring communities to peace so that good governance can be established. Except, to avoid the sensitivities of democratic ideologues, it wasn't dressed up like that.

EUROPE

BOSNIA – Democracy's Trial

He let the rain run down his face as we watched a bus pull up at the cemetery gate. Schoolchildren piled out and gathered under the covered meeting area for a lesson on the massacre that was commemorated there. He turned and stared across the rows of headstones.

Želko Vidovic's eyes were colourless, seemingly without life. His concentration span lasted only a few seconds. His expression changed constantly and seemed to totter on the brink of a furious outburst. Fifteen years ago, his political leaders were telling him that he was fighting to create a Greater Serbia, which would rebuild the former glory of his nation. It was catastrophic nonsense, of course. Yet it had been a heart-felt motivation by millions of people and persuaded them to go to war against their neighbours, spill blood and sacrifice homes and families.

Now, in early summer of 2008, Vidovic was the police chief of a small town called Srebrenica in eastern Bosnia and Herzegovina where in July 1995 some 8,000 people were killed in the worst atrocity in Europe since the Second World War.

The murderers were Serb militia. The victims were Bosnian Muslims. Both communities lived there, and Vidovic was showing us around a memorial that lay at the bottom of a wooded hill just outside the town. White headstones of simple Islamic design stretched back through summer grass from an open-air meeting area near the main gate that doubled as a mosque – with kneeling places facing Mecca. It was an unfussy structure where the townsfolk and their loved ones could come to grieve, remember and try to relieve the trauma. Today schoolchildren were there being taught their country's modern history.

The Srebrenica massacre was the turning point of the Bosnian war that had been raging since 1992 as Yugoslavia disintegrated. The Bosnian capital Sarajevo had been under siege and divided street by street between Muslim and Serb areas. In other parts of this small country of about 4 million people, the Croatian and Muslim communities fought each other. In some towns members of one besieged community would hunker down for months on end in pockets of just a street or two.

The view from the hills overlooking many Bosnian cities is one of church towers, mosque minarets and a fair number of cemeteries. Some moments you can hear the call to prayer mingle with the ringing of church bells because for centuries the country had been a melting pot and frontier between the Islamic East and Christian Europe.

In the early 1990s, it was as if an African tribal feud or the Israeli–Palestinian issues had been parachuted into modern Europe, tearing apart societies that were not short of food, shelter, money or basic freedoms.

The causes might by now sound familiar. A cohesive author-itarian government collapsed, and ethnic violence filled the vacuum. The direct cause of the Srebrenica massacre might also sound familiar. Western institutions, particularly the European Union, malfunctioned and failed to intervene in time. From early 1992 to late 1995, snipers killed children; militia raped women; men of fighting age were put in con-centration camps and starved and killed; villages were burnt; towns besieged; roads blockaded; and Western leaders negotiated with those carrying out the atrocities, as if there were an acceptable limit to murder that had yet to be reached.

The solution, and again we are on known territory, came from the White House. America intervened to stop the killing in a faraway land. Within six months of the Srebrenica massacre, the United States had pushed through a peace formula that was negotiated and signed not in Paris, London or Rome, but in Dayton, Ohio.

When I visited Srebrenica there had been more than thirteen years of imposed peace in the country, underwritten by the United Nations, the European Union and an international military force. The aim was to retain the state of Bosnia and Herzegovina and mould it into a modern democracy. The first step was to stop the violence. The second was to build institutions. So Bosnia's sovereign power was forfeited to an international administration. Underneath that structure, Bosnians were encouraged to practise democracy and test their hand at good governance.

But because each faction demanded a voice, the upshot of the 1995 Bosnian peace agreement was that the 4 million population would be represented by five presidents, four vice-presidents, fourteen separate cantons each with a government and parliament, and each raising different levels of taxation with conflicting sets of rules. There were also two larger areas known as entities. One was Bosnia Herzegovina and the other was Republika Srpska, which took in Srebrenica where we were now.

There was also constant speculation that the Serb community, unbowed by the stigma attached to its murderous militia, still wanted to separate off from Bosnia, either to form yet another small independent nation or merge with Serbia and be governed from Belgrade.

The last person I had expected as my guide to this memorial to murdered Bosnians was a Serb, although when I asked Vidovic how he felt being here, he made clear he had not been in the town at the time. 'I was fighting another army in another part of the country,' he said.

'But you supported the cause?'

'Of course I did,' he said softly, his eyes darting off to the hillside. 'Each side did and we have to say the war has left scars in our souls.'

'There is talk again of Bosnia breaking up,' I said, 'and the Bosnian Serbs breaking away to join Serbia proper.'

'I'm not entitled to give my private opinion,' he answered. He gaze fell on me for a second, then to the ground. 'But, of course, the official stand is that we now have to live and work together to join the European Union, so there is nothing else we can do, we have to cooperate.'

'But can you, after all the killing?'

'Yes. We must.'

While the Serbian Vidovic ran the police force in Srebrenica, the deputy mayor was a Muslim, whose father had been killed in the massacre. We arranged to meet them both later to see how these two communities, so recently at war with each other, were now working together on relatively mundane issues such as traffic regulation, petty crime and town planning.

Their partnership was part of the dogged detail set out in the American peace plan that was, in fact, an incredible social experiment on how to turn an ethnically bloodied war zone into a thriving modern democratic society. It was a foreign policy extension of the American Dream.

The concept was far from new. America had used it in post-Second World War Europe and in East Asia with great success, and my meeting with the Muslim deputy mayor and Serb police chief showed exactly how the smallest issues can blot the big picture and prevent anyone moving forward.

Deputy mayor Ramo Dautbasic, his hair cropped to the skull, his eyes squinting in the sunlight, strode purposefully down the town hall steps to greet me. He wanted to show me his plans to bring tourists to Srebrenica. He shook my hand and pointed to a gutted building next door, still charred and pockmarked with bullets and shrapnel from the war. 'We are turning all this into a luxury hotel,' he said proudly, pointing to scrubland behind. 'And here we'll have the car park for tour buses.'

Up in his offices, adorned with scruffy old government furniture, he told how his father had been killed by the Serbs, and he himself spent six days running and hiding in wooded hillsides to guide other members of his family to safety. He produced a photograph of an elderly man with shining blue eyes and a kind, weathered face. He laid it on top of a pile of administrative documents from which he brought out a sheet of paper.

'You should look at this before Vidovic comes,' he said. 'The police are constantly holding up projects crucial to the city. See here, the Turkish government gave us two brand-new ambulances. But Vidovic has only agreed to register one. Why? The other is sitting idle while the sick go without transport.'

He flipped through his pile of papers and drew out another document. 'And see this one . . .' he began, when, suddenly, without a knock, the door opened and in strode Vidovic, giving us each a handshake, his eyes skipping around the office, absorbing what was there.

He wore the same light-blue police uniform as in the cemetery, but the way he came into the room, or that he was simply there at all, changed the atmosphere completely.

'We must show this television crew that we're working

together,' Vidovic barked, with my interpreter, Rialda, whispering the translation into my ear.

'But it's a lie,' retorted Dautbasic. 'Because we don't.'

'We must,' said Vidovic, sitting down heavily in an armchair across the coffee table from Dautbasic. He was physically smaller than the deputy mayor. But he exuded power, while Dautbasic, in his dark crumpled jacket, the old photograph of his murdered father in front of him, showed a mix of surprise and anger.

The tension in the room became edgy and suffocating. Dautbasic verbally laid into Vidovic with a string of complaints starting with an accusation that three years ago Serb extremists tried to blow up the memorial built for victims of the massacre.

'You found explosives,' he said. 'But why have you closed the investigation when no one's been arrested? Are you covering up a war crime?'

Vidovic shook his head. 'We only have normal crimes in Srebrenica,' he countered. 'There are no ethnic crimes and we're working closely together on it.'

'That's rubbish. The explosives were found near the memorial just before a ceremony for Muslims.'

'Is that right?' I asked Vidovic.

'Yes. But we haven't found who was responsible.'

'Because you haven't looked for them,' snapped Dautbasic, bringing back out the ambulance documents. 'And why don't you register this ambulance?'

'We've sent in the papers . . .'

'That's a lie. I checked.'

Vidovic shrugged and said nothing. Dautbasic turned to me. 'This man is the chief of police. Turkey gives us two ambulances and we ask for them to be registered. This is strictly a police job. But he only registers one. Not two.'

'You're talking rubbish,' muttered Vidovic. 'I have to send the papers to my ministry.'

The sharp exchange went on, until I interrupted. 'Hold on! I just want to be clear about something. How often do you two guys actually meet, because you're meant to be running the town together . . . aren't you?'

Vidovic said nothing. He stared ahead as he had done in the cemetery. Dautbasic's face switched from fury to sheepishness. 'This is the first time,' he said.

'All right, then,' I continued. 'What can you each do to make the other's job easier?'

'He needs to implement the decisions of the city council,' said Dautbasic, jabbing his finger across the table. 'And he doesn't.'

'We do our best,' Vidovic shrugged.

'Maybe we should meet more often,' continued Dautbasic.

'Maybe we should,' retorted the Serb police chief, getting up to leave.

'He is really angry,' whispered Rialda. 'I will have to follow him out and explain.'

Vidovic began shaking hands with us, Rialda, then Simon Smith, who was filming, then myself. He was about to leave, hesitated, turned and held his hand out to Dautbasic. The Muslim deputy mayor did not respond. He kept his eyes locked on the documents and the picture of his father.

For a few unpredictable seconds, no one spoke. Then Dautbasic looked up and took the police chief's hand, his expression reflecting the huge and complex personal decision that he had just taken – one that is being replicated time and time again throughout Bosnia, Europe, the Middle East, Africa and elsewhere as societies painfully opt to patch up their differences and try, as difficult as it might be, to move on.

Srebrenica came to symbolize Europe's shame. This small rural community had been promised it would be a United Nations safe haven from civil war atrocities, and that promise was broken. Yet Bosnia went on to be a key player in the search for that elusive philosopher's stone of how to make a failed state become stable, peaceful and viable. I am convinced the Bosnian story will end up addressing the main challenges facing the West's global democratic mission.

Dautbasic and Vidovic were not role models in municipal efficiency, and shortly after that they both moved to new jobs. But at least they were not killing each other and by shaking hands they accepted that it was up to them to make things work.

Bosnia was one of the six new nations that tried to peel away from Yugoslavia at the end of the Cold War. The Yugoslav nation had been held together by the strongman Josip Tito, who not only managed to balance his historically feuding subjects, but also kept his country at arm's length from Moscow, giving people more freedoms and a higher standard of living than most in Eastern Europe.

But once its umbrella administration began to unwind, the Yugoslav identity became superseded by ethnic ones, where people trusted their own tribes and families rather than the state. Many interpreted the onset of full democracy as a land grab with an opportunity to settle grievances dating back centuries.

The American-sponsored peace plan imposed on Bosnia an authority higher than any national sovereignty being claimed by any of the groups. It was headed by an internationally appointed public servant known as the High Representative who held enormous powers to sack ministers or deploy military force to trouble spots. This is a process that will only work if the general population is compliant. If it is not, there will be civil war or insurgency against the foreign troops and often both.

The communities in Bosnia, although tired of war, might well have kept fighting for generations, as has happened between Israelis and Palestinians or Tamils and Sinhalese in Sri Lanka. But they were given an option. They had to put their trust in institutions made up no longer of themselves, but of officials from the international community. Despite reservations, they did have an overarching trust in the High Representative and his administration.

Under his guidance, Bosnians were being trained to run their own democratic institutions that would raise taxes, police communities and elect leaders without corruption and violence. It was a slow process – Vidovic and Dautbasic were barely able to work together on the basic issues of running a civil society.

Bosnia's ethnic fighting ended in 1995 and it is estimated that it will not be fully self-governing until about 2015 or 2020. That would have allowed up to twenty-five years for institution building. But even time alone might not have worked indefinitely. Muslims, Croats, Serbs and others in Bosnia needed a shared purpose, a reason to sort out their differences, rather than pick up a rifle and kill a child.

That goal, being sold hard to them every day, was that if they stayed the course they could become European Union citizens with all the benefits that go with it. And they bought it.

Here lies the irony. During the civil war, the different communities in Bosnia fought in order to protect what they had defined as their national and ethnic sovereignty. They then agreed to surrender that sovereignty to international powers. The upshot was that Bosnia would move seamlessly from being under the control of the High Representative to being accountable to the European Union. Its power would never be absolute. But then nor was it for any of the European Union members, including the big-hitters such as Britain, France and Germany.

During my 2008 visit, the job of High Representative was being done by a forty-five-year-old Slovakian diplomat, Miroslav Lajčák. Internationally educated, fluent in several languages, Lajčák was a child of post-Cold War nation-building. Czechoslovakia, the country into which he had been born, was itself dissolved in 1993 into the Czech Republic and Slovakia, but without violence. He knew exactly what his role was and what Bosnia needed to achieve.

'I am here to build state institutions,' he told me, 'to make the country politically stable and economically viable and embark upon the European journey.'

'But you have the powers of a colonial governor,' I probed. 'You can fire the prime minister. You can call in the army.'

'I like to describe my powers as that of a football referee with a yellow and red card. Everybody knows it is here. Everybody knows I can use it. Everybody knows I will use it, and I do use it whenever necessary. But the best game is the one when the referee doesn't have to use it too often.'

'What about building those institutions, then?' I asked. 'To what extent have you got rid of the type of nationalism that leads to ethnic cleansing?'

'The most difficult challenge we have is the psychological and mental challenge of getting people to understand the role of the state, to agree on priorities that basically put European integration and EU membership on the top of all agendas.'

'Would it be possible to rebuild Bosnia if there was no goal of European Union membership?' I asked.

'There must be a vision, and the only possible vision for Bosnia is the European Union.'

'So you need that beacon.'

'Yes,' he said. 'You do.'

When George W. Bush was selling the Iraq invasion, he had used the same idea, talking about creating a 'beacon of democracy' in the Middle East. But while Iraq had no role model within its own backyard, Bosnia did. Democratic, wealthy Europe was not only all around it, but its public servants were in the country showing how a society could be run for the benefit of its people.

'The Bosnian politicians need to change their mindset and move away from the nationalistic and ethnic card,' said Lajčák. 'They must stop saying "Vote for me and I will protect you from them." They need to talk more about jobs, the economy and social issues.'

'So right now if there was no beacon?'

'If we didn't have this beacon, it would be very difficult and the negative tendencies that lead to ethnic cleansing would become more visible.'

Before the Second World War, Europe had been a constant battleground of warring states. The peace treaty brokered by the European nations after the First World War was seen by many as being so vindictive towards Germany that it was partially blamed for giving rise to Hitler just twenty years later. Yet the American-brokered peace after the Second World War in 1945 led to the immense prosperity and stability Europe enjoys today.

In post-war Europe, America forged working democracies with policies similar to those it used in East Asia. Japan was kept under US military occupation for seven years until 1952 and any future military ambitions were strictly limited alongside security guarantees by the United States. Germany was kept under Allied military occupation for ten years while allowing new institutions to take root. By then, the Cold War was brewing. Germany and the rest of Europe relied on America to keep it safe.

Among the institutions created at that time was the European Coal and Steel Community, set up in 1952, a Franco–German organization, focusing on trade and designed to find common ground in wealth-creation in order to prevent future conflict. This was the founding body of the European Union (EU) that more than fifty years later has grown to twenty-seven members, many from the former Soviet bloc.

The EU has such a proven record of guaranteeing freedoms and raising living standards that, for tens of millions of people, the prospect of EU membership overrode other goals once pursued through violence and ethnic cleansing.

But the European project, as it is known, comes with a twist. Whether the issue is how to grow vegetables or how to define human rights, European Union nations have agreed to forfeit the authority of their own democratic institutions to institutions within the European Union that are not subjected to direct elections. The EU parliament has powers of veto that are rarely used and it rarely initiates legislation. The real power lies with the European Commission.

Nevertheless, the EU has become a club that even countries outside Europe are queuing up to join: Morocco in North Africa, Georgia in Central Asia and Turkey, once the heart of the great Ottoman Empire, all want in.

Diminished sovereign power and club membership has become the fashion rather than the exception. It has helped deliver good governance and allowed people to believe they had a stake in their future. It has given them a higher body in which to put their trust should suspicions of their own politicians emerge. It has created a goal to put people's livelihoods at the heart of the global economic supply chain so that tribalism and violence become too costly to contemplate.

Part mentor, part stick, the idea of a beacon is something to which a young, new democracy can aspire and keep heading towards, even when the going gets bumpy. Time and again, whether in Kosovo, Croatia, Estonia, Poland or little Montenegro, I've detected a sense of purpose and optimism because people knew that European Union membership is where they were heading. It is where they want their children and grandchildren to go, and they are confident they will be able to achieve it.

But, as in Latin America, other forces are also involved. The expanding European Union was creeping towards a Russia still bruised from losing its empire and still working out which political system was best to govern its own 140 million restless people.

At the same time, Europe's guilt over failing to stop the massacre in Srebrenica led to fast intervention in another place on the cusp of being ethnically cleansed. In 1999, four years after Srebrenica, NATO aircraft and troops forced Serbia out of its southern province of Kosovo, populated mainly by Albanians.

It was a final, decisive action by the West to end almost a decade of Yugoslav-inspired war. Many of the causes could be sourced back to the ultra-nationalist ambitions of the Serbian leader Slobodan Milošević. Fighting began in 1991 when Croatia, Slovenia and Macedonia declared independence, followed by Bosnia's declaration in 1992 that led to all-out civil war. Now, Milošević had turned his sights toward the small Serbian province of Kosovo.

Kosovo had a perfect set of ingredients for him. Ninety per

cent of the 2 million people were of ethnic Albanian origin, dwarfing the small number of Serbs there. Yet many Serbs considered Kosovo legendary territory in their nation's history, dating back to the Battle of Kosovo in 1389 when Christian Serbs fought but lost to the advancing Muslim Ottoman armies.

Kosovo suffered from years of underinvestment. Many Albanians felt they had no stake in its future under Serbian rule so it had become a landscape of drab Eastern European buildings, streets littered with plastic bags, the young fired up and resentful, and the old keeping their heads down as greater powers braced themselves to advance through the Kosovar landscape once again.

The Albanians were no innocents. Money, weapons and uniforms poured in from the diaspora in Europe and the United States amid claims that they would fight for a 'Greater Albania'. It was yet another historical notion of re-creating a golden age that – in modern geographical terms – would have taken in Kosovo, parts of neighbouring Macedonia and Albania itself.

The Kosovar Albanians formed a guerrilla group, the Kosovo Liberation Army, and sensed that history would be on their side because of Serbia's record of abuse in Bosnia. They were right. Their attacks on Serb forces in Kosovo led to reprisals that raised fears in the West that the Serbs would once again sweep through, killing and ethnically cleansing a part of modern Europe. It could not be allowed to happen.

After negotiations broke down, NATO aircraft bombed Belgrade, Kosovo and other targets from the end of March to mid-June 1999. After that, Kosovo was administered by the UN and began travelling a similar path to that of Bosnia. But it was different from the other breakaway parts of Yugoslavia in that it had not been one of the six republics within the

Yugoslav federation. It had been a province within the republic of Serbia. Its separation from Serbia would be comparable to Yorkshire separating from England, as opposed to Wales splitting from Britain.

Russia was a reluctant NATO ally for the 1999 military operation. But eight years later, when the West was encouraging Kosovo to declare formal independence, Russia was furious. The EU and NATO had already taken in at least seven territories that the Soviet Union had formerly controlled and had its eye on many more, including Ukraine which remained home to Russia's Black Sea Fleet. NATO missile defence shields were being planned for Poland and the Czech Republic. Rhetoric and relations between the Russian president Vladimir Putin and George W. Bush were hostile.

Russia chose to make a stand over Kosovo's independence, declaring that it had drawn a 'red line' on the issue that should not be crossed. The Kosovo–Serbia border became the testing ground of the strategic goals of Moscow and those of Washington.

Draga Polovina wasn't meant to be our interpreter for our journey from the Serbian capital Belgrade to Kosovo. Nor did she naturally involve herself in the day-to-day politics that at that time in late 2007 focused on the looming separation of Kosovo from Serbia. She led a busy, young lifestyle and her day job was as a receptionist in a car showroom. She was with us because her friend, who was a professional interpreter, had suddenly been called away for higher-paying work elsewhere.

In her mid-twenties, Draga was only a child during the 1990s when the Balkan wars left Serbia a nation stigmatized by war crimes. Even now its people were split equally as to whether it should move on and try to join the European

Union, or lean toward a more sympathetic Moscow and see if in the long run Russia would offer more than Europe.

Like all Serbs, she knew about the bombing in 1999 of Belgrade's main television station during NATO airstrikes aimed at forcing Serbia out of Kosovo. Sixteen people died. They were on night shift – technicians, make-up artists, journalists – and I remember holding back my personal fury when a NATO spokesman tried to argue that a television station in Belgrade was a legitimate military target.

This was not a missile silo. Nor did it have anti-aircraft guns on its roof. The dead were my colleagues. A television station was a place where we would go to look for film archive or to send a piece on a satellite feed. The victims just happened to be on night shift at the time. Their job was to put out the news about the airstrikes that were turning millions of Serbs against the West. Welcome to our vision of the New World Order, I thought.

The television station had been left as a charred shell with a memorial to the dead nearby. Just down some steps was the Church of the Holy Trinity, a small, white Russian Orthodox building, set back from the streets in grounds where a gardener was sweeping up autumn leaves.

The dome had also been damaged in the attack and the once magnificent murals that had decorated its ceiling were destroyed. It was now just covered in white paint. Draga stepped quietly across to the church entrance where she dropped coins into an honesty box, took a candle, lit it and watched pensively as the flame settled and gained strength. By the door was a list of donors who had given money for repairs. At the top was the name Vladimir Putin.

'What's it like, seeing this now?' I asked Draga.

'A church is meant to be a place of peace,' she said softly. 'How would you feel if your church was bombed?'

She lowered her head, giving a hint of the confusion and emotion that later emerged when we reached Kosovo itself. She must have been going through the same personal conflict as Vidovic and Dautbasic in Srebrenica. Many of us have been through it in some form or another, that confluence of emotion, fury at our own impotence, often followed by a peace of mind that we have to accept reality and keep going.

We had lunch at the Korchagin, which was fast becoming one of Serbia's most fashionable restaurants. Its decor was retro-communist memorabilia from Che Guevara, to Lenin and Tito. The staff kept Marxist songs as their cellphone ringtones and customers discussed how the good old days could one day return. But unlike, say, ten years ago, when this would have been mere nostalgia, it now had the whiff of reality about it.

The owner, Vladimir Cucic, used to be in academia, a political scientist, but then spent years helping Serb refugees who had been expelled from their homes because of war. Now he had opened a restaurant that was a more intricate and lavish version of the coffee shop with the hammer and sickle flag in the small Argentine farming town of Casilda. It delivered similar sentiments, too. In Argentina, the catalyst was the financial crash. In Serbia it was Kosovo.

By now, Russia had openly abandoned its experiment with Western-style democracy and, under Vladimir Putin, had turned back to authoritarianism. It was feeling more confident and less humiliated and was once again emerging as a nation with global muscle. It was taking stands on energy supplies and missile defence and a couple of months earlier had thrown down the gauntlet to the West with the 'red line' over Kosovo.

'Let me make it very simple,' said Cucic. 'You are pushing

us to Russia. If you recognize Kosovo we don't have a choice. So far Russia is doing nothing. Maybe they would like to have us back. In this case, if you push us back, Russia will be a protector. This will be an irreversible process.'

I pointed around the restaurant to portraits of Marx, Lenin, Tito, Mao Zedong, even one of the North Korean leader Kim Il-sung. 'Are these icons of the past or the future?' I asked.

'They are of a time when we really had an equal chance,' he said. 'They remind everyone here of the free health care, free education, proper housing, the possibility to be educated and work in other countries. You know in those days our passport was one of the most stolen passports around the world because everyone wanted to be a Yugoslav citizen.'

'So, we're looking at the past here, are we?'

'No. This is also the future. It might be far, far away – a hundred years perhaps. But globalism, or whatever it is, will lead us back to this idea, that we all have equal rights and equal chances that we do not have now under this new system.'

Cucic introduced us to the Ristanovic family who were having lunch. The father, Dusan Ristovic, was a machine engineer who had fled to Russia in the 1990s so that he didn't have to fight in the Balkan wars. There he met his Russian wife, Marina, a nurse, and they had now moved back to Belgrade. They had two children: Nikita, five, and Jevgenije, who was fourteen.

Jevgenije had thick blond hair, a young sportsman's physique and the bored expression of a teenager trying to stay polite in front of his parents. Dusan and Marina were busy ordering, and Jevgenije spoke some English.

'Can I ask you a few questions?' I said.

'Sure,' he nodded.

'OK. Number one. Who is Vladimir Putin?'

He squinted at me, unsure as to whether or not I was crazy. 'Putin,' he said deadpan. 'He's the Russian leader.'

'OK, and you know who George Bush is?'

He nodded.

'Gordon Brown?'

His face went blank, then he shook his head.

'Karl Marx?' I asked.

He pointed at a large picture of a bearded Marx on the wall. 'That old man, there.'

'Vladimir Lenin?'

This time he let out a big laugh. 'Everybody knows who Lenin is,' he said. 'He was a great man.'

With the food ordered, Dusan turned and asked me what I thought about the Kosovo problem. I gave an opaque answer, then pitched the question back. 'Why is Russia drawing a red line over Kosovo?' I asked. 'There's no need to pick a fight.'

'It's not picking a fight,' objected Dusan. 'It's a matter of principle and I don't think Russia could have dealt with it in any different way. It has to uphold international law.'

'Isn't it more about politics than international law?'

'If by politics you mean, should Russia help us, my answer is "yes". Throughout history Russia has been an ally to Serbia and right now we need their help. We'll never accept Kosovo's independence, so if you force it, you push us into the arms of Russia,' he said, using exactly the same words as Cucic had a few minutes earlier.

The CV of the Serbian deputy prime minister, Božidar Djelić, read like the early career of a man well placed for the task of building Western-style democracy. He studied economics at the Paris Institute of Political Studies, took a masters in business administration at Harvard, then went on to study at the prestigious Kennedy School of government. He had advised on the democratic transitions in Poland, Romania and Russia and now over the issue of Kosovo found himself pitted against the very system that had educated him.

Dressed in a finely tailored dark suit, he agreed to meet us in an ornate stateroom of a Serbian government building. He was a slight man, in his mid-forties, with a curious, intelligent face, familiar with the art of advocacy, and he knew his argument well.

'Let me ask you this,' he said. 'Why are you punishing Serbia because of the misrule by Milošević for twelve years? Time has passed. I am not Milošević. Our country is no longer run by a dictator. We are a democracy. We are ready to compromise. We have already given an enormous amount of concessions. We are ready to play ball. But you have to remember that for Serbia, Kosovo is its Jerusalem. We will never accept the independence of Kosovo.'

'But there has to be a solution sometime,' I said.

'In Northern Ireland you waited twenty-three years to find an appropriate solution. It has been decades in the Middle East, and Cyprus has been divided between the Greek south and Turkish north since 1974. I don't see anyone rushing to solve that problem. So why us and why now? I cannot see the strategic interest of doing something that will not only destabilize Serbia, but also the region, and it may reopen many Pandora boxes around the world.'

'So are you, too, throwing down a red line?'

'No,' he said angrily. 'I am saying wait. Let Serbia move toward joining the European Union. Give us time to bring our people with us so that there is no more being pro-Serb or pro-Albanian. Wait until we are all pro-European.'

Kosovo was about three hours' drive south along a motorway which fell into increasing disrepair the further from Belgrade we got. Close to the border with Kosovo, we stopped at the Serbian town of Kurshumliza, a monotonous, dreary place of potholed roads, unimaginative shop displays and clusters of men hanging around because there was no work.

'Kosovo?' I asked a middle-aged man at a newspaper kiosk. 'Can Russia help?'

'We really think they will,' he said. 'Russia is our only hope.'

'They are heavily armed and they're a strong world power,' said another man nearby. 'We are almost the same nation. They've helped in the past and they'll help now.'

A few miles away we reached the border and found a line of trucks on a road nestled among mist-shrouded hills. Their engines were switched off. Drivers smoked and litter had been dropped everywhere. In the distance was a weed-covered railway line linking Belgrade to the Kosovo capital, Pristina – except no trains had run along it for years.

Both the Kosovo and Serbian governments had declared themselves modern European democracies. Both said their end goal was membership of the European Union. Both accepted that in the EU national sovereignty was diminished and borders were flung open. Yet both were stuck in a rut over who owns what territory.

We walked with Draga toward this new 'red line' thrown across Europe. The immigration and customs posts were in white portable cabins. Pedestrians could get across quickly but cars and trucks could take hours. Our driver Simon Smith, who was filming, Draga and I carried the luggage but as we got closer Draga's mood suddenly changed. I failed to notice at first. Through the mist across the no-man's-land on the other side I had seen our Kosovar Albanian interpreter and waved. He waved back, but stayed with his vehicle.

'Can you manage?' whispered Draga, dropping a bag she was carrying.

'But it's only just over there,' I said naively.

'I don't think it's safe,' she replied. Her face had drained of colour. She turned away from the border to look back towards Serbia. Her hand was cupped around her chin. Our driver put his hand on my elbow.

'We'll go back,' he said, tilting his head protectively toward her. 'She thinks she may be killed if she crosses over.'

Draga had never been this close to Kosovo. She was frozen with a fear that had been instilled into her since childhood. It would take years to dissolve. Deputy prime minister Djelić understood it. This was what he meant when he asked for time to take the people with him on his journey towards modern Europe.

Much evidence surrounding the Balkans suggested that the fear engulfing Draga remained widespread, regardless of which ethnic community you belonged to. In Novi Sad, in the north, when we went there, nationalists had been desecrating Catholic churches, vandalizing synagogues and warning anyone who was not Serbian to leave the country.

'They rang my intercom and told me I was a Croatian whore,' a pro-European television presenter, Marcina Fratucan, told me. 'It's crazy, because I'm actually a Serb, and now I'm terrified and don't know where to go. This is my town, my country. My son, my husband, my family are all here.'

That evening she found graffiti sprayed on her garage door, warning that she was on a target list of people who should leave Serbia or be killed.

Serb nationalists frequently held rallies brandishing portraits of the deposed president, Slobodan Milošević together with wanted war criminals from Bosnia Radovan Karadžić and Ratko Mladić, the man directly responsible for the Srebrenica massacre.

Elections were due in a few months and the opposition leader, Tomislav Nikolić, was a conservative ultra-nationalist campaigning not on a platform of the European Union but the old vision of a Greater Serbia. 'Serbia will be a sovereign free and democratic country,' he told me. 'We don't need missionaries dictating to us who should be in power. We will not allow anyone to make slaves of us.'

Refugee camps in Serbia still held the homeless, who had been expelled, or fled, from Croatia, Kosovo, Bosnia and elsewhere as ethnic divisions had swept away their lives.

On a previous trip to Belgrade, I met an elegant, educated middle-aged woman, Tintor Lubica, who used to live a busy middle-class life in the Croatian capital, Zagreb. She now lived in a camp just outside the city and we arrived there at the end of a brilliant winter's afternoon. As we drove inside, the sky darkened suddenly. The wind started up. Solitary figures, distant and tiny against the violent white backdrop, slowed and hunched themselves up. Bitter gusts of wind blew clumps of snow off roofs. The huts stood in row after row and in the dimming light the camp threw off the appearance of a Siberian Gulag from another age.

Although a Serb, Tintor said she used to work as a personal assistant to a former Croatian prime minister. She mixed in the corridors of power, living in a government apartment close to the centre of Zagreb, its walls lined with an art collection and a library of books. In 1991, without notice, they were told to leave because they were Serbs – not pack and leave, but just get out, amid the mad panic and fear that then gripped the Balkans. More than fifteen years later, Tintor was still living in one room in a hut in a refugee camp just outside Belgrade.

She didn't want us inside her hut. Her mother was bed-ridden and two sick relatives were also in there. She told her story standing in the snow and, when we said we were going to Zagreb, she asked if we would check out her old apartment. She gave us the address.

When we got there, we found that her neighbourhood was a residential suburb of tenement blocks where children were sledding down slopes in the road. We couldn't tell by looking at them which ethnic group they belonged to.

'They could be Bosnians,' said Marco, my interpreter. 'Or Croats. Not Serbs, though, because they haven't come back.' We found the block number, filmed as we walked up a flight of stairs, then pressed the bell of Tintor's old apartment. A petite, friendly blonde woman opened the door, her face full of curiosity and welcoming.

'Hi,' said Marco, 'we just wanted to know who was living here before you.'

Before she could answer, a man appeared, tall with dark, shoulder-length hair. His hand was on the door, closing it before we could get any further.

The Croatian prime minister, Ivo Sanader, was, like Djelić in Serbia, urbane and multilingual and on a quest to make his country a member the European Union. One of the bench-marks he had to meet was the successful return to Croatia of refugees like Tintor Lubica.

'The war is behind us,' Sanader said optimistically. 'The return of refugees was one of the first announcements of my administration. Croatia is facing a great future and everyone must help. Right down to every office in every village. They must make sure it works.'

But the results were not good. Human Rights Watch esti-mates that of the up to 350,000 Serbs who were expelled or fled, only about 70,000 have gone back. Serbs used to make up more than 12 per cent of Croatia's 4.4 million population. In 2007, they only made up 4.5 per cent.

We went back to the refugee camp near Belgrade to see Tintor. She wanted to see our film of her Zagreb neighbourhood, so she invited us to set up the viewing equipment in her room. It was cramped with her mother in a bed pushed against a wall, a table and chairs in the middle, a sink and stove by the window and two bunk beds up against the other wall. Two relatives, a young woman with a child, sat on the bottom bunk.

She recognized her neighbourhood immediately. The woman and child moved round to get a better view of our small screen. Her mother propped herself up in bed. Tintor reached for a tissue and clasped her hands together. She peered closer as the camera followed us up the stairs and Marco's finger pressed the bell. When the door opened, Tintor's hand went to her mouth. The camera concentrated on the petite woman's face, then pushed in to try to pick up the inside of the apartment, until the door was closed on us.

'Can I see it again?' said Tintor. We spooled the tape back. 'Stop there, please,' she said. For a long time she looked at the frozen picture and the blurred and indistinct image of an apartment entrance hall and corridor that led back into a world that used to be her home.

She turned to Marco. 'Did you see my art collection?' she said. 'Were there any pictures from my collection on the wall?'

We hadn't.

'Do you know who they were?' she asked. 'The people inside?'

'They didn't want to tell us,' said Marco.

'The prime minister says you can go back,' I said. 'They will find you a new apartment. It may be a better one.'

Her mother reached out her hand. Tintor took it. 'No. I will stay in the camp,' she said, shaking her head miserably. She pressed the edge of the tissue to her eyes and looked at her mother. 'There is no life for us back there.'

A few years later, I would be talking to Ibrahim Salaymeh in the Israeli-Arab village of Turon, suggesting, as I had to Tintor, that he go back and live in his home village of Segera, or Ilaniyya, from which his family had been expelled.

He and Tintor had similar reactions. It might be technically possible, but the Serbs and Croats and the Israelis and Palestinians came from different races with many historical grievances. Serbia, Croatia and Israel were not like London or New York. It just wouldn't work.

At that time, there were many places on the ethnic and religious cusp like Serbia. Even within the European Union, the insurgents in Northern Ireland and in the northern Basque area of Spain were trying to see through an uneasy peace. The Russian war-front of Chechnya was quieter but still dangerous. In swathes of the former Soviet Union from the Caucasus to the Baltic states millions of ethnic Russians, whose homes had been there for generations, were feeling threatened by pro-European nationalist movements now in power. In Iraq, Sunni and Shia were fighting. In Sri Lanka Tamil and Sinhalese were at war. Ethnic divisions in Pakistan were pushing it towards becoming a pivotal global threat. India was being rocked by Islamic terror attacks, and Buddhists and Hindus were fighting in Thailand.

Against that backdrop, Serbia and Kosovo's problems might have seemed manageable. Both were working. Both were edging their way to becoming functioning democracies. Both were following that beacon path towards European Union membership. But ending ethnic cleansing is one thing. Convincing different communities to live side by side is another. As in Serbia, there were Kosovo Albanians with the same equally nihilist racist views.

Yet, those in power in Washington, London and many other European countries rejected Djelić's view that things should be allowed to move at a slow, but positive pace. They argued that, whatever the reaction from Moscow and Serbia, this was a boil that needed lancing and Kosovo must be granted its independence and quickly.

We left the terrified Draga at the border, carried over the equipment and loaded it into our new car. We headed straight to Kosovo's Drenica Valley, once the stronghold of the armed insurgency against Serbian rule. It was dark and spitting rain. Our headlights lit up patches of rolling green countryside swathed in black with the lights of farmhouses in the distance. We slowed on the outskirts of the small town of Skënderaj and turned into a parking lot behind a restaurant. We had been told to wait inside for a contact who would lead us to a Kosovo Albanian militia group that was threatening to start a violent campaign for independence if the West didn't grant it.

Above the restaurant bar were pictures of Kosovo Liberation Army leaders, decked out in camouflage uniforms and weapons from when they were NATO allies in the 1999 campaign. Many of the sullen customers around us would have been signed-up members.

A phone call came and we left. On a street corner, heading out of town, we picked up an intermediary who directed us back out into the countryside, then along a narrow road to a junction with a dirt track. A middle-aged man, head shaved, dressed in jeans and a black T-shirt got in. We drove up the track and stopped at a derelict building. I thought he was our guide, taking us to the insurgents' hideout. But when we stopped, he put on a balaclava so he would not be identified on camera. He claimed he was a member of the Albanian National Army, a guerrilla group banned by the UN administration. He said we should use his military name, Kacak, borrowed from a legendary Albanian fighter. In his day job, he ran a local hardware shop and lived with his wife and five children.

'If we see that we are not going towards the goal of independence we will start implementing our military plans,' he said pompously. 'We will protect our land from Serb forces.'

'But Serb forces aren't here,' I said. 'NATO's here. The UN's here.'

'We have information that Serb militia units have entered Kosovo,' he answered. 'We are recruiting in large numbers to protect our people.'

'Is it really worth it after nearly ten years of peace to bring back this spectre of violence?'

'Not only for ten but even for twenty years it is worth it to start a struggle and fight against those who do not want Albanians to live on their own land.'

With his pot belly and his slogans, he might have cut a laughable figure. But on his wrist was a shrapnel wound from fighting in the 1990s, and as in many societies emerging from conflict, war was his comfort zone.

'But if you do this,' I asked, 'what about America who liberated you?'

Through the black wool of the balaclava, his eyes, lit up from the side by our vehicle headlights, were sharp and uncompromising. He spoke without hint of the paradox he was creating. 'America,' he said, 'America is our biggest friend and ally.'

The Kosovo capital, Pristina, is a shabby, ugly little town. Slowly, the roads were being repaired and the litter collected.

The schools had rewritten the curriculum to erase inflammatory anti-Serbian stories. Institutions were being rebuilt. But after eight years of being separated from Serb rule, Kosovo society was still far from reaching the transforming visions of East Asia, the Gulf States or even other countries in new Europe. The EU and UN were trying to wean themselves away from day-to-day government and security, but their main tasks so far had been to stop ethnic violence and chase after corruption and organized crime.

One of Pristina's key landmarks was a huge hoarding of Bill Clinton, the man seen as the liberator. It covered the outer wall of a city centre building. Nearby a replica of the Statue of Liberty stood high up on the roof of a hotel.

I wanted to see if the sentiments of the wannabe insurgent Kacak were supported in some part by the mainstream politicians or, indeed, if they agreed with Serbia's Djelić that independence could wait. The latter, I quickly found, was a question not worth asking at all.

We went to see a huge figure of Kosovo's independence movement. Veton Surroi, who had founded an activist newspaper in the late 1990s, played a big part in the failed negotiations in 1999 and had now set up a left-leaning party to compete in the upcoming elections.

'Russia says it's drawn a red line over Kosovo's independence,' I said. 'So what's your message to the Kremlin?'

'This isn't an issue in which Russia should have any definite say,' he said.

'In Serbia, they're asking for more time. They're saying that independence will push them into the arms of Russia. So why press for it now?'

'We can't afford generation after generation to go on through periods of legal uncertainty.'

That caught me for a moment. Then I replied: 'If you declare independence, because of Russia, you will not have UN recognition, so the legal uncertainty will continue.'

'If we accept a lesser position than independence we would have continuous conflict and conflict by definition is legal uncertainty.'

'Why would you have continuous conflict?'

'We have gone through a period of domination by Serbia and it has not functioned well. But we have seen that to establish a functioning state means establishing democratic and independent states outside of Yugoslavia, so in our case outside of Serbia.'

'I don't understand. You have de facto independence now. There is certainty about your status through the European Union and the United Nations.'

'We don't want intermediary forms of authority,' he countered. 'We want sovereignty.'

'Then it's going to be a mess.'

'Yes. It doesn't look like a pretty picture.'

'Why create a nasty picture when everything is going fine at the moment?'

'It's not going fine at all. What you see here is simply a place waiting for a decision. Unemployment is above 50 cent. We have had eight years of this dual (UN) administration. We can spend another hundred years with international administration and it won't create better than what we have right now. And this is insufficient for a society.'

Surroi looked tired. He had the air of a seen-it-all patriarch, bored with explaining the obvious. He could easily have passed for a man twenty years older, but he was only in his mid-forties. I was unconvinced by his argument. I recognized the emotional need, but I hadn't yet heard him address the key point made by Serbia's Djelić: give it time.

'How is it that other societies can get themselves out of this ambiguity as you call it and you can't?' I said.

'Like who?' he challenged.

'Taiwan,' I said, referring to China's wealthy and democratic breakaway province that has no real international recognition at all. 'It's barred from all major international institutions. It has no seat at the United Nations and its legitimacy is recognized by very few governments. That is far more legal ambiguity than you have.'

'Taiwan has a totally different historical perspective,' he retorted, and with the word 'historical' he began heading into the area of past grievances and insoluble ethnic differences. Instead of running with the idea of successful, democratic, bustling Taiwan we headed back into a well-worn political comfort zone. I could have been talking to someone in Israel, Lebanon, Sri Lanka, Iraq or God knows how many other bloodied places. I let that run its course, then asked: 'What have the people of Kosovo done to prove they're ready for independence and democracy?'

'They have gone through the process of elections,' he said. 'They have built a civil society with an independent media and they've done it from a vicious conflict and years of apartheid. This means we are now a functioning electoral democracy.'

'What then is your policy on, say, health care? Do you advocate free health care?'

'Yes. It's within the electoral plan. We advocate health care in which there's a system by which you contribute to a health-care fund.'

'How much will that cost?'

'We have to create a fund first for every employed person.'

'What will the budget be?'

'We haven't made a calculation for the transformation.'

'Even though there's an election coming up?'

'Even though there's an election.'

'Why not?'

'It is within the programme of people who are dealing with health care.'

'But as leader of the party you are not aware of it?'

'I am aware of it. It is coming.'

'But you can't give me a figure.'

'Not now. No.'

He sent us into his staff to get the figures, a group of twenty-something men who were sitting around a large table talking about the election. They were mostly graduates from American and European universities, steeped in think-tank and conference-circuit language. They didn't have the health-care figures, so I put to them the question that has been at the heart of this book from Iraq to Cuba and now to Kosovo.

'If you had to choose between independence and health care, which would you choose?'

'All Albanians would die for independence,' said one, firmly tongue in cheek, his accent mimicking that of men like Kacak in the Drenica Valley.

'No,' I insisted. 'This is serious. Which is your priority?'

'We can't answer,' said another from the end of the table. 'It's like asking a Manchester United fan to choose between his team and health care. It is not a possible choice.'

We headed out to the countryside where we found an eighty-year-old farmer working on a vegetable patch in his garden. His name was Aleksander Krstic, a Serb, one of the minority who had stayed behind after the NATO intervention, when tens of thousands of others had fled.

'What do you think about Kosovo getting independence from Serbia?' I asked.

He stood up from his work and wiped his face with the scarf tied around his neck. 'Why's it so important?' he said. 'Life here was dreadful with the Italians in the Second World War. The communists weren't much better. What does it matter who owns the place and what they call it? Serbia, Kosovo. They can call it Fantasia for all I care.'

Amid huge celebrations, Kosovo declared its independence in February 2008. The United States immediately recognized it, together with a raft of other Western governments. Russia led the refusals, which included heavyweights from the Second World such as China, India and Brazil. Even the European Union was divided. Britain, France and Germany led the supporters whereas Spain, Greece and Romania were among those who opposed.

Serb rioters broke into the American embassy in Belgrade, setting fire to offices and one protester died. At the border Serb soldiers pelted NATO troops with stones and rocks.

The EU agreed to disagree and provided the infrastructure to take over from the United Nations, which no longer recognized Kosovo's status. The EU's job was to mentor the building of Kosovo's institutions. It also had executive powers to step in if necessary in a role similar to but less powerful than that of the High Representative in Bosnia. Apart from a new flag, jubilation in Kosovo, resentment in Serbia and fury in Moscow, not much changed.

In February, Serbia held knife-edge elections in which the pro-Russian candidate Tomislav Nikolić won the first round, but not enough of a majority, and was beaten in the second round by the pro-European leader Boris Tadić. It was seven years after the downfall of Slobodan Milošević and still almost half of Serbia believed in something of the vision of a Greater Serbia.

Kosovo came to represent one of the central issues surrounding the causes and solutions of many modern conflicts.
Given that most violence was rooted in ethnic, religious and
tribal divisions – as opposed to ideological – Kosovo's independence was seen as a step too far for many governments
who became distinctly nervous. This was why support for
recognition was limited.

At the time, there were more than fifty claims from various
groups for independent statehood. It is impossible to know
the real number because of the groups within the groups, and
the ability of only a few people to punch above their weight
by using violence to make their point.

Some of the better-known ones include Tamils in Sri Lanka,
Kashmiris in India. Papuans in Indonesia, Scots in Britain,
Basques in Spain, Pampans in Brazil, Texans in the United
States, Tibetans in China and – for one few have heard of –
Transnistrians in Moldova. It was because of these frictions
that Spain and China agreed with each other in refusing to
recognize Kosovo's independence. Spain had the rumbling
Basque problem and China had Tibet and its restless western
Muslim area of Xinjiang.

With a pro-European government scraping into office in
Belgrade and the protests dying down, Kosovo fell from the
headlines. Yet far to the east in the Caucasus, an area that
divides much of Europe from Asia, Kosovo's repercussions
were beginning to be felt.

Among the many small countries that the West was mentoring towards becoming a developed democracy was Georgia.
On the Black Sea, with Turkey to its south and Russia to
its north, Georgia was familiar with living under alternate
spells of colonization and independence. It was taken into
the Russian empire at the beginning of the nineteenth
century, had a brief period on its own after the 1917 Russian

revolution then was swallowed up by the Soviet Union. In 1991 it became independent again, after which, much to Russia's irritation, it lined up to join the European Union and NATO. From Moscow's standpoint, Georgia was nowhere near Europe and had little connection with the Atlantic region that NATO had been created to protect.

The West, though, held up Georgia as a model for meeting its democratic and free-market criteria. Hundreds of advisers were there, including military ones training up the fledgling army. The Georgian president Mikheil Saakashvili ticked many positive boxes. He was fluent in English. He had a law degree from Columbia University in New York. He had a diploma from the International Institute of Human Rights in Strasbourg, and in 2003 he had led a bloodless 'people power' revolution against Georgia's Soviet-era leader Eduard Shevardnadze.

But, Saakashvili was also a Georgian, living in the Caucasus amid feuds and hatreds stretching back centuries. Within Georgia itself lay two communities that wanted independence, South Ossetia with a population of about 70,000 and Abkhazia with one of 200,000. In the early 1990s as the Soviet Union broke up, fighting broke out between the communities. A ceasefire was agreed in 1992, policed by Russian and Georgian troops together with a mission from Europe to oversee peace-keeping.

It lasted until the summer of 2008 when violence broke out between Georgians and South Ossetians. Who started it and where blame lies is hotly debated, but Georgia deployed its troops against South Ossetian fighters and Russia reacted by sending in its army.

The international repercussions were momentous. This was the first time Russia had used its forces against a foreign country since the end of the Cold War. Coincidentally or not, the war began on the 8th of August, the same day that China staged the spectacular opening of the 2008 Olympic games. It was as if two circling superpowers were sending strong and but separate messages to the West that the global balance was getting a makeover.

The US presidential candidate John McCain described the Russian invasion as the first serious international crisis since the end of the Cold War. He also famously announced that it had made every American a 'Georgian'. The Russian president, Dmitry Medvedev, said his country was ready for a new Cold War, and promised to protect the interests of Russian citizens wherever they were in the world. The British conservative leader David Cameron, who travelled to Georgia at the height of the war, took up the point, writing in a British newspaper: 'History has shown that if you leave aggression to go unchecked, greater crises will only emerge in the future. Today, Russia says it is defending its citizens in South Ossetia. Where tomorrow? In Ukraine? In Central Asia? In Latvia?' Britain's Foreign Secretary David Miliband accused Russia of 'redrawing the map of Europe' and said the crisis 'marked a clear end to the relative calm enjoyed by Europe'.

By mid-August a ceasefire was in place and shortly afterwards South Ossetia and Abkhazia declared independence. Three days later, citing the Kosovo precedent, Moscow recognized the two new nations. The world was left with an unsavoury taste that ethnic divisions had forced hostile rhetoric in superpower rivalry with images of politicians polishing their warheads for a new Cold War.

During those summer weeks, I found myself in Moscow watching television pictures of men, their identities hidden by balaclava masks, proclaiming Russia to be their greatest friend and ally – just as Kacak, who ran the hardware shop in

Kosovo, had claimed for America. Each day, either Russia or the West was ratcheting up the stakes, as if both sides were relieved to get away from the nihilism of Islamic terror and work on something that they could get their teeth into. Russia even spoke of tensions resembling the eve of the First World War.

But it didn't quite work. When people talked of 'war' in Iraq, you could see it on the streets. When they used the word 'tensions' for the communities in Bosnia, you could sense it in the way people dealt with each other. But I couldn't see anything that seemed to lead towards a looming Cold War in Moscow.

The bus stop near my hotel was decorated with posters for *The Dark Knight*, then the new batman film. Hoardings advertised global brand names, and the skyline was speckled with cranes putting up new high-rise office blocks to keep pace with Russia's economic growth. From cellphones to cars to Russian editions of the celebrity magazine *Hello!*, it was pretty impossible to envisage how a new Cold War would actually work.

The US aircraft maker Boeing, for example, had a huge factory outside Moscow. Russia's Gazprom, the conglomerate much feared for its ability to turn Europe's gas supplies on and off, was one of the biggest companies listed on international stock exchanges.

When the European Union was called together to discuss sanctions on Russia, the meeting quickly became the material of farce. Would they mean, for example, that the Russian billionaire Roman Abramovich would have to sell Chelsea Football Club? And what to do with the millions of other Russians who lived in London, Paris, Rome and the rest of Europe? In the last Cold War, Russians were isolated behind their Iron Curtain. Their technology was ropy and the subdued population was subjected to meaningless statements from monosyllabic leaders.

Now you could barely stop Russian leaders talking and emailing on BlackBerrys, as they ferried between twenty-four-hour news-channel chat shows. Senior officials would arrange on-the-record telephone news conferences with the foreign press. To get through you had to call a number in New York.

Ringing around contacts in think tanks and embassies, I found a variety of views of which only a small number adopted the Cold War mindset.

I asked a British diplomat then seconded to a think tank if he accepted any of Russia's view – not only on Kosovo and Georgia, but also its wider argument advocating its authoritarian style of government. 'Utter bollocks,' he said. 'This country's run by a bunch of corrupt dictators and we've got to get that message through to them so they shape up.'

I checked that Cold War view with a Spanish official who had worked in Bosnia and was now sorting out more autonomy for Catalonia, the Spanish province that had its own independence movement. His European view of sovereignty in the twenty-first century was very different.

'The concept of the nation state is much weaker now,' he said. 'So the Kosovo, South Ossetia and Abkhazia issues are more smoke and mirrors than substance. The nation state does not exist as it did before. The frontiers are soft. The economies and cultures and education are entwined. You can be Catalan, Spanish, European, a member of NATO, the World Trade Organization. You can have your education at Harvard, the Sorbonne and the University of Beijing and Moscow. You can have your Facebook group, your alumni, your family. Tell me, where does your loyalty lie?'

'So what happened in Georgia, then?'

'If you want a thousand years of historical hatred, I'll give it to you. But I'll tell you this. If Saakashvili's government was being kept in check by a higher power like in Bosnia and Kosovo, there would not have been a war.'

I called a senior Indian official in Delhi and asked what he thought of the Georgia crisis and why India hadn't recognized Kosovo. 'Russia and America are using ethnic rivalries to strengthen their ideological positions,' he said. 'My God! Haven't we been through enough of that?'

From my many conversations, the Cold War spectrum came mainly from the establishment in the United States and Britain. The more textured view came from those in Russia and the Second World. In a nutshell, Russia had tried democracy and it had failed, leading to the Chechnya war, organized crime and economic collapse. Russia was now retreating into an environment with which it felt more comfortable. It understood that its old-style dictatorship would not work, but it wasn't sure what would. Therefore, thought the Second World voices, leave it be while it worked things out. While the overarching view was shared by most Russians, many had little but scorn for their present government which they regarded as corrupt, inefficient and bereft of policy. But the EU and NATO expansion, coupled with Kosovo and then Georgia, pushed Russia into a situation where it had acted in a predictable way – by lashing out in a show of force.

The swift resolution in Georgia came because of factors that have been a constant in Europe's own development since the Second World War. Trade between Russia and the West had reached a point that where was too much to lose to make things worse. The neutralizer of economic Mutually Assured Destruction had kicked in to keep complete polarization at bay.

Yet, as I discovered a few weeks later, Russia was still far from the point that China had reached.

*

The Narva river marks the border between Russia and the European Union. Half the river is in Russia. Half is in the small Baltic country of Estonia that had once been on the western edge of the Soviet empire. There are castles on both sides, and the day I was there, the national flags of each country flew in a strong wind that whipped up white river water, making a scene from a medieval epic.

The border post was marked by a small flow of people walking across and a stationary truck that would stand for an hour or more before being allowed across. That hour was the end of a wait that lasted days. The line of commercial vehicles went back into a huge car park where the trucks were lined up in rows. From there a queue stretched back along the main road for five or six miles outside the town of Narva itself.

The drivers waited a week to ten days before being allowed through. The hold-up was on the Russian side, ostensibly because of what the Russians called technical complications. But the drivers knew it was because Russia was being bloody-minded over the Georgia crisis.

'Every time there are political problems we get queues,' said a Russian driver who had been waiting for eight days.

'Whose fault is it?' I asked.

'The politicians. Who else?'

Another driver shouted out from his cab: 'We do our work. They should do theirs and come to an agreement.'

'How much is it costing?'

He opened the door and jumped down. 'Just work it out. Someone has to pay for us and for the time the truck is off the road doing nothing and bringing in no profit. It costs a lot and it's completely unnecessary.'

It was a view shared by the US ambassador to Estonia, a North Carolina republican businessman named Dave Phillips.

The night before he had been to a concert with the Russian ambassador and the two routinely dined together. But their friendship counted for nothing in the larger stakes at play.

'The situation in Narva is just ridiculous,' said Phillips. 'It's harassment. It's incompetence. It just makes Russia look silly.'

In economic terms, what Russia was doing didn't make sense at all. Apart from an ugly queue of traffic outside an otherwise pretty little town, Estonia was barely suffering at all. The trucks were carrying goods needed by Russian companies, which would now be having difficulty meeting their orders, thus putting the livelihoods of their staff at risk. In the longer term, what foreign investment would go anywhere near this border area, if every time there was a political spat supply lines shut down?

Like Georgia, Estonia's history reflected the ebb and flow of wars with tiny states being swallowed up then spat out by a succession of larger ones. It had been controlled by Denmark, Sweden, Germany and Russia with brief periods of independence in the early twentieth century, but it ended up being absorbed into the Soviet Union, then made independent again, and was now a part of the European Union.

The Estonian view of the Second World War is evidence of how political loyalty is defined by personal experience. For many Estonians, Nazi Germany is seen as a liberator and the Soviet Union the oppressor. Estonia's heroes were those who fought, not Hitler, but Stalin. Germany's Second World War defeat was mourned, and the seeds of today's deep suspicion of Russia were sown when Stalin deported tens of thousands of Estonians to Siberian labour camps and sent in Russians to take their place. In the 1990s, Estonia launched its own war crimes campaign, not against Germans, but against Russian civil servants responsible for the deportations – however lowly their jobs.

It is against the backdrop of hostility between Estonians and Russians that Narva was such a symbolic town. Not only was it on the Russia–Europe border, but also more than 80 per cent of its population was Russian. When President Dmitry Medvedev talked about protecting Russian citizens wherever they were in the world, it was referring to places like Estonia where 30 per cent of the 1.4 million people were Russian.

Unlike the Cuban activist Hector Palacios or the wedding photographer Usama Rehda in Iraq, who had no real choice about the environment in which they lived, Estonia's Russians did. They could, if they wished, pack their bags and walk across the Narva river into authoritarian Russia and build a new life there. It was, in short, a test to see to what extent Russia was offering a genuine alternative in its system of government.

We headed to the offices of Juri Mishin, who ran the Union of Russian Citizens in Narva. He was also an adviser to the Russian parliament with a brief to alert Moscow if its citizens living outside Russia were being mistreated in any way. In short, a word in Moscow's ear could bring Russia's wrath down on Estonia.

Dressed in a neat light-grey suit, Mishin was a short, energetic man. He walked purposefully across the room to greet us and ushered me to a seat, keen to explain his position in the new global order. The room was decorated with busts of Stalin and Lenin. A red hammer-and-sickle flag stood in the corner and from the window there was a view down to the Russian border. I pointed to it and asked whether Russians in Estonia were looking towards Moscow or the European Union for their future.

'Right now, after what happened in Georgia, where Russia protected life, human rights and citizenship, people are in favour of the Kremlin again. Now we know that Russia isn't the collapsed state it was ten years ago. She's risen from her knees and has become a country that we can rely on. As Russians, wherever we live we can now ask for its support.'

It wasn't quite the answer that addressed my question, although I suspected he knew that, too, and that his views would not be black and white.

'You mentioned human rights,' I said. 'Are your rights being violated here?'

'Of course, and we expect the Estonian government to do more. There are problems to do with language, citizenship, schools and funding for cultural activities.'

'But not enough to make you want to leave?'

'Probably a lot of people would like to live in Russia; many consider Estonia to be their home. We would like to live in Estonia but have equal rights.'

'And if you didn't, would you ask Russia for protection?'

'We don't have to because Russian law provides protection for its citizens and this is one of the key policies of President Medvedev.'

Mishin's leadership could be crucial as the West and Russia staked out their new relationship. Russia was already accused of using instability among its expatriates as a possible weapon. A year earlier, Estonia was shaken by riots believed to have been inspired by the Kremlin. A few weeks later, its Internet system came under cyber attack – also traced back to Moscow.

'If Russia asked you to cause trouble for Estonia, what would you do?'

'We're already worried about statements from some not

very wise Western politicians that there should be NATO military bases in Estonia. We think that would cause provocations on both sides. But we would like to retain peace here in Estonia by having regard for human rights in accordance with international and European Union law.'

I liked Mishin. He was a canny Russian apparatchik, playing all sides of the game and doing his damnedest to make sure he would keep having the best of both worlds.

'What advice would you give the Russians, South Ossetians and Abkhazians who have just broken away from Georgia, or for that matter any other people in similar situations, so that their villages don't get burnt and their loved ones don't get killed?'

His answer was to get up and ask us to lunch. There was a man he wanted us to meet who might explain the problem better. We got into our minivan and drove the short way to the Narva Hotel in the centre of town, where an old Soviet soldier, standing ramrod straight in a dark blazer, was waiting for us. Bargrat Djikayev was seventy-five years old and had originally come from the now newly independent South Ossetia. Many of his family were still there. He used to go back regularly until, he said, it became too dangerous.

The waiter laid out the table with a selection of starters – potato salad, crab sticks, pork in jelly, meat pancakes, mushrooms in cream and other dishes. Mishin ordered us all a beer and I asked Bargrat Djikayev what had happened to his family in the recent conflict.

He began by explaining how his brother's house had been damaged by Georgians, then he went on hurriedly, ignoring my attempts to interrupt. He didn't touch his food, but kept both palms down on the table as he spoke. His face became tense, with his eyes welling up.

Our interpreter, racing to keep up, translated in bursts of

half sentences: '. . . dragged away . . . executed . . . burnt alive . . . children raped . . . the whole village burnt.'

'Hold on,' I shouted eventually, cutting through his flow. 'Are you saying this is happening now?'

Our interpreter translated. Bargrat faltered and tried to keep going. She put her hand on his arm. He looked confused. They fell into a short conversation. 'No,' said the interpreter. 'He says all that happened in the twelfth century.'

'Twelfth century,' I blurted in disbelief. 'But why does it make you so angry?'

He started talking again, cutting his hands through the air to make his point. 'He says it started long before that,' translated the interpreter. 'They have been attacked by the Georgians since the second century.'

'But that's not now,' I suggested.

He shook his head. 'I want to go back and kill Mikheil Saakashvili,' he said quietly referring to the Georgian president.

Mishin had stayed quiet, listening silently because he wanted me to understand his point. He chose this point to intervene. 'He's influenced by this feeling of blood revenge that's common in the Caucasus,' he said. 'His brother's house was damaged. But his family is safe. These stories that happened so long ago are very real to them. They tell them again and again so they become vivid as if it all happened yesterday.'

I looked across to Bargrat. 'What advice, then, do you offer him?'

'A bad peace is better than war,' said Mishin. 'They should talk and reach a consensus. We have our differences with the Estonian government but we always manage to negotiate.'

'Did Bargrat agree?'

'Yes,' he said, looking at Mishin. 'He is a wise and good man. I've known him for forty-five years.'

'All right then, Mr Djikayev. Can I ask you again?' I said. 'What do you want to do now about Georgia?'

The old Soviet soldier from South Ossetia sat up, deep in thought, his hands clasped together. We waited silently for his response. We could almost feel the conflict between reason, emotion, loyalty and honour. Then he laid his hands on the table, dropped his eyes to the table and shook his head. 'The same,' he said. 'I want to go back and kill Mikheil Saakashvili.'

Once again, here was the beacon of the European Union playing its part. The instinct of Bargrat Djikayev, at seventy-five, was to pick up his rifle and kill. But Mishin, his mentor, was keeping him at bay and persuading him there was another way. Mishin himself had credibility because of his connections to Moscow, although he was determined to keep one foot firmly in the camp of modern Europe.

For the 25 million Russians living outside their country, players like Mishin would be crucial if more Georgia conflicts were to be avoided, just as players like the police chief Vidovic and deputy mayor Dautbasic would be for Bosnia to succeed, and deputy prime minister Djelić in Serbia.

Estonia was already a European Union member, so any racist anti-Russian movement, if not stopped by the government, would be held back by the umbrella authority of the EU. This was happening in a more overt way in Bosnia and Kosovo. Georgia was far behind, so were many countries in Africa, the Middle East and elsewhere.

In Georgia, while it was being courted by both NATO and the EU, there was no official mentoring authority to stop Mikheil Saakashvili from sending his troops into South Ossetia. Had any senior figure in the United States or the European Union told him unequivocally to keep his men in barracks pending a diplomatic solution, he would no doubt have complied.

But they didn't. Either the West wanted a showdown with Russia, as has been suggested by some. Or its eye was off the ball and it didn't realize how dangerous tensions had become. Or it did know, but refused to impinge on the sovereignty of a democratic nation – even though Georgia's institutions, including the president himself, were arguably too immature to be allowed to handle hostilities with Russia on their own.

Estonia, smaller than Georgia, with fresh memories of Russian atrocities, had managed to forge an uneasy peace with Moscow and a workmanlike relationship with its potentially hostile Russian community.

One of the key figures in guiding it through that process was Mart Laar, who had twice been prime minister and turned up for our meeting in an open-necked shirt, jeans and trainers. He helped us pull up a couple of chairs and find a quiet place in the wide, panelled hallway of the historic parliament building.

'During the Soviet period of the 1970s and 1980s there was real hate in Estonia. This was a practical hate and permanent sense of conflict between Russians and Estonians that you could feel on the street and at the bus stop.'

'So what happens now with Russia's warning to protect its citizens?' I asked. 'Couldn't that be really harmful here?'

'If Russia wants to become aggressive it will always find its reasons, and its citizens abroad are one. Unlike before we are protected now by the European Union and NATO, so we feel safe. But the faster we can integrate the Russians into modern European society the faster we will end this problem.'

'So is that hatred you spoke about still there?'

'Luckily it is not,' said Laar. 'That is one of the best achievements of an independent Estonia. This hate has gone, and this tension is not in the air. So my children, thank God, are living in a very different situation from the one in which I grew up.'

On the Estonian coast is a bleak town called Paldiski that used to be a top-secret closed Soviet city and naval base. Just outside the town, down a wooded lane, is a high wire fence behind which is the entrance sign – an old concrete sculpture of the hammer and sickle. The grounds are covered with weeds and huge pieces of rusting metal. In the middle is a building looking like a gigantic shipping container, painted bright yellow and maroon. Inside it, encased in layers of concrete, is a nuclear reactor that was used for training naval recruits serving on submarines.

The radiation given off by the reactor is still lethal and it will stay entombed for at least another fifty years before it is safe enough to dismantle. Like hundreds of other Soviet facilities, the Paldiski base was abandoned virtually overnight and made safe with European Union money.

One of the staff, Valeri Baryrkhanov, used to be an instructor at the base. He now worked as the radiation protection adviser. He took us into one of the training areas that was built to replicate a submarine – old pressure and radiation gauges, thick hatch doors and huge slabs of metal held together with massive bolts.

'This is exactly as it was,' he said, letting his hand run down the polished metal. 'But when we went to sea, you know, we all thought: "Oh God, please that we don't use our weapons. Just, please, because it would be horrible for everyone."'

In his late fifties, Baryrkhanov was close to retirement, but when I asked about the talk of the new Cold War and Russia's offer to protect him, he laughed.

'Maybe some people are thinking about this, but not me, and none of my friends. There's a submariner friend I know who's now living in San Francisco and he says everything is fine. I've lived in Paldiski for many years. My wife is here. My daughter is here. My granddaughter is here. We're very happy.

Telling people you must be on this side or that side is from another time. It's not good. I am now a free man living a free life.'

What Baryrkhanov has achieved by seeing himself as a 'free man, living a free life' is the universal aspiration of billions of people. The mechanisms through which they can achieve that are also pretty much universal, as are their reactions to success or failure.

Even after building its institutions to a high degree of sophistication, Europe still fought the Second World War, and another half-century was needed to get it to where it is now. Even then there were such obstacles as Yugoslavia.

Across the other side of the world in East Asia, another place that has also clawed its way towards peace, wealth and democracy. East Asia is not yet as advanced as Europe, but their paths have been remarkably similar.

EAST ASIA

TAIWAN – Democracy's Prize

Tall, thin, gangly, and absorbed in his workshop at the back of his store, knife-maker Wu Tseng Dong snapped on a cigarette lighter to start up a welding flame. Along one wall were machine tools, lathes, sharpening blocks and along another were stack upon stack of old artillery shells, caked with soil and rust, dug up from fields on the Taiwanese island of Kinmen – barely a mile from the Chinese mainland.

As a boy, Wu spent hours cowering in shelters. 'It was really scary,' he said. 'They kept bombing and bombing every night, sending over these shells to let the Taiwanese people know they were the enemy.'

'So should China now say sorry?' I asked.

'Why?' he retorted, pulling his protective glasses onto his forehead to get a better look at the person who asked such a ridiculous question. 'If they say sorry, we have to say sorry. It was war. It's time to work together now.'

He pulled the glasses back down again, and started work, fast and purposefully. Outside a bus pulled up and a tour group from China got out. Wu's knives had become a sought-after tourist memento.

'What would happen if there was war again?' I said when I saw he was finishing.

'There won't be.' He turned off the flame. 'War is cruel, you know. It's not like a movie. It's not exciting.' As the freshly moulded metal was cooling, he began to inscribe Chinese characters into the blade. 'Ordinary people like me can't see any reason for there to be war. Our leaders are cooperating and opening a new chapter in our history.'

He wiped the blade with a cloth and presented it to me like a cutlass. It was actually a large, shining cooking knife inscribed, jokingly, in Chinese characters that translated: *War and Peace, Love From Mao Zedong.*

The last time I had visited Kinmen was in 1996 when Taiwan was about to hold its first-ever direct presidential elections – and China was actually threatening war. The last thing the world's greatest surviving communist state needed was a successful democratic election right on its doorstep and one carried out by a breakaway rebel province.

Beijing declared that its missiles were primed to fire on Taiwan, and the United States sent an aircraft carrier into the Taiwan Straits, the hundred-mile-wide stretch of water between the main island of Taiwan and the Chinese mainland.

But Kinmen is much closer than that. At low tide, landfall to landfall the Chinese and Taiwanese-controlled territories are barely a mile apart. Technically part of China, Taiwan was occupied by the defeated nationalist armies in 1949. They swept in with 2 million refugees, taking over the once-sleepy province and setting up a pro-American stronghold just off the coast of China. After Mao Zedong's victory, Kinmen, together with other offshore islands, bore the brunt of Asia's Cold War. The shelling Wu talked about lasted from 1958 to 1978. The island itself reminded me of the Scottish Hebrides, with panoramic seascape vistas and a sense of its own pace and isolation.

If China was ever to invade, this would be one of the first places it would secure. So, for years, stakes with sharpened tips rose out of Kinmen's lush agricultural fields in order to impale Chinese paratroopers. Concrete machine-gun posts, camouflaged in green, stood on high points of the gently rolling countryside. The coastline was a closed-off military zone where tanks and gunboats were hidden in tunnels and artillery lined the beaches.

For many years, Taiwan represented a pro-American flash-point where war could break out at any moment. During much of that time, Taiwan was governed by a dictatorship. But slowly, mentored by America, it reformed and developed a rough blueprint of how to move from dictatorship to democracy without violence.

South Korea trod a similar path, living under threat of attack from the north, governed by a dictatorship that gradually transformed into a fully fledged democracy. Both Taiwan and South Korea began their journeys in the 1950s, far poorer than many African countries at the time. As reference points for creating democratic societies, both are remarkable successes. South Korea was first in 1993 and Taiwan followed three years later.

It is Taiwan that makes a nonsense of Veton Surroi's argument that his community in Kosovo was incapable of progressing without a formal declaration of independence.

In 1971, Washington switched its diplomatic recognition from Taiwan to China and many other governments followed suit. Taiwan lost its seat at the United Nations and was refused access to any key global institutions of which China was also a member.

Taiwan, therefore, encompassed many of the triggers that in other parts of the world are blamed for war. It lived cheek-by-jowl with a large, hostile neighbour that wanted to conquer it and impose its own extremist ideology. Millions of its people had lost their homes and loved ones in the Communist Party takeover of China. The defeated nationalist government promised to take back power on the mainland. Its soldiers had weapons and motivation that could have started an insurgency. Taiwan could have taken provocative action to prompt a Chinese invasion, thus drawing America directly into the fighting. It could have kept its people in run-down settlements and called them refugee camps and promised that war would continue until the Communist Party was destroyed and the nationalist government was back in power. The nationalists could have refused to accept the causes for their defeat: corrupt leaders and policies that had failed to deliver to their citizens. They could have blamed everyone else except themselves.

But they didn't. They brushed themselves off to become one of the worlds' fastest-growing economies and then a new democracy.

In 2008, Taiwan's per capita income was more than US$30,000 a year, edging close to that of Britain's US$36,000 and within reach of America's US$47,000. Its infant mortality rate was 5.35 deaths per 1,000, slightly better than those in Cuba, which we looked at earlier, and comparable with those in the West. The average lifespan at seventy-seven years reached similar levels. Its health care is also world class. Every Taiwanese is entitled to a biometric card that contains basic medical history and means they can be treated in any hospital at any time. Taiwan's average cancer survival rates are higher than those in Britain.

This has been achieved without the diplomatic recognition that Kosovo claimed was needed to extract it from 'legal ambiguity'. Taiwan had no access to the World Bank, the IMF, or those other international institutions that are awash in the developing world. It was only given observer status at the World Health Organization in May 2009.

As hostilities thawed, there was no peace treaty between Taiwan and China, and Beijing's threat of invasion remained – should Taiwan ever make a formal declaration of independence. Yet, Kinmen's gun emplacements and secret military tunnels became tourist museums because at some stage and unannounced, both governments simply accepted that war was out of the question. Instead of bolstering their strategic coastal positions, the Chinese military began to lease them to Taiwanese businessman, one of whom planned to build a funfair and theme park where the gun batteries had been.

At Kinmen's small, modern airport, the television screen was showing more killings in the Palestinian territories and a bombing in Iraq. In just over an hour we were in the Taiwanese capital Taipei, which, far from being barricaded up like Baghdad or seething with impoverished humanity like Abidjan, was a vibrant, energetic Asian megacity. And like Dubai and Malaysia it has laid claim to its success by building a record-breaking high skyscraper, Taipei 101, with a shopping centre called New York, New York across the road and a replica of the Statue of Liberty outside.

Taiwan's dictator was Chiang Kai-shek, leader of the Chinese Nationalist Party or Kuomintang, whose corruption and openly pro-West policies had been no match for Mao Zedong's new ideas and international Marxism.

For many years Chiang Kai-shek's regime in Taiwan was repressive and paranoid, held in place by secret police and threats. He was, however, surprisingly honest about his own weaknesses and aware of his place in history, once famously musing to an American congressman: 'When I die if I am still a dictator, I will certainly go down in the oblivion of all dictators. If, on the other hand, I succeed in establishing a truly stable foundation for a democratic government, I will live forever in every home in China.'[1]

---

1 Jay Taylor, *The Generalissimo: Chiang Kai-shek and the Struggle for Modern China* (Harvard University Press, 2009).

In Taipei, Chiang's larger-than-life statue presided over a vast room in a building once named after him. It was now called National Democracy Memorial Hall with some exhibits both of Chiang as dictator and of the protests carried out by those who fought to change his system. Among the young faces, bandannas on their heads, sitting in the streets and holding up democracy placards, were leaders holding office and competing in elections now.

'Why do you keep Chiang's statue up there?' I asked my host, Dr Edgar Lin, who headed Taiwan's Council for American Affairs.

'Why not?' he replied, curious at my question.

'Well, he was a dictator. They pulled statues of Stalin and Lenin down, and they pulled Saddam's statue down.'

'And look what happened in Iraq,' he countered. 'Chiang Kai-shek is part of our history and you can't change history.'

Like thousands of other Taiwanese, Dr Lin had been educated in the United States as part of America's policy to build strong institutions in Taiwan. At one time, 90 per cent of Taiwan's cabinet had graduated from American universities. It could have been his people-friendly manner, or the ease with which he fielded conversation, but as he showed us around things began to fall into place.

America's security umbrella confined China's hostility to rhetoric and trade blockades while the Taiwanese themselves got on with building their civil society. Even today Washington maintains its role as mentor, telling Taiwan to pull back when it believes it is becoming too vocal about its independence from China – ensuring that Taiwan's plans do not supersede the good of the global community. This is exactly the type of mentoring that was denied Mikheil Saakashvili in Georgia in the summer of that year.

The complaint among many Taiwanese, including Dr Lin,

was that America was now siding with autocratic China against democratic Taiwan.

'It's very sad,' said Dr Lin. 'Here we are, a model, not only for China, but also for the rest of the world, and Washington is trying to repress Taiwanese democracy by giving in to Chinese demands.'

The issue was coming to a head when we were there in 2007 because the ruling Democratic Progressive Party (DPP) was fighting an upcoming election on a pro-independence platform that was irritating China. The United States was making no secret that it wanted the opposition KMT to win the election. After losing militarily to Mao Zedong in 1949, the Chinese Nationalist Party KMT guided Taiwan towards its first presidential election in 1996 – which it won. It then lost power for two consecutive terms to the DPP and was now campaigning to win it back on a platform of better relations with China.

Before checking out the election campaign itself, we went to the offices of a hi-tech company called D-Link, which began twenty years ago with less than twenty staff in an old warehouse. Now it was a multinational conglomerate with offices all over the world.

I wanted to find out how Taiwan's trading psychology had contributed to its transformation to democracy. After all, 40 per cent of Taiwan's trade was now with China. Put that up against the 0.01 per cent of trade between Israel and its two main Arab neighbours.

'It's about leadership,' explained D-Link's young chief executive, J. C. Liao. 'Even when Taiwan was non-democratic, it was run by technocrats who understood that economic development and global trading were the only way to raise people's living standards.'

'But just about all we hear in the press is that there could be a war with China.' I said.

'No,' he laughed. 'There won't be one.' He swept his hand around the D-Link showroom where we were talking. It was filled with computer gadgets that have become part of our everyday lives. 'Taiwan and China, between us we control the world's computer supplies. Think what would happen if there was a war. The technology is designed in Taiwan and made in factories in China.'

'What, more than 50 per cent?' I asked.

'Ninety per cent in some form or another,' said Liao, 'and in the field of wireless routers it's 95 per cent.'

We went on to discuss a comical scenario where Taiwan and China begin going to war, but call a ceasefire because the rest of the world is crying out for Internet equipment. Then neither side has enough soldiers because they're too busy making Wi-Fi routers.

'And for what exactly would we be fighting about?' asked Liao with a smile. 'A declaration of independence? To have something written on a piece of paper that everyone knows exists anyway about something that happened before most of us were born?'

I wanted to take the idea further so dropped in on the Taiwan Institute of Economic Research with a specific question about when a society is ready to begin the path to Western-style democracy. If the first stage was economic development, then was there a specific economic point at which a society was rich enough to begin the journey? Dr Paul Collier had set the level at about US$2,700, but he was referring to the poorest in the world that he described as the 'Bottom Billion'. In the 1960s the Taiwanese would have been included in that group. So was there a figure when it was safe to launch the democratic vision?

'It was around 1985,' said the institute director, Dr David S. Hong, 'our economic growth per capita reached a certain threshold, around US$5,000, and that was the point when we were able to move from a government-planned to a market economy that led to the first political freedoms.'

'And if you had brought in democracy before that?' I asked.

'In the early stage of development, that kind of political system is not really efficient because you have different interests competing together. So our progress would have been slower.'

'All right, then. Let's look at Cuba, Iraq, Afghanistan, even China. The West keeps pressing for democracy, but what should they do?'

'The rule of thumb is that in the early stages of development stability is the most important factor. You mustn't forget that it's possible to have a government that is not democratic but has good leadership.'

A veteran of Taiwan's democratic transition was Dr Su Chi, whom we found campaigning for the KMT in a small, chaotic election office in the middle of Taipei. I had met him before in the early 1990s when he was the government information minister and as Taiwan was beginning to open up. I asked him to lay out the stages needed to create a full democracy.

'The first stage was economic development,' said Su, 'which made people conscious of the need to protect private ownership. With that came taxation that created the pact of responsibility between the government and its citizens. The second step was pluralization when people began to organize themselves into civic groups. The third was liberalization, meaning press freedom, travel, freedom of speech and, of course, the people's freedom to constrain the government's power. The fourth step was the institutionalization of various laws to regulate behaviour. We went through all of these stages through the decades. It took a long time, but this was why our democracy was achieved without bloodshed. After the first presidential election in 1996, people felt that nothing had changed but all of a sudden we were a democratic country.'

'Has anybody in Washington asked you about this process?' I asked. 'I'm thinking particularly in respect to Iraq.'

Su shook his head. 'No. No one.'

In April 2004, I was asked to join a BBC Radio 4 programme called *What If?* in which we discussed what would have happened after the 1989 Tiananmen Sqaure protests if the Chinese government had negotiated a settlement with the students that led to democratic reform. In the chair was Professor Christopher Andrew of Corpus Christi College, Cambridge, and with us was Steve Tsang, a China expert at St Anthony's in Oxford, and Dr Jonathan Mirsky, an academic and journalist who had reported for the *Observer* from Tiananmen Square at the time. I had been asked as I was the BBC's Beijing Bureau chief during the 1990s.

China's decision to use the army against demonstrators in Tiananmen Square in June 1989 was a pivotal moment in the debate between democracy and dictatorship. The protests began in April 1989 with the death of the reformer Hu Yao-bang, the former general secretary of the Communist Party who had called for more openness. He was much loved by the younger generation and his death acted as the catalyst that drew first students, then assorted groups to Tiananmen Square to protest. International television crews were in Beijing in any case for the visit of the Soviet president Mikhail Gorbachev, and the world was treated to polarizing images of the students facing down the Chinese security forces day in day out. The confrontation was perhaps best encapsulated when a huge replica of the Statue of Liberty, known as the Goddess of Democracy, was paraded in front of the portrait of Mao Zedong staring down from the entrance to the Forbidden City.

For many weeks, the protesters and government were at a standoff until China's leader Deng Xiao-ping gave orders for Tiananmen Square to be cleared. Late in the evening of 3 June 1989, the army went in. No one knows the exact number of dead, but it's estimated that up to 800 civilians were killed together with about 50 soldiers and police. The killings jolted the West out of its innocence that China was on an inevitable path toward reform.

Western democracy felt let down. It imposed sanctions, and investment slowed to a trickle. East Asia, too, was left foundering. It yearned for a lead and was hoping that China, emerging from the destructive era of Mao, would fill that role. That now seemed to be impossible.

The discussion began with Christopher Andrew asking what would have been the global reaction if the Chinese leadership had accepted the students' demands.

'The United States would have been extremely pleased with that result,' said Tsang. 'It would have been the first serious win of the Cold War. It would have caught the imagination of Americans and you would have seen an injection of Western capital as well as assistance and aid.'

The discussion continued on a fairly gentle course until Andrew asked Tsang if the onset of more democracy in 1989 would have led to chaos – 'the disintegration of central authority, the return to the age of warlords and trouble in China and trouble for the rest of the world'.

'I don't think so,' said Tsang, 'and I'm working on the assumption that communism didn't collapse in the Soviet Union and Eastern Europe later in 1989.'

'We can't assume that,' interrupted Andrew.

'Then,' said Tsang, pausing for thought, 'how I see it is that if communism collapsed in Eastern Europe, your good-humoured, reasonable Chinese students, that had been persuaded in the summer of 1989 to withdraw, would come back with a vengeance. They would push and push, and if Deng Xiao-ping had agreed [to a settlement] because there was no way out in the summer and because he was concerned about causing bloodshed, he would not have had that concern then. He would have come back with even stronger determination and if necessary a wider use of force in order to prevent that from happening.'

'So your point', said Andrew, 'is that if we had avoided a bloodbath in June 1989 there would have been a massive and even bigger bloodbath in 1990.'

'Yes,' said Tsang. 'I believe, regrettably, that would have been the most likely scenario.'

'If that happened, it would have been the end of the Chinese state,' said Mirsky. 'Instead of having some kind of widening of democracy you would have had a serious civil war in China.'

When we had walked into the recording studio that day, none of us knew how the alternative scenario Andrew would be coaxing from us would turn out. Yet we all concluded that nothing but bloodshed would have emerged from an instant transition to democratic government – even though Mirsky was a fervent pro-democracy campaigner.

China saw what had happened with Communism's collapse in Europe and firmly decided against it. It reacted to the Tiananmen Square killings by focusing on its economy. The result was international praise for its poverty alleviation, the creation of a vocal middle class, with a degree of freedom that would have been unimaginable before with radio and television chat shows, investigative journalism into corruption and other issues and an ease to move around because of improved infrastructure. During my years there in the mid-1990s we routinely switched our travel plans because a new highway or airport had opened in a place where there was none before. Yet, if you spoke out against the government on issues it did not like you could end up in jail.

As we teased some of this out in the *What If?* discussion, Christopher Andrew remarked that the scenario we were painting was 'deeply hostile to Western conventional wisdom. But', he added, 'that doesn't mean to say it's wrong.'

Tiananmen Square in June 1989, with that stark image of a man standing in front of a column of tanks, came to symbolize dictatorial repression. The shock and horror of the killings were felt throughout the world, yet twenty years on China was being hailed as a model of economic success and the beacon that East Asia and much of the world has been looking for. It had been elevated to the role of an economic engine the world depends on, eclipsing that of Japan. It had also set a global example in alleviating poverty.

In Taipei, we headed off to the anti-China DPP campaigners, the party that was presently in government. The streets were adorned with political bunting. Minibuses cruised around, decked in ribbons and posters, with candidates appealing through loudspeakers for votes. A cartoonist sketched the two candidates as pro- and anti-China warriors brandishing flags across the Taiwan straits.

We found Bi-khim Hsiao on the pavement with clusters of pensioners, dressed in yellow, stuffing pamphlets into envelopes. A horn blared from a passing election van. Bi-khim Hsiao stood up and waved. An elderly couple came up and greeted her. She gave them a pile of pamphlets and envelopes, set them to work, then turned her attention to us.

Bi-khim Hsiao is the daughter of a Taiwanese father and American mother, with a masters degree in political science from New York's Columbia University. Dressed in a white top, she cut a striking figure at the hectic election office. She reached under a trestle table piled with leaflets to pull out two stools for us to sit on.

'A lot of people believe that democracy isn't suitable for some societies, like China, the Middle East and Africa,' I said.

She smiled, was about to answer and was immediately interrupted by a party worker who wanted her to check the design of a brightly coloured poster. She cast her eye over it and nodded. The poster was calling for Taiwan to be given a seat at the United Nations – a move that America had publicly condemned. As she turned her attention back to the interview, I quipped: 'America doesn't like this UN idea.'

Bi-khim Hsiao stiffened. 'China is run by an authoritarian government,' she said sharply, 'and we've worked for decades to get rid of authoritarianism in this country. All we are asking is for our achievements to be recognized. We see the Americans praising the people of Iraq for having the courage to go to the polls and vote. Yet at the same time they're condemning us for holding a vote to express our desire to be part of the international community.'

She pointed across the road to a huge green banner also calling for UN recognition. Two minivans passed from the rival KMT Party with loudspeakers broadcasting music. Three young girls paused to say something to her as they headed into the office.

'What about democracy as a whole,' I asked, returning to my first question. 'Is it suitable for some cultures and not for others?'

'Democracy is applicable to everyone,' she replied. 'But you have to do it properly. We have created our democracy with our own hands and our own hard work and what we've done here counters the argument that democracy is not an Asian concept, that it is not applicable to Asians. We've proved that wrong. We cherish our democracy and it can be applied everywhere whatever the culture, race or religion.'

Bi-khim Hsiao was young, telegenic, passionate and educated. Her childhood and upbringing ran parallel to Taiwan's slow and peaceful transformation from dictatorship to democracy. Her DPP lost the election. Naturally, she was disappointed, but one thought did not cross her mind – or that of millions of others in Taiwan.

No one was going to strap explosives to their chests and head off to kill. There was too much else to live for.

CONCLUSION

I asked Simone Apel of Publishers Research Services to see if she could find out how many people had died around the world due to conflict since 1989, when Western-style democracy has had an almost free rein to prove its worth. We both knew that it could only ever be a rough guess, because of the overlaps between war, poverty and disease. She came up with a figure of just over 10 million deaths, with 9 million of those in Africa.

Ten million dead on the twenty years of democracy's watch might not be the failure it first seems. The First World War killed 35 million people. In the Second World War 70 million died. Stalin's Great Terror and Mao's Great Leap Forward caused the deaths of an estimated 30 million people each. American, British and other allied troops killed in Iraq and Afghanistan are a fraction of those who died in the earlier wars in Korea and Vietnam.

The world is becoming a safer and more trusting place. But that doesn't mean we should not be constantly looking at ways to do things better. The common thread in the stories in this book is that poverty, ethnic and religious differences, corruption, land disputes, history and venal leaders make full electoral democracy a very risky system for some societies. Yet, at the same time, people want their governments to deliver and they want to be able to speak out without fear of punishment. It is that transition from poverty and oppression to wealth and freedom that has proved to be so difficult to manage.

One lesson learned since 1989 is that elections are limited – and often damaging – in what they can deliver. The success of democracy depends on many other factors, including leadership, institutions, trade, mentoring and – perhaps the most crucial – time.

Firstly, leadership – whether it comes from Saddam Hussein or Nelson Mandela – is crucial in setting the course for a society. South Africa's relatively peaceful democratic transition was successful in no small part because of the role Mandela played as a guiding force. Iraq buckled into war because of Saddam's autocratic intransigence. If leaders are ideologically hostile to democracy, as many can be, then the changes must be finely managed. The stick and carrot formula of aid and sanctions has failed too often, and the idea that the foreign armies of democratic powers will be met with jubilant scenes of celebration was buried in the deserts of Iraq.

Second, the holding of elections, even those that lead to a peaceful transfer of power, is often used as a smokescreen for success. It gives legitimacy to the elite, while little improves for the poor. The really tough part is building the institutions. There needs to be a free and responsible press; uncorrupt and efficient public services; an independent judiciary that closes cases and makes decisions; a disciplined police and military; a strong election commission; a banking authority; and education, health and transport organizations, all of which can be held to account. There is no such thing as a perfect institution, and developed societies are constantly modifying their own. Nor is all of that needed before a society can begin the path to democracy. But a minimum degree of institutional quality is essential, and much damage can be done by dealing with a society on the assumption that its institutions are strong. In Ivory Coast, weak institutions were unable to fill the vacuum when the long-standing leader stepped down. In Argentina, they failed to regulate the banking system. In Morocco, there was no institution to look after an eleven-year-old boy abandoned by his parents. In Iraq, they were destroyed in America's de-Baathification campaign.

Ideally, institutions are built up over time by the people themselves and not on Western prescriptions sweetened by aid packages. While aid can be used to build infrastructure, supply medicine and distribute food in emergencies, it cannot directly buy good governance. The ongoing debate about aid has an embarrassing core. Much of the fastest poverty reduction in the past twenty years has been in China, Vietnam and Cuba, primarily as a result of home-grown reforms and not through Western aid.

A third element is the need for mentors – individuals or nations that can guide and support a country's development over the years. This is a very different concept from the maligned and often cited return to colonization and imperialism. Colonization was for the benefit of the colonizer. Mentoring, as for example in Bosnia, is for the benefit of the country. Mentors, unlike aid donors, are not driven by the need to spend their budgets. Mentors are critical-friends: they support, but have the authority to criticize, and in some cases control. Bosnia has powerful and extensive mentoring. Taiwan's mentoring by the United States came through a political reality of dealing with its huge neighbour. In Georgia, mentoring failed – at least to prevent the 2008 war with Russia. In the European Union, mentoring is planned and systematic with benchmarks that produce specific rewards. In Africa, the concept is often shunned for being a return to colonialism. In Iraq, the mentors were rejected because the Iraqi dream conflicted with the American dream which, in any case, was too foreign and unimaginable.

A fourth element is the need for trade, which leads to integration and a better understanding of how other societies think and operate. Israel barely trades with its Middle Eastern neighbours and remains on a war footing. But increased trade between Russia and the West helped ease the 2008 Georgia crisis and trade between Taiwan and China has made war there almost unthinkable. Trade also forces through institutional reform. Companies will not invest in a place that is insecure and where corruption is endemic. It encourages the creation of umbrella organizations whereby governments are willing to swap some independence for the benefits that membership will bring. Regionally, they will join Mercosur in Latin America or ASEAN in South East Asia. Globally, they will be members of the United Nations and the World Trade Organization and NATO or other defence and economic groupings that set standards of behaviour. Countries within these organizations act as beacons or examples for others to follow, and once a government joins it accepts its responsibility as a member of the international community. Trade and integration create wealth that in turn bring demands from a more confident and educated population. People who own their home and wish for a good education for their children will temper their demands so as not to destroy the mechanism that is bringing them wealth and security. In exchange, well-run governments will stay ahead with reform in order to keep their citizens happy.

A fifth element is time. Building institutions needed to make a country safe for democracy should be counted in decades not years. The Allies waited ten years after the Second World War before returning sovereignty to Germany and seven years for Japan. It could easily take Bosnia a quarter of a century from the end of its war in 1995. It took almost fifty years for Taiwan to hold its first direct-presidential election and more than forty years for South Korea.

The purpose of democracy is to provide good governance and dignity. The repercussions of the loss of dignity and self-esteem can be catastrophic, for both the individual and society. Therefore, we should not be wedded to elections unless they lead directly to what is needed. Instead, such as in Bosnia, we should find an acceptable alternative with which to handle the delicate transitions from instability and dictatorship.

Over the next few years, we may see transitions beginning in countries that could either go smoothly or erupt into global crises. They include: Burma or Myanmar, which has been under military rule since 1962 – its beacon of freedom Aung San Suu Kyi has spent much of the past twenty years there under arrest; North Korea, one of the world's most closed countries governed by a brutal dictatorship; Cuba, which will come under increasing pressure to hold elections as relations with the United States thaw; Zimbabwe, when it begins recovering from the misrule of Robert Mugabe; Sri Lanka, which has to find a lasting peace with its Tamil community; and Iraq and Afghanistan, where the transitions are far from over and the lives of soldiers from Western democracies are being lost.

This book began with a question and an imaginary story. The question – 'What's so good about having the vote' – is one that needs to be answered by anyone standing for office and advocating full elections – specifically in a society with weak institutions. It is a question, not a statement. It requires an answer, not a response. Churchill's maxim that democracy is 'the worst form of government except all those other forms that have been tried' no longer does the business. We have to do better than that.

The scenario I painted at the beginning was that the world was on the brink of destruction and that you have a choice to save your family by escaping either to Cuba or to Haiti.

Supposing the impact of your choice extended far beyond your family and you had to make the decision for billions of people from all walks of life from all over the world, with their loved ones, their sick, their children and their hopes and dreams to be somewhere safe that they could build their lives for the future.

Which one would it be and why?

AUTHOR'S NOTE

I would like to thank all the people who helped me gather the material for this book over the many years. From Jolo Island in the Philippines to Harvard University in the United States, from the shopping malls of Malaysia to the bomb shelters of Iraq, I have been privileged to talk to people from all walks of life and political leanings, many of whose views have fed into the stories and what they reveal. There are too many to name individually, but I have a huge debt of gratitude to those whom we know in our trade as fixers. These are people who for a short time and often at great risk work with us in their own societies in order to give us access and insight. I would also like to thank the BBC for allowing me to report from far-flung places where few other broadcasters ever tread. This book is about building institutions, and the BBC is a great British and global institution.

SELECT BIBLIOGRAPHY

Chanda, Nayan, *Bound Together: How Traders, Preachers, Adventurers and Warriors Shaped Globalization* (Yale University Press, 2008)

Chandrasekaran, Rajiv, *Imperial Life in the Emerald City: Inside Baghdad's Green Zone* (Bloomsbury, 2007)

Collier, Paul, *The Bottom Billion: Why the Poorest Countries are Failing and What Can Be Done About It* (Oxford University Press, 2007)

Collier, Paul, *Wars, Guns and Votes: Democracy in Dangerous Places* (The Bodley Head, 2009)

Friedman, Thomas L., *The World is Flat: The Globalized World in the Twenty-First Century* (Penguin, 2005)

Fukuyama, Francis, *The End of History and the Last Man* (Penguin, 1992)

Fukuyama, Francis, *Trust: The New Foundations of Global Prosperity* (The Free Press, 1995)

Gause, F. Gregory, 'Can Democracy Stop Terrorism?', *Foreign Affairs* Sept./Oct. 2005

Ghani, Ashraf, and Lockhart, Clare, *Fixing Failed States: A Framework for Rebuilding a Fractured World* (Oxford University Press, 2008)

Hakim, Peter, 'Is Washington Losing Latin America?', *Foreign Affairs* Jan./Feb. 2006

Hourani, Albert, *A History of the Arab Peoples* (Faber & Faber, 1991)

Huntington, Samuel P., *The Clash of Civilisations: And the Remaking of World Order* (Simon & Schuster, 1997)

SELECT BIBLIOGRAPHY

Khanna, Parag, *The Second World: Empires and Influence in the New Global Order* (Allen Lane, 2008)

Meredith, Martin, *The State of Africa: A History of Fifty Years of Independence* (The Free Press, 2005)

Muller, Jerry, 'The Clash of Peoples: Why Ethnic Nationalism Will Drive Global Politics for Generations', *Foreign Affairs*, March/April 2008

Off, Carol, *Bitter Chocolate: Investigating the Dark Side of the World's Most Seductive Sweet* (Random House, Canada, 2006)

Zakaria, Fareed, 'The Rise of Illiberal Democracy', *Foreign Affairs* Nov./Dec. 1997

INDEX